Justice and the Way of Jesus

Justice and the Way of Jesus

*Christian Ethics and
the Incarnational Discipleship of Glen Stassen*

Edited by David P. Gushee and Reggie L. Williams

Maryknoll, New York 10545

Founded in 1970, Orbis Books endeavors to publish works that enlighten the mind, nourish the spirit, and challenge the conscience. The publishing arm of the Maryknoll Fathers and Brothers, Orbis seeks to explore the global dimensions of the Christian faith and mission, to invite dialogue with diverse cultures and religious traditions, and to serve the cause of reconciliation and peace. The books published reflect the views of their authors and do not represent the official position of the Maryknoll Society. To learn more about Orbis Books, please visit our website at www.orbisbooks.com.

Copyright © 2020 by David P. Gushee and Reggie L. Williams

Published by Orbis Books, Box 302, Maryknoll, NY 10545-0302.

All rights reserved.

The scripture quotations contained herein are from the New Revised Standard Version: Catholic Edition, Copyright © 1989 and 1993, by the Division of Christian Education of the National Council of the Churches of Christ in the United States of America. Used by permission. All rights reserved.

No part of this publication may be reproduced or transmitted in any form or by any means, electronic or mechanical, including photocopying, recording, or any information storage or retrieval system, without prior permission in writing from the publisher.

Queries regarding rights and permissions should be addressed to: Orbis Books, P.O. Box 302, Maryknoll, NY 10545-0302.

Manufactured in the United States of America

Library of Congress Cataloging-in-Publication Data

Names: Stassen, Glen Harold, 1936-2014, honoree. | Gushee, David P., 1962- editor. | Williams, Reggie L., 1971- editor.
Title: Justice and the way of Jesus : Christian ethics and the incarnational discipleship of Glen Stassen / edited by David P. Gushee and Reggie L. Williams.
Description: Maryknoll : Orbis Books, 2020. | Includes bibliographical references and index. | Summary: "Eighteen Christian theologians and ethicists offer a rich engagement with the theological ethics of Glen Stassen (1936-2014)"— Provided by publisher.
Identifiers: LCCN 2019048271 (print) | LCCN 2019048272 (ebook) | ISBN 9781626983663 (paperback) | ISBN 9781608338306 (ebook)
Subjects: LCSH: Christian ethics. | Stassen, Glen Harold, 1936-2014. | Catholic Church—Doctrines.
Classification: LCC BJ1191 .J87 2020 (print) | LCC BJ1191 (ebook) | DDC 241—dc23
LC record available at https://lccn.loc.gov/2019048271
LC ebook record available at https://lccn.loc.gov/2019048272

In Memory of Glen Harold Stassen

The editors gratefully acknowledge the extensive efforts of each contributor to this volume, as well as the generous financial support of Kathleen Stassen Berger, whose grant to Mercer University's Center for Theology and Public Life, directed by David P. Gushee, made this project possible. We are also grateful to Peter Goodwin Heltzel for his attendance at the consultation and significant engagement with this project.

CONTENTS

PROLOGUE
   Testing Ethical Method in the Laboratory of History
      Glen Harold Stassen   ix

INTRODUCTION
   Incarnational Discipleship and a Thicker Jesus
      David P. Gushee and Reggie L. Williams   1

1. Incarnational Discipleship, Christian Eschatology, and "Realistic Hope"
      Lisa Sowle Cahill   9

2. Toward an Incarnational Theology of Identity
      Jacob Alan Cook   25

3. Rejecting Stassen's Thick Jesus
      Miguel A. De La Torre   39

4. My Jesus Is P-H-A-T: A Womanist Response
      Stacey M. Floyd-Thomas   55

5. Fidelity: A Sexual Ethic for Christians and Other Aliens in a Strange Land
      George Hunsinger   70

6. Covenant as a Historical Drama for Incarnational Discipleship
      Hak Joon Lee   86

7. America's Cultural Ethos of White Supremacy
    Peter J. Paris   105

8. Friendly Amendments
    Larry L. Rasmussen   119

9. A Thicker Jesus and Democracy
    Ron Scott Sanders   135

10. Seeing Jesus: The Muslim Refugee Crisis
    Peter M. Sensenig   149

11. Race
    Reggie L. Williams   163

12. An Enduring Legacy for Christian Ethics
    David P. Gushee   178

CONTRIBUTORS   203

INDEX   207

PROLOGUE

Testing Ethical Method in the Laboratory of History

Glen Harold Stassen[1]

H. Richard Niebuhr wrestled with historical relativism—with postmodernism before we were using the term. Instead of flinching at how our historical context and social location influence our ethics, he made that historical relativism fully clear in his first book, *The Social Sources of Denominationalism*.[2] Then *he used the awareness of historical context as a way of testing the faithfulness or unfaithfulness of our theological ethics*: he advocated using history as the laboratory in which our theological ethics is tested. In *Kingdom of God in America*, he investigated the history of American Protestantism, looking for "faith which is independent, which is aggressive rather than passive, and which molds culture instead of being molded by it." He identified the early Puritan period, the Great

---

1. This January 2014 paper was originally titled, "With Cahill, Testing Ethical Method in the Laboratory of History." The paper was more than fifteen hundred words longer, as it contained a lengthy section engaging the then-recent work of our contributor and distinguished ethicist, Lisa Sowle Cahill, as further confirmation of incarnational discipleship. We have cut this section for brevity, and thus also have changed the name of this essay. Note: all further footnotes were in Stassen's original text.

2. Lisa Cahill aligns with Niebuhr's case for social contextualization or historical relativism in this book in her *Global Justice, Christology, and Christian Ethics* (New York: Cambridge University Press, 2012), 7.

Awakening, and the Social Gospel as movements that had such transformative faith. Had he written later he surely would have included the Civil Rights Movement.

I am looking for faith that stands the test of faithfulness—that leads Christians to do what is right when others are being seduced by an unfaithful culture. One historical time of testing that we all recognize was the Third Reich, when most pastors were seduced into going along with the horrible violence of Hitler, or simply being passive bystanders. Dietrich Bonhoeffer and Karl Barth led the church resistance against the Nazis. So did André Trocmé in Le Chambon, who led that French village to rescue more than three thousand Jews. We almost all recognize that Bonhoeffer, Barth, and Trocmé passed the test while others failed. We can ask whether they shared key themes in their ethics that helped them make the right witness when so many others failed.

Another historical test was the U.S. Civil Rights Movement. Many Christians supported segregation or were mere bystanders. Martin Luther King Jr. and the white Southern Baptist Clarence Jordan passed that historical test in dramatic ways.

We should add the mid-century Catholic activist Dorothy Day and Muriel Lester (her Baptist friend who took similar action in England) in the struggle with economic injustice and poverty.

And we need to know the history of the people movement, the "Revolution of the Candles" in East Germany, in order to give honest credit to the churches and the people who brought down Communism there.[3] The people accomplished what Germans in the Third Reich could not accomplish: they toppled the violent dictator, and the Berlin Wall, and they did it nonviolently—because they had schooled themselves in the ethics of Bonhoeffer and Barth and Martin Luther King.

Church leaders organized two interdenominational conferences, developing a book-length document demanding specific changes for "More Justice in East Germany." The Communist government

---

3. See John Burgess, *The East German Church and the End of Communism* (New York: Oxford University Press, 1997) and Jörg Swoboda, *The Revolution of the Candles: Christians in the Revolution of the German Democratic Republic* (Macon, GA: Mercer University Press, 1996).

threatened the churches with retribution if they were to publish that document, but they courageously proceeded. It became the consensus demand for the changes that people agreed were needed. Since meetings were illegal elsewhere, all the planning meetings were carried out in churches, where people had studied the writings of Martin Luther King, had posted his pictures on the church walls, and had prayed that their demonstrations would stay nonviolent.

On the morning of Friday, November 10, 1989, the Berlin Wall was suddenly opened. East Germans came flooding into West Germany through the several gates between East and West. The very evening before the Berlin Wall was opened, I was staying in the Dietrich Bonhoeffer House in West Berlin, preparing to engage in a two-week speaking tour on themes of peacemaking and justice in different towns throughout East Germany. At 10 PM Thursday evening, the television suddenly announced that the Wall would open the very next morning. As you can imagine, the next two weeks of dialogues made a deep impression on me. I had not expected they would pass the test.

The leaders of the Revolution of the Candles were disciples of Bonhoeffer and Barth, and the people were modeling their movement on Martin Luther King. On Sunday in Bitterfield perhaps two thousand people gathered in the town cathedral, as was their custom. After the service, they moved out to the town square for an open-mic gathering, which they climaxed by singing "We Shall Overcome" in English. They had not only studied the strategies of Martin Luther King, they had learned the civil rights songs in English! I was so moved that I went up to the platform and the main microphone. They stayed to hear what I would say, since they recognized me as one of the speakers in the cathedral two hours previously. I said only three sentences: "I was deeply engaged in the U.S. Civil Rights Movement. What you have accomplished is what we were trying to accomplish. I am deeply moved, and deeply grateful." They gave me the biggest applause I have ever received. They had been locked in, isolated, but were modeling their movement after the U.S. Civil Rights Movement. For me, an American deeply engaged in that movement, to make the connection directly was exactly what they wanted to hear. They were modeling their movement on Bonhoeffer, Barth, and King—with the same themes in their theological ethics.

The Question for Our Ethics

The question for our method in Christian ethics is whether the ethics of these Christian leaders shared distinctive features that help explain their faithfulness in contentious times, and that we can learn from.

1. Strikingly, they all wrote books digging deeply into the way of Jesus. Bonhoeffer wrote *Discipleship*, exegeting the Sermon on the Mount concretely and specifically, taking each unit as concrete guidance for our action. He charges that other kinds of ethics are cheap grace, and he calls for costly grace that follows the way of Jesus concretely. "It is not ultimately important to us what this or that church leader wants. Rather, we want to know what Jesus wants."[4] Trocmé wrote *Jesus and the Nonviolent Revolution*, not only exegeting Jesus concretely, but also setting him in his historical context over against the traditions of the Sadducees, Pharisees, Zealots, and Essenes, and examining with innovative attention the Jubilee tradition that he saw in Jesus' political ethics. His *Jesus and the Nonviolent Revolution* became the central influence on John Howard Yoder's *Politics of Jesus*, which has influenced our generation's beginning recovery of the way of Jesus for Christian ethics. Clarence Jordan wrote *The Sermon on the Mount*, with concrete and specific exegesis similar to Bonhoeffer's, directly calling on us to do specifically what Jesus teaches. Martin Luther King wrote *Strength to Love* and made Jesus' way of nonviolence the way of life for the Civil Rights Movement. Day and Lester wrote articles, not books, but their articles advocate following Jesus' way thickly, as practical and necessary guidance, not as high and distant ideals.

Barth wrote Christ-centered doctrine. The Barmen Declaration, which he drafted, says:

---

4. Dietrich Bonhoeffer, *Discipleship*, Dietrich Bonhoeffer Works, vol. 4 (Minneapolis: Augsburg Fortress Press, 2001), 37, 43–46.

The inviolable foundation of the German Evangelical Church is the gospel of Jesus Christ as it is attested for us in Holy Scripture and brought to light again in the Confessions of the Reformation.

"I am the way, and the truth, and the life; no one comes to the Father, but by me" (John 14:6).

"Truly, truly, I say to you, he who does not enter the sheepfold by the door, but climbs in by another way, is a thief and a robber.... I am the door; if anyone enters by me, he will be saved" (John 10:1, 9).

Jesus Christ, as he is attested for us in Holy Scripture, is the one Word of God which we have to hear and which we have to trust and obey in life and in death.[5]

It is truly striking that all these heroes of the faith wrote books thickly exegeting Jesus. Few theological ethicists were writing such books then. Why not? In the Middle Ages, most church members were not literate; they learned their Christian ethics from art, from traditional teaching, and from a church more-or-less aligned with political authorities. The art portrayed Mary and baby Jesus and Jesus crucified, but not Jesus' ministry and teaching. The Magisterial Reformation tended to draw its public ethic from natural law or common grace, and to distance itself from Anabaptist movements that focused on following Jesus. Nineteenth-century German Protestant theology—Schleiermacher, Hermann, Ritschl, Troeltsch—tended to focus on one ideal or another. Early twentieth-century theology was highly skeptical of the historical Jesus. As a result, the giants—Bultmann, Brunner, Barth, and the Niebuhrs (my mentors), who shaped our predecessors—tended to have a thin Jesus. Reinhold Niebuhr initially saw Jesus as teaching an impossible ideal.

H. Richard Niebuhr, by contrast, advocated Christ as the Rosetta Stone by which we can interpret what God is doing in history. Yet in the 1950s, he rebelled against what he labeled Barth's "Christomonism" and adopted radical monotheism, with God almost

---

5. Barmen Declaration, article 1; Arthur C. Cochrane, *The Church's Confession under Hitler* (Philadelphia: Westminster Press, 1962), 239.

infinitely distant from ethics, and with his own prophetic ethics temporarily losing much of its content. Yet, as I argued in *Authentic Transformation: A New Vision of Christ and Culture*, he was recovering his more Christ-centered and prophetic ethic in his last two years. Dietrich Bonhoeffer's *Discipleship* and his advocacy of Christ-centered revelation in his *Ethics* argue against ethics with a thin Jesus. His two drafts of "History and Good" describe how he wanted to revise his interpretation of the Sermon on the Mount so it would be useful for political ethics.

This history, including nineteenth-century thin idealism and early twentieth-century skepticism about the historical Jesus, created an inadequate interpretation of Jesus by the giants who have shaped us and our traditions. Becoming aware of the historical causes that have skewed our theological ethics alerts us to the need for our own process of recovery.

The heroes of the faith whom I have named were not so confined by this thin-Jesus tradition. As Reggie Williams shows in his *Bonhoeffer's Black Jesus: Harlem Renaissance Theology and an Ethic of Resistance*,[6] Dietrich Bonhoeffer was freed by his experience in Harlem and Abyssinian Baptist Church. Trocmé, King, Jordan, Day, and Lester were influenced by other traditions. My own seminary studies included not only a highly skeptical course on the historical Jesus taught by the elderly Henry Joel Cadbury but also an influential New Testament Theology course with W. D. Davies, who pioneered in setting Jesus and Paul within their own Jewish context. The contrast of those two courses symbolized the turning of the aeon in mid-twentieth-century New Testament studies. E. P. Sanders's *Jesus and Judaism* (1985) cites numerous "fresh attempts to give a general account of Jesus' teaching and activity." Sanders comments: "The dominant view today seems to be that we can know pretty well what Jesus was out to accomplish, that we can know a lot about what he said, and those two things make sense within the world of first-century Judaism."[7]

---

6. See Reggie L. Williams, *Bonhoeffer's Black Jesus: Harlem Renaissance Theology and an Ethic of Resistance* (Waco, TX: Baylor University Press, 2014).

7. E. P. Sanders, *Jesus and Judaism* (Philadelphia: Fortress Press, 1985), 2.

One dramatic illustration is James J. Megivern's *The Death Penalty: An Historical and Theological Survey*.[8] The church of the first two centuries quoted the Sermon on the Mount more than any other passage and opposed the death penalty. But the more the church grew in power and involvement in secular society, the more it became entangled in capital punishment. It shifted from an ethic rooted in Jesus' life and teachings to an ethic based on Roman law, philosophy, and other secular norms.[9]

Clement of Alexandria was the first Christian writer to articulate theoretical grounds justifying capital punishment. He appealed to no biblical or Christian source, but instead argued that as a doctor amputates a diseased organ that threatens the body, evil individuals are executed if they threaten society.[10]

After Constantine became the first pro-Christian emperor in 312, at least sixty-six imperial decrees were issued against Christian heretics, and another twenty-five against paganism.[11] The Middle Ages and Renaissance/Reformation periods witnessed horrible instances of violence by Reformers, popes, and other Christian leaders, assigning the death penalty to multiple thousands of Christians, including Jan Hus, Joan of Arc, Albigensians, Waldensians, Franciscans, Knights Templars, and Anabaptists.[12]

Before and during the Enlightenment and Reformation, the Waldensians, John Wyclif, and the Quakers strongly objected to the death penalty as a violation of the way of Jesus. The Anabaptists were convinced that following Jesus was fundamental to Christian discipleship; no societal or state agenda could trump the clear and authoritative witness of Jesus' life and teaching.[13] Invariably, protests against capital punishment were fueled by reform movements that translated and distributed the Bible to the common people.

---

8. James J. Megivern, *The Death Penalty: An Historical and Theological Survey* (New York and Mahwah: Paulist Press, 1997).

9. Ibid., 20–22.

10. Ibid., 22–23.

11. Ibid., 27–28, 45–46, 191.

12. Ibid., 123–29.

13. Ibid., 192–206.

And here is the main point. The mid-twentieth century saw a dramatic turn of Catholic teaching toward articulate attention to the Gospels and the way of Jesus as normative for ethics and life. The result was the dramatic turn of Catholic teaching to opposing the death penalty. Megivern's history of Catholic teaching on the death penalty shows a decisive correlation between ethics based on nonbiblical bases and support for the death penalty, and then the turning in the twentieth century toward a thicker Jesus and resultant opposition to the death penalty.

2. The second theme that runs through the work of these theologians who stood the historical test was the sovereignty of God or Lordship of Christ through all of life, not only in a private or inner-ecclesial realm. H. R. Niebuhr in his *Christ and Culture* worries that the dualistic type sometimes sets Creator against Christ and lets norms from the Creator dominate our public ethic while marginalizing norms from Christ. (He dedicated *Christ and Culture* "to Reinie," and here I think he was in part subtly criticizing his brother.) "Transformative faith selects appropriate ethical understandings in the culture and makes temporary or dialectical coalition with them, thus increasing the concreteness and persuasiveness of its advocacy." But their appropriateness is measured by the normativity of Jesus' way.[14]

Here we see the second meaning of *incarnational* discipleship: the ethic is *embodied* incarnationally in public ethics by making tactical alliances with those particular themes in its surrounding culture that move society in a direction toward the ethics of the incarnate Jesus.[15]

W. A. Visser 't Hooft named the problem that Barmen was confronting. He wrote that, prior to the Third Reich,

---

14. Glen H. Stassen, Diane M. Yeager, and John Howard Yoder, *Authentic Transformation: A New Vision of Christ and Culture* (Nashville: Abingdon, 1996), 171.

15. "'Christ Jesus, whom God made our wisdom, our righteousness and sanctification and redemption' (1 Cor. 1:30).... We reject the false doctrine, as though there were areas of our life in which we would not belong to Jesus Christ, but to other Lords." Barmen Declaration, article 2, cited in Cochrane, *Church's Confession under Hitler*, 240.

The general tendency of Protestantism becomes... more and more to describe the reign of Christ as an invisible, spiritual and heavenly reality located in the souls of men. This shift of emphasis from the universal, all-embracing sovereignty of Christ over the whole world to a purely inward sovereignty leads inevitably to the pietistic conception that the affairs of this world are the sole concern of the secular powers and that the church has no word for the world but only for individuals who are to be saved out of this world.... Christianity becomes more and more introspective and the church knows less and less what to do with the world-embracing and world-shaking affirmations of the Bible.[16]

John Howard Yoder's own historically self-critical theological ethics is a call to repentance for the captivity to ideologies that results from this systematic naiveté, this limiting the gospel to inner-church matters without a public ethics. Yoder has been badly misunderstood and stereotyped by those mainline ethicists who have offered self-justifying rationalizations for their own slothful failure to read Yoder by subsuming his theological ethics under their negative readings of Stanley Hauerwas, whom they interpret as offering sectarian withdrawal from having a public ethic. Yoder explicitly rejects that reading of his own ethic in the early pages of his *For the Nations*. He devotes five footnotes to explaining that Hauerwas, the author of *Against the Nations*, had urged him to write as a sectarian without a public ethic. Yoder rejected this urging, and instead wrote *For the Nations*. Throughout his last decade of writing he was distancing himself from this Hauerwasian tendency.[17] Yoder's argument for the lordship of Christ through all of life has been his impact on Mennonite ethics.[18]

---

16. W. A. Visser 't Hooft, *The Kingship of Christ: An Interpretation of Recent European Theology*, The Stone Lectures for 1947, Princeton Theological Seminary (New York: Harper & Brothers, 1948), 24–25.

17. See John Howard Yoder, *The War of the Lamb: The Ethics of Nonviolence and Peacemaking*, ed. Glen Stassen, Mark Nation, and Matt Hamsher (Ada, MI: Brazos Press, 2009), "Introduction," 11–15.

18. See Ervin Stutzman, *From Nonresistance to Justice: The Transformation of Mennonite Church Peace Rhetoric, 1908–2008* (Scottdale, PA/Wateloo, ON:

3. The third theme is repentance for becoming engaged in unfaithful ideologies. Barmen says:

> In opposition to attempts to establish the unity of the German Evangelical Church by means of false doctrine, by the use of force and insincere practices, the Confessional Synod insists that the unity of the Evangelical Churches in Germany can come only from the Word of God in faith *through the Holy Spirit.* Thus alone is the Church renewed.... The Christian Church is the congregation... in which Jesus Christ acts presently as the Lord in word and sacrament through the Holy Spirit. As the Church of pardoned sinners, it has to testify in the midst of a sinful world, with its faith as with its obedience, with its message as with its order, that it is solely his property.... We reject the false doctrine, as though the Church were permitted to abandon the form of its message and order to its own pleasure or to changes in prevailing ideological and political convictions.[19]

A major theme in Dietrich Bonhoeffer's writings is *Schuldübernehmung*, taking guilt upon oneself. In 1933, he co-authored the Bethel Confession, which included a confession of sharing responsibility for Germany's guilt on the Jewish question, but when the committee removed the confession of repentance, he removed himself from that confession.[20] He wrote a forceful eleven-page passage of confession of guilt and repentance for himself, the church, and Germany in his *Ethics*.[21]

Herald Press, 2011), and Leo Driedger and Donald B. Kraybill, *Mennonite Peacemaking: From Quietism to Activism* (Scottdale, PA: Herald Press, 1994).

19. Cochrane, *Church's Confession under Hitler*, 237, 240–41. Italics added.

20. Eberhard Bethge, *Dietrich Bonhoeffer: A Biography*, rev. ed. (Minneapolis: Fortress Press, 2000), 302–5.

21. Bonhoeffer, *Ethics*, Dietrich Bonhoeffer Works, vol. 6 (Minneapolis: Augsburg Fortress Press, 2005), 134–45. The Confessing Church published the Stuttgart Confession of Guilt in 1945. "Although many of the authors actually opposed the Nazi regime and suffered for it, they acknowledged solidarity with the nation and the church in sin and suffering, they confessed guilt, and called for a new beginning." Cahill, *Global Justice, Christology*, 239. President Richard von

Jennifer McBride's recent book, *The Church for the World*, proposes that Bonhoeffer's theme of repentance is what churches need in our pluralistic culture to make their witness more palatable.[22] She demonstrates that Bonhoeffer's interpreting repentance through the person of Christ directly challenges the assumption that repentance primarily concerns sorrow about one's individual standing before God; instead, as participation in Christ, repentance constitutes existence for others.[23]

André Trocmé published *The Politics of Repentance*. He calls for repentance for letting truth be subverted by the ideology of our society, such as "the worship of free enterprise."[24] And "of all the deceptions of history, war is the most monstrous. It enrolls the noblest of men in the service of a tragic illusion."[25] Though he also writes of Catholic churches, as a Protestant his strongest call to repentance is aimed at Protestant churches. Ministers' "Bible commentaries are dialectical; often they shrink even from preaching on Gospel texts. They have made the tension between law and grace, justice and love, the object of their studies. The result is that the Protestant churches are adapting themselves to the world,

---

Weizsäcker and Chancellor Willy Brandt, as well as *Aktion Sühnezeichen Friedensdienste*, issued dramatic and specific confessions of Germans' sins. The result was an ethically and spiritually healthier Germany and a much improved relation between Germany and other nations.

22. Jennifer McBride, *The Church for the World: A Theology of Public Witness* (New York: Oxford University Press, 2012).

23. In *Discipleship*, he links *metanoia* with the church's conformation to the crucified Christ. In *Ethics*, he links repentance to the church's this-worldly activity when he defines the church's repentance as preparing this "penultimate" world for its redemptive transformation. In *Letters and Papers from Prison*, he defines metanoia as "living completely in" this world's tasks, questions, successes and failures, experiences, and perplexities, taking seriously the suffering of God in the world. As the acceptance of divine judgment, repentance is energized by hope for the world and humanity, animated by joyful expectation as much as lament, and oriented toward future transformation as much as past and present sin.

24. André Trocmé, *The Politics of Repentance: The Robert Treat Paine Lectures for 1951*, trans. John Clark (New York; Fellowship Press, 1953), 35; André-Pascal Trocmé, *Collection de Souvenirs: Une Autobiographie*, (n.d., n.p.), 199–216. Trocmé's writings are found in the Swarthmore College archives.

25. Trocmé, *Politics of Repentance*, 14.

betraying their true nature as churches of a continuous reformation wrought by the Word of God itself."[26] He warns against the pride of self-righteousness. "All men are guilty, the elect even more so than the rest."[27]

When you read through Trocmé's *Autobiographie*, you are struck by his pietism, his experience-based faith, and his sharing faith and testimonies with a group of students. "I was probably better than the others immunized against doubt. My faith was pietist in origin and not rationalist. Even stripping off certain dogmas let it subsist without pain." Learning of some "contradictions in the Gospels did not raise problems for the living presence of the person of Jesus."[28] But he was a Huguenot, in the Reformed tradition, who by no means separated his pietistic faith from repentance for societal sin. When he writes of "Jésus et La Revolution," around 1970, he says Jesus must be interpreted in the prophetic tradition of Isaiah, Jeremiah, Hosea, and Jubilee; otherwise we reduce him to doing charity rather than justice.

Martin Luther King Jr. may have called the United States to repentance more effectively than anyone. His "Letter from Birmingham City Jail" calls "moderate" pastors to repentance for claiming to support justice while criticizing the practices needed to move the nation away from segregation and toward justice. His 1967 Riverside Church Address, "A Time to Break Silence," gave seven reasons for repentance for the Vietnam War. The first was:

> A few years ago there was...a real promise of hope for the poor—both black and white—through the poverty program. There were experiments, hopes, new beginnings. Then came the buildup in Vietnam and I watched the program broken and eviscerated as if it were some idle political plaything of a society gone mad on war, and I knew that America would never invest the necessary funds or energies in rehabilitation

---

26. Ibid., 64.
27. Ibid., 68.
28. Trocmé, *Collection de Souvenirs*, 91.

of its poor so long as adventures like Vietnam continued to draw men and skills and money like some demonic destructive suction tube.[29]

Already as a seminary student, Clarence Jordan was calling on fellow Southern Baptist Theological Seminary students to repentance for their economic privileges in a Louisville with many people living in poverty. They joined in sharing their income with each other and participated in ministry to the poor of Louisville, black and white, especially in the Haymarket area. Jordan was called "The Bishop of the Haymarket." Upon graduating, he returned to south Georgia, the most segregated part of Georgia. He founded Koinonia Farm, with blacks and whites living and working together, sharing their income, and teaching south Georgians more effective farming. They were boycotted, shot at, discriminated against by the neighboring whites. Jordan's whole life as well as his writings were a call to repentance for racism, segregation, and economic injustice. He is the hero of the faith for Southern Baptists who have committed themselves to opposing racism.

Dorothy Day is well known for her similar witness and action against economic injustice and poverty.[30] The Catholic Worker communities which she founded continue their witness of repentance in many cities. Less well known is Muriel Lester. Eileen Egan writes:

> Two revolutionary women, Muriel Lester and Dorothy Day. They were not only rebels, but prophets, having lived lives that pitted them against injustice, poverty, colonial oppression, racism, and above all, against war, preparation for war, and the vengeance that is the legacy of every war. They had

---

29. Martin Luther King, Jr., "A Time to Break Silence," in James M. Washington, ed., *A Testament of Hope: The Essential Writings and Speeches of Martin Luther King, Jr.* (New York: HarperCollins, 1991), 232–33.

30. See *Dorothy Day: Selected Writings*, ed. Robert Ellsberg (Maryknoll, NY: Orbis Books, 1983 and 1992); and *On Pilgrimage: Dorothy Day* (Grand Rapids, MI: Eerdmans Press, and Edinburgh: T&T Clark, 1999).

both known the inside of prison for their convictions and actions.[31]

Lester organized a community of support for the poor, and her witness spread widely. Both Day and Lester were calling Christians to repentance for becoming part of a culture of privilege that oppresses the poor.

The book published by the interdenominational conference of churches in East Germany is a call for repentance by an administration practicing widespread injustice—which they specifically name.

4. These heroes of the faith each advocate specific community practices that embody what they advocate incarnationally. Barth and Bonhoeffer supported practices of the Confessing Church in rejecting the Aryan clause that excluded Jews from churches, and Bonhoeffer especially advocated justice for Jews outside churches as well as inside. He devoted himself to the practice of teaching in the underground seminary at Finkenwalde, and there developed community disciplines, described in his *Life Together*. André Trocmé is well known for the remarkable discipline he developed among all church members and residents of Le Chambon, enabling them to rescue more than three thousand Jews from the Nazis. Martin Luther King is known for the discipline of nonviolent action that he spread to millions of demonstrators, beginning in churches, and that succeeded in achieving civil rights laws and a major turning in the nation—as he said, "to save the soul of the nation," even though we know much more turning is yet needed. Clarence Jordan is known for his development of the Christian community of Koinonia Farm. Dorothy Day is known for the Catholic Worker communities, and Muriel Lester for her development of the community of Kingsley Hall. The Revolution of the Candles is known for what its name names—a nonviolent movement modeled on Martin Luther King's movement—and again, it was all based in churches.

I define "practices" in dialogue with H. Richard Niebuhr and John Howard Yoder, emphasizing response to God's grace in Christ

---

31. Eileen Egan, "Foreword," *Ambassador of Reconciliation: A Muriel Lester Reader*, ed. Richard Deats (Philadelphia: New Society Publishers, 1991), vii.

and shared community action, first in churches and then by analogy in societal action:

> Normative Christian practices are performed by social selves, shaped in community, responding to what God has done in Jesus Christ as rooted within Jewish prophetic tradition and described in the New Testament, and what God in Christ is now doing in our historical context, through the Holy Spirit, so they are participation in grace (as Bonhoeffer emphasizes). Practices are readily observable, as are baptism, the Lord's Supper, conflict transformation, community discernment, calling out the gifts. By contextual analogy, as Yoder explains in *Body Politics*, they can be commended to any society as a healthy way to organize. Baptism crosses racial divisions; the Lord's Supper feeds the hungry, conflict transformation is self-evident, etc.[32]

By contrast, the definition of practice in teleological ethics is criticized by H. Richard Niebuhr for its focus on human effort toward ideal perfection of the doer and its lack of grace. It is hard "to reconcile this with the Christian conviction and experience of the primacy of *God's* action."[33] This applies directly to Alasdair MacIntyre's Aristotelian definition of practices:

> Any coherent and complex form of socially established cooperative human activity through which goods internal to that form of activity are realized in the course of trying to achieve those standards of excellence which are appropriate to, and partially definitive of, that form of activity, with the result that human powers to achieve excellence, and the human conceptions of the ends and good involved, are systematically extended.[34]

---

32. Stassen, in *Authentic Transformation*, 172–73.

33. H. Richard Niebuhr, *The Responsible Self: An Essay in Moral Philosophy* (New York, Evanston, and London: Harper & Row, 1963), 134–35.

34. Alasdair MacIntyre, *After Virtue: A Study in Moral Theology*, 3rd ed. (New York: Bloomsbury, 2013), 218.

By contrast with the Hebraic God who hears the cries and sees the needs of the needy and oppressed and is moved to deliver them within history, Aristotle's God was an Unmoved Mover who did nothing active. There is no grace in an Unmoved Mover, or in MacIntyre's definition of practices. Christian practice has the objective of community relations with compassion and justice for the marginalized, faith in God the Compassionate Deliverer, and hope in future deliverance. Oddly, those who quote MacIntyre's definition of practices almost never analyze its implications and explain how it is compatible with the Gospel.

Nor does it catch what is important about the practices of the heroes of the faith. Their objective was not self-improvement; not extension of their own powers, but deliverance of others in need. Virtue is developed best not by focusing on one's own skills, but by focusing on compassion and justice for those in need. The definition developed in dialogue with H. R. Niebuhr and J. H. Yoder fits what we have observed in the heroes of the faith far better.

Let Us Join with Pope Francis

A recent *Sojourners* blog by Jim Wallis focused on Pope Francis:

> The remarkable acts of kindness and grace we see with Pope Francis are the natural response from a disciple who has known the kindness and grace of Christ in his own life. The pope's moments of Christ-like compassion and love point not to "a great man," but rather point to Jesus. He is not asking us to follow him, but inviting us to follow Christ.

Let us join with Pope Francis. He is pointing toward the tradition of incarnational discipleship; people are giving him their praise and loyalty. They recognize a follower of Jesus.

INTRODUCTION

Incarnational Discipleship and a Thicker Jesus

David P. Gushee and Reggie L. Williams

Glen Harold Stassen (1936–2014) was at first simply the most compelling professor we had ever met. David met Glen at Southern Baptist Theological Seminary in 1984. Reggie met Glen a generation later, in 2005, at Fuller Theological Seminary. For both of us, Glen introduced the academic discipline, Christian ethics, that so utterly consumed him and which we both came to adopt as our own vocation. There are few people in anyone's life of whom it can be said, "My life is fundamentally altered because I met you." For both of us, Glen Stassen was such a person. Many of the authors in this collection can say the same thing.

For David, Glen moved from compelling professor to primary mentor, professional advocate, and very dear friend. After earning a doctorate in Christian ethics at Union Seminary (New York), which Glen recommended and to which Glen helped open the doors, David became a colleague of Glen's at Southern Baptist Theological Seminary (1993–96) and eventually co-author of the widely used textbook *Kingdom Ethics*.[1] Today, David is Glen's literary executor and the primary custodian of his professional memory.

---

1. Glen H. Stassen and David P. Gushee, *Kingdom Ethics: Following Jesus in Contemporary Context* (Downers Grove, IL: Intervarsity Press, 2003). The second edition was published by Eerdmans in 2016 after Glen's death.

For Reggie, Glen's impact also included being mentor and advocate. Reggie studied with Glen at the doctoral level at Fuller Seminary, and Reggie's dissertation became the widely cited book, *Bonhoeffer's Black Jesus*.[2] In the end, along with his other roles, Glen became something of a father figure to Reggie.

Our ties to the late Christian ethicist ran very deep, and we feel them very deeply to this day.

The origin of this collection goes beyond personal loyalty. Glen's last completed book before his death was called *A Thicker Jesus: Incarnational Discipleship in a Secular Age*.[3] It was published in 2012, and it represented a major effort on Glen's part to offer a methodological statement and overall approach to the discipline of Christian ethics. Glen believed that he had found an approach better than the major existing alternatives, that it could be named "incarnational discipleship," and that it needed to be considered in any serious conversation about Christian ethics methodology.

It is easy for this drive on Glen's part to be misunderstood. It was not fundamentally motivated by personal or academic ambition, but by a wholehearted belief that so much was (and always is) at stake in Christian ethics. In particular, Glen believed that his approach could strengthen faithfulness to Jesus Christ in the contemporary church and could equip the church with a stronger public witness in American society—and both were desperately needed, because American Christianity, according to Glen, was deeply compromised both in its fidelity to Jesus and in its Christian witness.

After publishing *A Thicker Jesus*, Glen wanted to attract other scholars to the serious study of his proposal and to join him in refining and advancing it. He had employed a similar approach over the previous two decades in gaining wide attention to and adoption of his breakthrough work on the theory and practices of just peacemaking.[4] He pulled together consultations of scholars, first Christian and

---

2. Reggie L. Williams, *Bonhoeffer's Black Jesus: Harlem Renaissance Theology and an Ethic of Resistance* (Waco, TX: Baylor University Press, 2014).

3. *A Thicker Jesus: Incarnational Discipleship in a Secular Age* (Louisville, KY: Westminster John Knox Press, 2012).

4. Glen Stassen's published books on peacemaking begin with *Journey into Peacemaking* (Memphis, TN: Brotherhood Commission of the Southern Baptist

then interfaith, to examine, refine, and advance this new approach to the ethics of peace and war. He wanted to do the same thing with his idea of a "thicker Jesus" and his methodology called "incarnational discipleship" (henceforth, in this book, we will consider these as terms of art and drop the quotation marks).

As Glen grew sicker from cancer in 2013 and early 2014, his primary professional project was still to bring together this meeting of scholars. Letters went out from the Just Peacemaking Institute at Fuller. For the historical record, here is an excerpt from one of Glen's invitation letters:

> Dear friends interested in joining together for incarnational discipleship:
>
> I have gone slowly, discerning who might have a common interest in joining together to advocate doing theological ethics as incarnational discipleship. "Incarnational discipleship" is the name we have chosen for those heroes of the faith who stood the test of faithfulness in historical test times like the Third Reich, the Revolution of the Candles in East Germany, the US Civil Rights Movement, and the struggle for economic justice a century ago. They are Dietrich Bonhoeffer, Karl Barth, André Trocmé, [and] the leaders of the Revolution of the Candles, all of whom were disciples of Bonhoeffer and Barth, Martin Luther King, Jr., Clarence Jordan, and Dorothy Day and Muriel Lester.

Convention, 1983, 1987). Then came Glen H. Stassen, *Just Peacemaking: Transforming Initiatives for Justice and Peace* (Louisville, KY: Westminster John Knox Press, 1992). He began building a coalition; thus Glen Stassen, ed., *Just Peacemaking: Ten Practices for Abolishing War* (Cleveland: Pilgrim Press, 1998/2008). Finally, after the expansion to an interfaith conversation came Susan Brooks Thistlethwaite, ed., *Interfaith Just Peacemaking: Jewish, Christian, and Muslim Perspectives on the New Paradigm of Peace and War* (New York: Palgrave Macmillan, 2012), a book based on a consultation Glen helped arrange and in which Glen has a chapter. This journey demonstrates many things, including Glen's deep commitment to just peacemaking and his intentional strategy of creating an ever-expanding community of co-practitioners. He intended the same trajectory for incarnational discipleship. Ironically, Glen's relentless and largely successful advance of just peacemaking may have hindered his ability to gain attention to incarnational discipleship. Just peacemaking was Glen's "brand"; could he develop another?

All these did ethics as incarnational discipleship, in three senses: (1) They all wrote with a thick, historically embodied, realistic understanding of Jesus Christ as revealing God's character and thus providing norms for guiding our lives. Bonhoeffer wrote *Discipleship*, Barth wrote the Barmen Declaration, Trocmé wrote *Jesus and the Nonviolent Revolution*, King wrote *Strength to Love*, Jordan wrote *The Sermon on the Mount*, Day and Lester's writings did exegesis of the way of Jesus as practical guidance for life. (2) They all wrote with a holistic understanding of the Lordship of Christ or sovereignty of God throughout all of life and all of creation. They opposed a two-kingdoms or body-soul or temporal-eternal dualism or sectarianism that blocks God's guidance in Christ from applying to public ethics. That required a tactical alliance with a tradition in the society, such as the human rights tradition. (3) They all wrote with a strong call for repentance [for] captivity to ideologies such as nationalism, racism, and greed. The Barmen Declaration roots this rightly in the Holy Spirit. We believe our focus should be on the ideology of laissez-faire capitalism, which since 1980 has changed income taxes, inheritance taxes, and reduced taxes on capital gains and dividends to 15%—the equivalent to low-level workers, not wealthy owners.

Our purpose is to join together as a group, first to refine our vision, and then to write with explicit reference to each other so that we strengthen attention to what each of us advocates, somewhat as Radical Orthodoxy does, but with a different vision. Thus we strengthen each other's voices.

We are following the method that developed the unanimous consensus for the new paradigm, Just Peacemaking, and the consensus support for Interfaith Just Peacemaking. It is not simply a discussion of papers, but a discussion of how to refine the vision and a plan for who will write papers for the book and for the second conference. In each of the previous efforts, we were surprised by how well we reached consensus among scholars who come from different traditions.

In each of those two previous projects, we have found it useful to have a leadership team leading the discussion, one focusing on the vision, and one focusing on relationships. ...I have enlisted stand-ins or substitutes for my own role.... The reason is that I have contracted prostate cancer, and my future strength is unknown. So you may be hearing from them about the conference.

The date was set for September 2014, at Princeton Seminary. Alas, Glen died on April 26, 2014, before the meeting could occur. The event, and the attention to his proposal, remained part of Glen Stassen's unfinished project in Christian ethics. This is said quite intentionally. Even though Glen died at the age of seventy-eight, his work seemed, to him at least, very much unfinished.

Death is almost always cruelly indifferent to the ambitions of scholars. Only very, very few thinkers in any field receive much attention after their pen has been stilled by mortality. But partly out of personal loyalty, and partly because we believed that Glen Stassen's late work was still unfinished and still worthy of engagement, five years later, the two of us called together a group of scholars in Atlanta to fulfill Glen's hope and discuss incarnational ethics and a thicker Jesus. This group included many of the same and some different participants from those whom Glen originally envisioned. We met in early April 2019.

We asked this group to interrogate the concept of incarnational discipleship as seriously as Glen wanted it done. We did not ask them to write encomiums of praise. We asked them to do what Glen had most wanted—to take his ideas seriously. For a true scholar, the greatest gift is to have one's ideas engaged, while the greatest offense is to have them ignored. Over a very full two days, a highly distinguished group of scholars, including several former presidents of the Society of Christian Ethics and American Academy of Religion, rendered that service of engagement to Glen's ideas of a thicker Jesus and incarnational discipleship, exchanging papers about it and discussing those papers intensively with each other. Now the results of this classic academic process are before you in this volume.

This collection makes little sense without readers having encountered what Glen meant by incarnational discipleship. Thus, besides the excerpt from the letter, we include in the prologue a much longer extract from Glen's final address at the Society of Christian Ethics, offered when he was quite ill with cancer, in January 2014. This text, edited for length, offers at least a glimpse of what it was that Glen was proposing, an incarnational discipleship tradition that he was still trying to name and deepen. Those of us who were in the room that day can never forget both how passionate, and how ill, Glen was that day.

The chapters that follow engage, from each author's perspective, what Glen called incarnational discipleship. What results is a true intellectual feast and a step forward for the discipline of Christian ethics. The reader will not discover mere endorsements of the man or his ideas, but they will find a dozen scholars advancing the conversation about those ideas in ways that we think matter very much today.

Catholic scholar Lisa Sowle Cahill examines Glen's social ethics, exploring what "realistic hope" looks like in Christian social-political ethics and considering the basis of a justice-oriented Christian social ethics in the New Testament depiction of Jesus himself.

Jacob Cook, who worked closely with Glen as a doctoral student at Fuller and ran the Just Peacemaking Institute at the time of Glen's death, notices that, for Glen, incarnational discipleship was fundamentally about the nature of Christian identity, and its corruption. This is where his searching theological-ethical-psychological inquiry begins.

Miguel De La Torre, who studied with Glen at Southern Seminary, examines Glen's thicker Jesus and concludes that Glen's Jesus was still too white, and that there is no redeeming a white Jesus. De La Torre's chapter initiates in this volume a searching examination of race in the work of Glen Stassen.

Stacey Floyd-Thomas offers a "vastly darker and a lot larger" PHAT Jesus as she engages Glen Stassen's thicker Jesus. This is christology, and biblical ethics, in a womanist vein, taking seriously Glen's Jesus but also pointing out limits tied to his social location.

George Hunsinger offers a biblical treatment of same-sex relationships and reflects on the potential and limits of incarnational discipleship in this regard.

Hak Joon Lee, Glen's colleague in Christian ethics at Fuller Seminary at the end of Glen's career (and life), carefully probes Glen's hermeneutics and rendering of the biblical story. He concludes that incarnational discipleship would be strengthened by a much stronger integration of the covenantal framework of the Bible.

Peter Paris examines white supremacy as the cultural ethos of the West, including the United States. Paris shows that the United States comprehensively, and therefore in culture, politics, and religion, is infected by white supremacism. This raises interesting questions for Glen's project.

Larry Rasmussen tests Glen's late incarnational discipleship ethics against the reality of human-induced climate change and the catastrophic threat it poses to humanity and the creation. This implicates questions of christology as well as social ethics.

Ron Sanders, a former doctoral student of Glen's, tackles his political theology and understanding of American democracy, arguing that, while Glen's overall approach to the origins of American democracy as well as his way of discussing the posture of the church in relation to public life constituted a serious engagement in the tradition of democratic discourse, it also needs to be challenged.

Peter Sensenig, another former doctoral student of Glen's, explores incarnational discipleship through consideration of Peter's on-the-ground ministry context in majority-Muslim Africa. This essay engages a different literature in missiology, and it also offers what might be described as a practical incarnational ethic.

Reggie Williams offers a searching examination of Glen's treatment of race. Reggie suggests that Glen's understanding of white racism was underdeveloped, and that Glen missed the opportunity to engage critical race theory as it was developing. Reggie suggests an anthropological-aesthetic corrective.

Finally, David Gushee reflects on Glen's life and work in light of all the essays, considering major themes that can be discerned in Glen's work and in the collection—including Jesus, scripture, church, politics, democracy, and race. David considers Glen's overall career trajectory as well as what he was trying to do with the concept of incarnational discipleship. In the end, David asks about the continued relevance of Glen's moral vision in these radical days, now more than five years since his death.

We are deeply grateful to you for having selected this book to read.

ONE

Incarnational Discipleship, Christian Eschatology, and "Realistic Hope"

Lisa Sowle Cahill

It has been a privilege and an education for me to participate in this project on the "incarnational discipleship" of Glen Harold Stassen. I have especially appreciated the occasion to interact intellectually and personally with so many of his former students, friends, and colleagues, many of them in the Fuller Theological Seminary network. This research group has challenged my ecclesiology, my christology, and my politics, while also reinforcing my conviction that Christian social ethics must be not only critical and prophetic but also a hopeful enterprise.

Perhaps the best contribution from the research seminar that preceded this book is that, while Christian ethics and politics should be centered on Jesus, the Christian experience of Jesus is, should be, and will remain pluricentric. This reality cautions against attempts to negotiate any one-consensus vision. That being said, faithful pictures of Jesus will share a family resemblance. Helpful here is Elisabeth Schüssler Fiorenza's distinction between seeing the New Testament as a "mythic archetype" or as a "historical prototype." Both archetype and prototype denote original models. "However an archetype is an ideal form that establishes an unchanging timeless pattern, whereas a prototype is not a binding timeless pattern or principle," but is "open to the possibility of its own transformation."[1] Whereas an archetype functions more like an architectural blueprint, a prototype is more like a bowl cast from a potter's wheel—it inspires more in the same style that are intentionally not duplicates. The scriptures themselves already treat Jesus and his ministry as prototypes. The Syro-Phoenician woman leads Jesus to recognize that his healing mission extends beyond his own people (Mark 7:24–30); Paul makes the mission to the Gentiles central to the emerging church (Acts 15:12–22); and the four Gospels present recognizably similar yet non-identical depictions of Jesus for different communities spanning a generation. Different Christian communities unite around different experiences of Jesus, but faithful understandings of Jesus and faithful mediations of his presence must be similar in some essentials. These must include his vivid and constitutive relation to God, whom he calls "Father"; his inclusive fellowship with sinners and outcasts; his prophetic challenges to religious and imperial elites; his acceptance of suffering and death in consequence of his steadfast union with God and dedication to fellow humanity; and the experience-tested conviction that the risen Jesus, who sends his Spirit to the church, still transforms and empowers Christian disciples and communities today.

A, if not *the*, critical question for Christian social ethicists today is: *Given that* we are formed and guided by the teaching and example of Jesus, *what do we envision as a "realistic hope"* that we can be agents of real political change? Just as experiences of Jesus are diverse, so are the possibilities and limits of Christian action, and therefore of concrete political hope. Glen Stassen's ethic of incarnational discipleship exuded confidence that "the Lordship of Christ through all of life" could challenge greed and militarism and expand the values of human equality and social democracy. But his project was framed mainly in terms of the (white) U.S. experience of the generation following World War II.[2] When more diverse and more recent experiences of Christianity are brought into view, that hopeful picture can change.

---

1. Elisabeth Schüssler Fiorenza, *In Memory of Her: A Feminist Theological Reconstruction of Christian Origins* (New York: Crossroad, 1983), 33–34.

2. See Glen Harold Stassen, *A Thicker Jesus: Incarnational Discipleship in a Secular Age* (Louisville, KY: Westminster John Knox Press, 2012), 16–17, 40–41.

Miguel De La Torre's revisionist theological program involves "embracing hopelessness," on the basis that the world is rife with violence and atrocities; that many of them are committed in the name of religion; that hell, the realm of hopelessness, "is where the vast majority of the world's oppressed currently live"; and that insisting on hope is a tactic of the privileged to blame the victims, justify apathy, and defuse resistance.³ Following De La Torre, David Gushee invokes a Jewish apocalyptic Jesus to challenge his own previous work with Stassen in *Kingdom Ethics* as too liberal, liberationist, and pseudo-inspirational, oriented as it is around "an immanentist, participative, certainly-coming Kingdom-of-God narrative."⁴ "If Christian eschatological hope is fixed on a happy outcome to history, it looks like a losing bet."⁵

Yet if we Christian ethicists give up hope, we are not only distancing ourselves from bourgeois, middle-class, armchair academic theology and churchgoing complacency with the status quo. We are also distancing ourselves from the testimony and lived Christianity of many people who are still trying to escape their assigned status as "the wretched of the earth" (to borrow Frantz Fanon's title). If we despair of any incremental social justice, we align ourselves *de facto* with two competing streams in our discipline of Christian theological ethics: the ethics of an ecclesiocentric world-denying theology that has given up on the power and calling of the church to ameliorate the conditions of human suffering in any systemic way (Stanley Hauerwas and, to a possibly lesser extent, John Howard Yoder);⁶ and the ethics of a "political Augustinianism" that takes a muscular, well-armed view of the responsibility of the church to rein in the sin of the world, accepting as tolerable costs moral compromise, "dirty hands," and a low bar

---

3. Miguel A. De La Torre, *Embracing Hopelessness* (Minneapolis: Augsburg Fortress, 2017), 137.

4. David P. Gushee and Codi D. Norred, "The Kingdom of God, Hope and Christian Ethics," *Studies in Christian Ethics* 31 (2018): 3.

5. Ibid., 15.

6. See for example, Stanley Hauerwas, *A Community of Character: Toward a Constructive Christian Social Ethic* (Notre Dame and London: University of Notre Dame Press, 1981), especially parts 1 and 2; and John Howard Yoder, *The Politics of Jesus* (Grand Rapids, MI: Eerdmans, 1972); but also Yoder's *When War Is Unjust: Being Honest in Just-War Thinking*, rev. ed. (Maryknoll, NY: Orbis Books, 1996).

of success.[7] Yes, ecclesiocentric Christian ethics is a salutary reminder that the church should be forming Christians counterculturally; and yes, Augustinians make it clear that despite Christian formation and our well-intentioned efforts, sin will defeat gospel-based politics a significant amount of the time. Still, I will cast my lot with the likes of #MeToo, #BlackLivesMatter, the Catholic Climate Covenant, the Kino Border Initiative, the Global Mennonite Peacebuilding Conference, the Just Peace advocacy of the World Council of Churches, the "evangelical peacemakers" given voice by David Gushee,[8] and the Catholic Peacebuilding Network. Christian political action, especially in concert with wider social movements, can accomplish political change a significant amount of the time too.

But envisioning a more confident yet still realistic hope of political change soon meets with reasonable objections. The historical track record seems not to be in our favor. Despite generations of teaching about love of neighbor, social justice, and inclusive community by Christians and the churches, not only do the members of these churches not practice these ideals themselves, but the world as a whole can hardly be said to be on an upward trajectory. For instance, while slavery and the disenfranchisement of women have been abolished in most if not all of the world's legal systems, slavery and the sexual instrumentalization of women have simply transmuted into other forms. While the floor of global poverty has been raised, the inequality gap between rich and poor is becoming ever vaster. Add to all this the continued incredible scourge and sin of direct and murderous violence, in extreme, cruel, and sadistic forms, inflicted by some human persons directly on their fellow human beings face to face. De La Torre's book *Embracing Hopelessness* details examples from Chile, Cuba, Budapest, and Korea; and I, personally,

---

7. See Jean Bethke Elshtain, *Just War Against Terror: The Burden of American Power in a Violent World* (New York: Basic Books, 2003); Nigel Biggar, *In Defence of War* (Oxford: Oxford University, 2012); James Turner Johnson, "The Broken Tradition," *The National Interest* 45 (1996): 27–37. See also Michael J. S. Bruno, *Political Augustinianism: Modern Interpretations of Augustine's Political Thought* (Minneapolis: Fortress Press, 2014).

8. David P. Gushee, *Evangelical Peacemakers* (Eugene OR: Cascade Books, 2013).

have listened to survivors of the Rwandan genocide and advocates for raped women in the Democratic Republic of the Congo (DRC).

Yet these undeniable realities do not validate or mandate a "political theology of despair." This is not the right time to renounce the idea that we can, should, and must participate in the advance of God's kingdom. Despair is low-stakes for academic theologians and other privileged Christians. We need *more* Christian action for gospel-informed justice, not less.[9] I don't know where we would get data confirming that the majority of the world's people are actually in despair (as De La Torre claims), but many who are barely surviving in terrible, soul-destroying conditions still testify to or even *create* hope through their very struggle, through their desperate cries to God, through their defiance of the fate that seems certainly to await them.

Let us consider three examples from beyond my own "social location" before turning to the problem of despair and hope for us privileged white Americans. A poem by Nancy Lynne Westfield (for which I have Stacey Floyd-Thomas to thank) depicts the resourcefulness and grit of women Westfield calls "the Hagars" and "the Celies." She gives voice to one of them in these words:

See something where others have thought everything worth
  taking was took
Create fresh possibilities in heaven & hell & the planets in-
  between
Stretch hope where anguish & misery thought it ruled
  supreme....[10]

---

9. De La Torre may ultimately agree with this, since despite embracing hopelessness, he asserts that "engagement in positive and liberative praxis, even when the situation is deemed hopeless, remains possible" (*Embracing Hopelessness*, 141). Gushee may agree too, as he still hopes for the "truly liberative Christian theology and ethics" that might still emerge from "richly diverse communities of scholarly conversation," in his "2018 AAR Presidential Address: In the Ruins of White Evangelicalism: Interpreting a Compromised Christian Tradition through the Witness of African American Literature," *Journal of the American Academy of Religion* 87, 1 (Spring 2019): 15.

10. "Nevertheless, in Stark Contradiction," in Stacey M. Floyd-Thomas, ed., *Deeper Shades of Purple: Womanism in Religion and Society* (New York and London: NYU Press, 2006), 209.

For María Pilar Aquino, a Mexican American feminist theologian, "hope is not a far-off ideal or a palliative. It is a deep spiritual force—because it comes from the Spirit—that encourages the poor in their struggles. It is an objective reality, an anticipation of God's justice and love as experienced in the life, death and resurrection of Jesus."[11] Danka Zelić is a Catholic woman who survived the ethno-religious violence in the former Yugoslavia. She is now a tireless peacebuilder, "bringing neighbor to neighbor" in one of the most forsaken regions of Bosnia and Herzegovina, where the ethnic communities are now even more divided than before the terrifying war and its rampant atrocities.[12]

One of the most moving and powerful books I have read in the past couple of years is *Born from Lament: The Theology and Politics of Hope in Africa*,[13] by the Ugandan theologian, Emmanuel Katongole. The uniqueness of this book lies in the fact that, while it ends on a note of Christian hope, it dares to confront the possibility that God is not a God of justice or mercy after all. Katongole writes about what he terms the seemingly endless "pathological" violence inflicted on the suffering peoples of the Great Lakes region of Africa (Burundi, the DRC, Kenya, Malawi, Rwanda, Tanzania, and Uganda), in which Congo is a region of especially "unimaginable violence"—rapes and massacres taking bizarre and inhuman forms. Katongole's special concern is to understand what specific concrete practices "rehumanize" human relationships and rebuild trust.[14]

Part of the answer is implicit in Katongole's title, *Born from Lament*. Lament has become an increasingly salient theme in theologies of protest and resistance.[15] Yet lament is often portrayed as the

---

11. María Pilar Aquino, *Our Cry for Life: Feminist Theology from Latin America* (Maryknoll, NY: Orbis Books, 1993), 107.

12. Zilkać Spahi Šiljak, "I Brought Neighbor to Neighbor: Danka Zelić," hapter 2 in *Shining Humanity: Life Stories of Women in Bosnia and Herzegovina* (Newcastle upon Tyne: Cambridge Scholars Publishing, 2014), 38–69.

13. Emmanuel Katongole, *Born from Lament: The Theology and Politics of Hope in Africa* (Grand Rapids, MI: Eerdmans, 2017).

14. Ibid., 15, 18–19, 80.

15. Emilie Townes, *Breaking the Fine Rain of Death* (Eugene OR: Wipf & Stock, 2006).

necessary first step to a course of action already assumed or begun, eliding the proximity of lament to real and justified despair. Here, Katongole distinguishes the Book of Lamentations from the psalms of lament. In the psalms, lament is a prayer to God that includes several elements: complaint, appeal to God, evidence for why God should respond, and *trust in or assurance of God's assistance*.[16] In the Book of Lamentations, however, "the people's prayer is bleak, bitter and without hope" (5:2–18). They have suffered atrocities and total destruction in the occupied land of Israel. The God of hope is a memory, not a presently encountered reality. The God encountered in lament is "contradictory," "at once liberating, abusing, silent, and indifferent."[17] This encounter is in *fact* a human dimension of the experience of God. The biblical recognition of a possibly abusive God is a consolation for those who "turn in and around God...in the midst of ruins," and are met only by divine silence.[18] Nevertheless, for Katongole, there are survivors of pathological violence whose stories bear out the possibility that hope can make a surprising appearance, fragile and unsteady, in the thick of despair. "There is no clear manual, no neat progression of steps, on how to move from lament to hope; no clear promise of going through lament and then living happily ever after." If hope comes in lamentations, it comes as "sheer gratuity."[19] Yet it comes.

Sometimes, those who are spared such suffering are counseled or exhorted to lament for and with those who are not, as a step in the way of repentance, deepened compassion, and resolute intervention.[20] But we also have good reasons to lament on our own behalf and even to despair. Here are two examples that resonate with challenges posed by other chapters in this volume. The first is the responsibility of white people for racism. Many have rightly named the need for white people to recognize the reality of white supremacy, and then for compassion,

---

16. Katongole, *Born from Lament*, 107–8.

17. Ibid., 58, cf. 111.

18. Ibid., 18–19.

19. Ibid., 55.

20. Bryan N. Massingale, *Racial Justice and the Catholic Church* (Maryknoll, NY: Orbis Books, 2012), 111.

repentance, and conversion.[21] Obviously, white people have been slow to heed this call. But the problem is worse than that. While the United States is well populated with conscious and unconscious racists, there are also a good number of whites who see that racism is a problem, are horrified by historical lynching and contemporary police violence against unarmed black men and boys, deplore the racially biased mass incarceration system, and relate positively to the #BlackLivesMatter movement. But even for them, racism seems like just too big and insidious a problem to take on systemically. There are too many complexities, too many irresolvable historical injustices, too many entangled causes, and too much knee-jerk residual bias even in those who sincerely abhor it. Our seeming paralysis is similar to the condition of constricted agency in the face of war and the application of just war principles that Paul Schulte calls by the French term *engranage*: "the condition of being enmeshed, at whatever scale of conflict, in a geared action-reaction system, which overrides or negates the possibility of individual reflection and judgement."[22] It also involves perverse incentives to evaluate incorrectly and make the wrong judgments. This makes it impossible to execute the considered and principled judgment on which just war tradition depends, just as it makes it difficult, if not impossible, for white people formed in a racist culture to get enough foothold outside it to evaluate it correctly and move to change. This is certainly cause for lament—and possibly cause for despair. Yet we have to ask whether and when despair is a luxury of the privileged. It is far more possible and even attractive for

---

21. In the words of Reggie Williams, "White supremacy defines white humanity as normative humanity in order to carve out space for whites only, to distribute goods, and to create systems and structures for the benefit of people racialized as normative white humanity. White supremacy is the historical pursuit of the idyllic community, framed by the social imaginary of an idealized humanity that informs politics, legal structures, how goods are distributed and how systems are created, and inspires the historical practice of terrorizing people of color into compliance as assimilated inferiors." See his "Empathic and Incarnational: A Better Christian Ethic at Fuller," *Fuller Magazine* 4 (2015): 54.

22. Paul Schulte, "Probing the Biggar Line: Strong Points and Vulnerabilities of an Anglican Defence of Britain's Latest Belligerent Century and of Wider Just War Theoretical Positions," *Studies in Christian Ethics* 28 (2015): 321. Schulte is a scholar of international conflict and peace studies and has served as a top official of the UK's post-conflict initiatives in Iraq and Afghanistan.

white people to "give up" on racism (emotionally and motivationally, if not intellectually) in a white supremacist society—than it is for those whose lives and those of their children are directly threatened by white supremacist violence. If "they" have hope, who are "we" to embrace despair? It is up to us to strengthen our resolve against injustice, especially if we are the perpetrators.

A second example reflects Larry Rasmussen's article on the environment, chapter 8 in this volume. As Rasmussen brings home with an overwhelming amount of evidence, our planet and its species are currently headed for an environmental apocalypse. The Union of Concerned Scientists does not exaggerate when it warns, "We have reached a tipping point on climate action—Scientists say we have roughly one decade left to avoid the most severe consequences of climate change."[23] Yet individual choices to adopt "greener" lifestyles fall far short of the massive changes that are needed. At the societal level, the political will to take decisive legal, judicial, and policy initiatives falls far short. The United States is withdrawing from the 2015 United Nations Paris Climate Accord, implementation by signatories is falling behind targets, and goals are continually under adjustment toward more "realistic" options. In such a situation, only those whose homes and families are immediately under climate assault seem energized and determined to change humanity's course. Yet their fates are no less disastrously entwined with the inaction of those for whom the apocalypse seems insuperable, distant, or avoidable—at least for the privileged few. Despair easily entices, but it is surely not the answer.

Instead, let me turn to the alternative of Christian eco-ethicist Willis Jenkins. His subject is the environment, but his approach applies equally well to other massive injustices that elude human resolve and resolution. In *The Future of Ethics: Sustainability, Social Justice, and Religious Creativity*, Jenkins's essential point is that some problems exceed what humans can understand and manage, given our limited abilities and our dysfunctional, unjust cultures. He calls

---

23. Union of Concerned Scientists, "Global Warming Impacts." https:// www. ucsusa.org/our-work/global-warming/science-and-impacts/global-warming-impacts.

these "wicked problems," and climate change is certainly among them. Wicked problems are so complex that they "outstrip a society's scientific and ethical competencies," leaving human agents in a state of "moral incompetence."[24] In response, Jenkins recommends a pragmatic, problem-based approach—not a theoretical analysis that begins with religious or philosophical premises, defines principles and norms, and takes these down to the level of "applied" ethics. The latter strategy is powerless in the face of wicked problems, yet it is one commonly adopted in religious and theological ethics. In Jenkins's view, religious ethics should adopt a "more pragmatic way of thinking" if it wants to play a more successful role in "adaptive social change."[25] Constructively, Jenkins argues that pragmatic reform projects, targeting specific ecological challenges, can be sources of creativity that expand cultural values and imagination, generating novel and innovative responses to global problems that, per se, exceed humanity's moral grasp. Religious worldviews, cosmologies, practices, and liturgies are particularly fruitful resources for limited and carefully targeted initiatives, which are potentially game changing because they can instigate change in a moral culture. Moral communities, especially when religiously inspired, can "open ways of practical hope from the midst of overwhelming problems."[26] Importantly, moral communities, themselves, are not only diverse and context-specific, even within Christianity; they learn and change by working across borders with other communities. Working concretely on a problem can "disrupt the complacency of a dominant-culture community," leading to a better and more just shared or at least overlapping politics.[27]

---

24. Willis Jenkins, *The Future of Ethics: Sustainability, Social Justice, and Religious Creativity* (Washington, DC: Georgetown University Press, 2013), 171; cf. 21–23 on moral incompetence.

25. Ibid., 20.

26. Ibid., 12.

27. Willis Jenkins, "Atmospheric Powers, Global Injustice, and Moral Incompetence: Challenges to Doing Social Ethics from Below," *Journal of the Society of Christian Ethics* 34 (2014): 78.

Glen Stassen's Incarnational Discipleship

Glen Stassen's paradigm of incarnational discipleship represents an insightful and useful way to envision Christian ethics in a transformationist, interventionist, and culture-changing mode. Yet, like any paradigm, it is limited in socio-historical origin, perspective, and range. Moreover, it was fallibly applied by Glen Stassen. Stassen did not consistently apply to or within his definition of incarnational discipleship the Niebuhrian lens on sin and social sin that Christian eschatology demands. This is because Christian eschatology, as "kingdom" or "reign of God" eschatology, envisions *both* that the Spirit of the risen Christ is already empowering historical transformation *and* that the historical realm is always an incomplete embodiment of salvation, remaining under the power of sin. This qualifies what can be meant by or expected of "incarnational discipleship" (Stassen) or "living as risen beings" (Jon Sobrino[28]). Relatedly, I will distinguish Christian eschatology from apocalyptic, noting that both have a place in the Bible and should continue to do so in Christian ethics. Christian social ethics premised on biblical eschatology demands both a world-engaging ecclesiology and a vision of hope that does not depend on certainty that "the arc of history bends toward justice."[29] Yet the reign of God does "break in" as dawn over a dark horizon.

A Christian ethics of hope is biblically valid and existentially necessary. But when Stassen argues that the Sermon on the Mount represents "transforming initiatives" that can actually transform situations of violence, and when he enumerates the practices that ensure this result, he can sound overly enthusiastic, optimistic, and naïve. In

---

28. Jon Sobrino, *Christ the Liberator: A View from the Victims*, trans. Paul Burns (Maryknoll, NY: Orbis Books, 2001), 1–16.

29. Dr. Martin Luther King is often quoted as saying "the arc of the moral universe is long, but it bends toward justice" (John Craig, "Wesleyan Baccalaureate Is Delivered by Dr. King," Hartford CT, *Hartford Courant*, June 8, 1964): 4. However, the origin of this saying has been attributed to others, including Theodore Parker, *Ten Sermons of Religion* (Boston: Crosby, Nichols and Company, 1853), 83–84.

A Thicker Jesus, Stassen has a chapter on "A Realistic Understanding of Sin and Selfhood," a necessary qualifier to his proposals for social action. But how much does the realism he calls for really qualify his own proposals? In the chapter on "War," Stassen claims that the ten peacemaking practices "actually are working to reduce wars." One piece of evidence is that the World War II generation "developed a number of practices like the spread of democracy and human rights, the Marshall Plan for rebuilding Europe economically, the unification of Europe, [and] the United Nations."[30] But objections immediately ensue. Today, democracy has brought us populist, xenophobic nationalism; we have seen a worldwide economic recession that left some European economies in tatters; the United Kingdom voted to leave the European Union; and the United Nations has no enforcement power and declining moral authority in an environment where international laws, accords and treaties can be disregarded with virtual impunity by superpowers. As more recent examples of the success of nonviolent action, Stassen gives the Arab Spring and initiatives of West Bank Palestinians—which in retrospect hardly prove his point.

In my view, Stassen's model of incarnational discipleship would have been more accurate and persuasive if he had, first, remembered with Reinhold Niebuhr (with credit to Augustine), that those whose interests are served by the status quo will rarely relinquish power or advantage unless they are directly or indirectly forced to do so. Second, Stassen's enthusiasm for the potential success of "transforming initiatives" got in the way of clarity about the fact that history is a series of some steps ahead, followed certainly by an indeterminate number of steps backward, sometimes in greater number than those already accomplished in the right direction. Moreover, success in any given area of justice often or usually involves negotiation and compromise, with the result that justice is always partial and in progress.

A more realistic assessment of the kind of resolution of armed conflict for which Christians can hope is offered by the Catholic peacebuilding theorist, Daniel Philpott. Philpott proposes an ethic of "political reconciliation" that takes as its point of departure the fact that conflict leaves deep social and personal "wounds" that never will

---

30. Stassen, *A Thicker Jesus*, 197.

be fully eradicated. Justice in the wake of conflict requires "the restoration of right relationship," a process that will never be unambiguous or complete.[31] This restoration is always "suffused with blemish." "If the practices were ineffectual, the ethic would be futile; if they did not involve partiality, compromise, and intractable dilemmas, the ethic would be pointless."[32] Nevertheless, just peace and just peacemaking or peacebuilding can and should be undertaken concretely, contextually and pragmatically, because they are bearers of human, Christian, and political hope; and because people devastated by conflict persevere in their cause. For Philpott and others, they can and should involve enforcement of the rule of law, reparations, and just punishment when necessary to avoid an ethos of impunity.

In his chapter on sin, Stassen grants that Christian ethics needs more "realism and honesty," including recognition that Christians and the churches are in solidarity with sin and sinful structures, not entirely outside them.[33] In Stassen's *Just Peacemaking*, the need for coercive power against sin comes through more clearly than in *A Thicker Jesus*, in the discussion of civil disobedience and the U.S. civil rights movement.[34] Nevertheless, Stassen does not really push the question of what forms noncooperation and resistance will actually need to take to be effective. He does not take up the difference between Martin Luther King and Malcolm X over strategies, for example, as does the Catholic ethicist, Bryan Massingale. At the end of the day, we may have to consider both whether Christian political action against injustices of many kinds can be as effective as Glen expected and whether it can be limited so thoroughly to means that are Christ-like and conversionary.

Nevertheless, Niebuhr himself did believe that love-informed justice can extend the "spirit of brotherhood" against the territory of

---

31. Daniel Philpott, "Reconciliation: A Catholic Ethic for Peacebuilding in the Political Order," in *Peacebuilding: Catholic Theology, Ethics, and Praxis*, ed. Robert J. Schreiter, R. Scott Appleby and Gerard F. Powers (Maryknoll NY: Orbis Books, 2010), 95.

32. Ibid., 106.

33. Ibid., 124.

34. Glen H. Stassen, *Just Peacemaking: Transforming Initiatives for Justice and Peace* (Louisville, KY: Westminster John Knox Press, 1992), 50–51.

sin,[35] and that it can change communities and structures to more nearly approximate justice. In fact, though every historical advance risks a historical contradiction, Niebuhr still urges, "We must [and implicitly can] seek to fashion our common life to conform more nearly to the brotherhood of the Kingdom of God."[36] This is the aim for which Stassen too hopes, and the possibility in which he trusts. In particular contexts, there can emerge *kairos* moments, and even *kairos* trajectories and eras, in which some definite outcome is either clearly to be desired or clearly to be repudiated, and in which we can and should invest our efforts—with hope.

Jesus and the Reign of God

The present century of biblical scholarship provides a surge of interest in Jesus' Jewish background, his inherent Jewish identity, and the ways in which early Christianity remained a Jewish movement and transmitted to later generations of Christians lasting aspects of Jewish faith and community. Jesus' eschatology is a form of Jewish apocalyptic, which he distinctively interprets.[37] When the Jewish people returned from exile in the sixth century BCE, they were to remain under foreign rule through the time of Jesus, and long after. While the hope that God would appoint a new political future for the Jews under a king like David waned, the hope for a final apocalyptic vindication by divine power at the end of history grew.[38] Jesus certainly shared the Jewish expectation that God would vindicate Israel with a future, decisive act. This type of future vision can be politically ac-

---

35. Reinhold Niebuhr, *The Nature and Destiny of Man*, vol. 2 (New York: Scribner's, 1944), 248.

36. Ibid., 308n10.

37. Sean Freyne, "Jesus the Jew," in *Jesus as Christ*, ed. Andrés Torres Queiruga et al. (London: SCM Press, 2008), 24–32; and E. P. Sanders, *Judaism: Practice and Belief, 63 B.C.–66 A.D.* (London: SCM Press, 1992). For a general definition of apocalyptic with Jewish and Christian examples, see Howard Clark Kee et al., *Cambridge Companion to the Bible* (Cambridge: Cambridge University Press, 2007), 306.

38. Daniel J. Harrington, *Jesus: A Historical Portrait* (Cincinnati: Franciscan Media, 2007), 22–23.

quiescent because it is historically hopeless in the face of powerlessness against dominant powers. This is why it is not the only strand included in the biblical canon. There are more revolutionary strands even in Jewish apocalyptic, for instance, Daniel 7. In Isaiah's vision of a renewed Jerusalem, "the servants of Yahweh" who have neither worshiped idols nor oppressed the poor already enjoy his blessings (Isaiah 65:1–15, 66:14).[39]

Nevertheless, the future-oriented apocalyptic dimensions of Jewish faith and in the outlook of Jesus still have relevance for Christian ethics. Evil is often victorious over righteousness in the historical sphere, and many of those who embody God's reign will be subject to suffering and death. The apocalyptic strands of biblical faith—incorporated in the Book of Revelation—offer consolation by assuring the faithful of God's power, providence, and prevailing justice.[40]

Jesus certainly retained the future expectation of his fellow Jews, as heard in his call to repent in view of the nearness of the kingdom (Mark 1:17); and in the prayer he taught his disciples, "Your kingdom come, your will be done, on earth as it is in heaven" (Matt 6:10).[41] Yet he also challenged and destabilized the authority of both imperial and religious elites, culminating in the action in the temple during Passover that led to his arrest and execution. As the earliest Gospel, Mark, announces, "Jesus came to Galilee, proclaiming the good news of God, and saying, 'The time is fulfilled, and the kingdom of God has come near; repent, and believe in the good news'" (Mark 1:14–15).

The kingdom or reign of God is a social and political metaphor and a key to Jesus' ministry. The renewed community to which Jesus summons his followers involves love of God and neighbor, open-table fellowship with socially disreputable sorts such as tax collectors and sinners, and—by extension—inclusion of other outsiders. As Jesus tells the Pharisees, "the kingdom of God is among you" (Luke

---

39. Freyne, "Jesus the Jew," 103–8.

40. See J. Matthew Ashley, "The Turn to Apocalyptic and the Option for the Poor in Christian Theology," chapter 7 in *The Option for the Poor in Christian Theology*, ed. Daniel G. Groody (Notre Dame, IN: University of Notre Dame Press, 2007), 132–54.

41. Ashley, "Turn to Apocalyptic," 23–24.

17:21b). The synoptic Gospels underwrite this vision through their narratives of Jesus' exorcisms, miracles, teaching "with authority" (cf. Luke 4:32), and even forgiving (cf. Mark 2:10, Matt 9:6). Jesus was not a social revolutionary in the sense of mounting a movement to overthrow imperial power. Yet, his teachings, actions, and community-formation are radically threatening to all oppressive historical structures.

It is not yet time to turn our backs on this-worldly Christian hope. Through his life, death and resurrection, Jesus inaugurates a new and divinely willed order in which we can participate. Our transformational efforts will be pragmatic, solidaristic, always limited, and not always successful. Yet God's reign dawns or is "incarnate" in Jesus' disciples when they embody compassion, forgiveness, reconciliation, and generosity—as well as when they actively resist and restrain injustice.

TWO

Toward an Incarnational Theology of Identity

Jacob Alan Cook

In our interactive age of densifying pluralism, can we name an ethic that will draw Jesus' followers into a faithful way of life? While his project has many moving parts, Glen Stassen describes his own aim for *A Thicker Jesus* in terms of two questions: (1) How do we "find a faithful and solid identity for faith and ethics"? and (2) How can that identity "be a compass in our rapidly changing and interactive age"?[1] He is looking for an ethic that avoids idealism in the epistemological sense (i.e., ferreting out all the changeless, timeless content of such an identity) and that realistically attends to the living, biblical, historical Jesus. In the West, by Charles Taylor's account, it is easier to live within a disenchanted, impersonal world than one in which God is a known, personal agent. Stassen's work, however, entails what Jim McClendon has called "the baptist vision,"[2] which makes us contemporaries with Jesus' first disciples in our experience of Jesus: what is before us is analogous to what was before them, the church then is the church now. So, as he did for his embodied contemporaries in the first century, Jesus meets us where we are, and from that point on, our identities and our responsibilities are made clear—or at least

---

1. Glen Harold Stassen, *A Thicker Jesus: Incarnational Discipleship in a Secular Age* (Louisville, KY: Westminster John Knox Press, 2012), 4.

2. James Wm. McClendon, Jr., *Ethics: Systematic Theology*, vol. 1, rev. ed. (Nashville: Abingdon Press, 2002), 17–44.

thrown into sharp relief. In this chapter, we will first encapsulate Stassen's ethic in *A Thicker Jesus*, then test it against the "incarnation" theme in Taylor's *A Secular Age*, and, finally, draw on these sources to suggest some new directions for a theological ethic of identity.

Stassen's Quest for an "Identity"

What especially worries Stassen about the secularizing forces in our world is their operations on, within, and through the church and the sense that the social orders of the day have captivated the hearts and minds of those who are otherwise identifying with Jesus. So, secularism defined as a social imaginary, in which the idea of God does not occur to many people and a personal God arises for even fewer, is not the only trouble; Stassen is concerned about the church's evasion of Jesus while identifying his kingdom with any number of sinful, worldly projects. This state of affairs represents a breakdown of Christian identity that facilitates a misshapen understanding of discipleship, neighborliness, and love of enemies as well as overall responsibility (to God and to others). Or, we might say, our thin discipleship in the church is quietly made thinner by a number of sinful, worldly discipleship programs—like the racism, capitalism, and militarism to which Stassen calls attention. As such, when bad gives way to worse, too many Christians are left without the capacity or resources to resist ideologies' call to arms, call to die for "the cause" as one has lived. Especially susceptible to this posture toward sinful structures are those who regularly enjoy the privilege and false security of identity-based power that regularly goes unnamed in modern societies—such that capital-I Ideologies and Influences need not announce their names in order to operate on, within, and through individuals. When such ethics come to be articulated as Christian ethics, they invariably comprise some number of convictions that come from other sources and run counter to Jesus' mission. One can assume that Stassen's intended audience may be found primarily among those who develop Christian ethics within the frames of Christendom (especially as wedded to partisan political agendas) and Capitalism. And we rightly mourn that

Stassen did not articulate a clearer picture of the machinations by which whiteness has hidden itself so lastingly in modern worldviews.

What Stassen has in mind in terms of "identity" is different from the conversation about Christian identity that we will argue can most faithfully set our compasses in our broken-but-cherished world, yet key elements on offer in *A Thicker Jesus* (especially the chapters on sin and the cross) might be refigured and recast in the light of other much-needed learning. When Stassen articulates the identity he has in mind, it is more specifically an *identifiable tradition*, namely "incarnational discipleship," which he hopes will unite those who share a certain set of convictions and practices to resist modern secularism—something like "Radical Orthodoxy" has done for John Milbank and company. This incarnational discipleship tradition, for Stassen, is a cord of three theological strands that takes seriously Jesus' incarnation and our own enfleshed lives: (1) heeding the practical guidance from a thick (i.e., the living, biblical, and historical) Jesus in which good exegesis is critical; (2) opening one's whole life to this guidance such that it permeates all sectors of life and not only one's inner life or most basic personal relationships; and (3) responding to the Holy Spirit who prompts repentance, processes of peacemaking, and progress toward truer ways of knowing God, self, and others. This last part, understood well, surely includes repentance for ideological principalities and powers of our own making that have expanded beyond our control as well as "the sin embedded within our own Christian traditions."[3] Stassen is concerned that we encounter the living, biblical, historical Jesus whose ministry entails not only compassion but also confrontation. Writing in the first person, Stassen argues: "In Jesus Christ, we are confronted by God, who enters into our place of evasion, deception, and shame and takes us with our sin into community. By this invasive work, God transforms us in Christ."[4] So, therefore, continuous repentance for our wayward allegiances entails dying to oneself by a thousand cuts. As a matter of discipleship, or *Nachfolge* (following-after), those who would identify (with) Jesus over time must pay attention to how Jesus identifies (with) both *us*

---

3. Stassen, *A Thicker Jesus*, 124.
4. Ibid., 150.

and *others*. And as we are implicated, as we are made responsible, we must choose ever and again to respond to the Holy Spirit as the axes of identity-based power pull their levers.

Charles Taylor's "Incarnation" Theme

With the kernel of Stassen's ethic in mind, I would like to highlight five distinct points around which Taylor himself, in *A Secular Age*, demonstrates his partiality toward a loose tradition in church history that he takes to be the beating heart of "orthodox Christianity" (his term)—namely, among those focused on the incarnation.[5]

First, Taylor observes that traditions motivated by Jesus' humanity have often risen in response to the trends of disenchantment and what he calls "excarnation" in the life of the church and its surrounding cultures. Taylor speaks of excarnation as a de-prioritization of bodily matters, along with the emotion and contingency of human existence in time and space.[6] In his own words, excarnation is "a transfer out of embodied, 'enfleshed' forms of religious life, to those which are more 'in the head.'... The issue is whether our relation to the highest... is mediated in embodied form.... Or looking to what moves us towards the highest, the issue is to what degree our highest desires, those which allow us to discern the highest, are embodied, as the pity captured in the New Testament verb 'splangnizesthai' plainly is."[7] By Taylor's account, the incarnation strand has emphasized several key points, including (a) the bearing of faith on all aspects of life (i.e., a holistic faith),[8] (b) the dignity of all human persons as particular individuals, and (c) an expansion of Christian community to embrace those who suffer oppression's many faces and, often relatedly, have been excluded from the prevailing institutional church's life. This assessment of an identifiable incarnation

---

5. For instance, Taylor glosses Christianity as "faith in the Incarnation" (*A Secular Age* [Cambridge, MA: The Belknap Press, 2007], 93).

6. Taylor, *A Secular Age*, 288.

7. Ibid., 554.

8. Ibid., 144.

strand is an account of *historical facts* for Taylor. His project is not as ambitious as Stassen's in terms of establishing a normative account of discipleship, but it should be noted well that the themes just named feature centrally in Stassen's account of incarnational discipleship. We should maintain a healthy skepticism about the extent and evenness of any supposedly attained inclusion or recognition of dignity—especially in white circles. But there is a connection here somewhere that might contribute positively to the conversation: encountering Jesus in his humanity (i.e., his particularity, his living personhood) opens us to the genuine divine-human communion that disrupts and liberates, to the God who sees with compassion and restores.

Second, when considering "the stress on the human suffering Christ,"[9] Taylor describes Jesus' incarnation as a divine initiative to enter into our experience and restore communion. He reads many traditional atonement theories as fitting Jesus' suffering "into an already existing framework of significance, whereby suffering was seen as punishment or pedagogy, the economy of which was altered by Christ's sacrifice."[10] But, Taylor continues:

> We could start somewhere quite different, see suffering and destruction as often themselves devoid of meaning, and see the self-giving of Christ to suffering as a new initiative by God, whereby suffering repairs the breach between God and humans, and thus has not a retrospective or already established, but a transformative meaning.... We start with the fact of human resistance to God, closure towards God who could heal the consequences of this resistance, which we call sin. This is the first mystery. God's initiative is to enter, in full vulnerability, the heart of resistance, to be among humans, offering participation in the divine life. The nature of the resistance is that this offer arouses even more violent opposition, not a divine violence, more a counter-divine one.[11]

---

9. Ibid., 93.
10. Ibid., 654.
11. Ibid.

Stassen is more willing than Taylor to construe the element of nonviolent resistance *as resistance*, but the commonality between the two thinkers is a way of explaining how Jesus' posture leading up to and through the cross accomplishes the work of atonement. By entering into human life, then loving and offering communion even in the face of opposition, Jesus evokes further resistance from the powers that seek to secure the world for themselves on their own terms. And by living a denial of the world's power to generate perpetual resistance and violence, "a path is opened of non-power, limitless self-giving, full action, and infinite openness."[12] Now, we have plenty of reasons to resist the idealization of limitless self-donation as central to discipleship to the detriment of those whose dignity is routinely challenged by others who have power in and around their lives. But in this moment, Taylor is framing Jesus' way of incorporating a catastrophe into the "providential story" of God; it is all in how Jesus responds to what human beings throw at him. As such, what matters is not so much what has *gone before* but what *goes forth* from the point of suffering. Stassen echoes this sentiment and adds, "But we still fear that we will disobey and distrust and be hostile once again, and therefore will be rejected. We fear trusting God. Therefore, we need God to receive our hostility in the cross and show that it does not cancel the offer of presence and incorporation."[13] In the face of our potential falling away again into idealist-teleological categories and measures of success or failure—and into the jockeying, coercion, and violence that often comes with them—the incarnate God continues to incorporate us into communion as persons. Several significant sub-points spin off of these first two in Taylor's work.

Next, or third overall, Taylor describes the primary objective in the incarnation as that moment in which God *brings communion to us*. As Taylor explains, salvation is (effected by) our being in communion with God through community with others (namely, the church), and salvation itself is subverted when God and self and others are treated as mere objects or concepts or mechanisms rather than persons.[14]

---

12. Ibid.

13. Stassen, *A Thicker Jesus*, 166.

14. Taylor, *A Secular Age*, 278–79.

"Body, heart, emotion, history; all these make sense only in the context of the belief that the highest being is a personal being, not just in the sense of possessing agency, but also in that of being capable of communion."[15] There is no excarnate, impersonal order to which we should relate, because God is a living being, a person; this is a theology of relationality, not an epistemology that empowers individual access to the rational order of the universe. If we want to know what it means to be human, for ourselves or for any others, Taylor tells us, we may only truly know in relation to the one, unique God-Man.[16] Only in communion are human beings integrated into their true nature, or *identities*, "as bodily beings who establish their identities in their histories, in which contingency has a place."[17] Contingency becomes a key element here, for salvation is worked out in the actual relations of humans as they bump into each other in this world. Unpacking the story of the Good Samaritan, Taylor explains, "My neighbor is someone I come across, bleeding in the road. It was sheer accident that I came along at just that time; but this accident can be the occasion for rebuilding a skein of human relations animated by agape."[18] Here, we might connect with Stassen's language of *participative* grace.

Fourth, and importantly tied to the last point, the eschatological horizon is where all individuals' stories in all their rich variety are ultimately worked out in the Great Story gathered together in eternity—none is negated, each is embraced and hallowed as the life-story of a real-life creature with limits.[19] The significance of particularity means recognizing the value of difference, not least in experiences with God in Christ. A focus on Jesus' unique incarnation ends up foregrounding the particularity of all individuals in their fullness, in their embodied context, in their incarnate selves; the particular is given "new status...as something more than a mere instantiation of

---

15. Ibid., 278.
16. Ibid., 94.
17. Ibid., 279.
18. Ibid., 277.
19. Ibid., 765–66.

the universal."[20] This focus on the particular also betokens a communion of grace that can take in an individual's whole story—all of which "belongs to the end," Taylor tells us, "not just the last state it arrives at."[21] He goes on to talk about the import of saints in these terms: "These are the paths to God of different people, and it is the paths which are being gathered, not just their upshots. The stories are also stories of sin, but the sin is also the occasion of mercy, of turning, and as such can be taken up."[22] Taylor's account of "history," if we want to call it that, is quite beautiful in this light: "The significance of history, which enters eternity as gathered story, entails the significance of the individuals whose identities are worked out in these stories."[23] The stories end well, to be sure, but not because they are scripted from the beginning; instead, by Taylor's account, "God's Providence is his ability to respond to whatever the universe and human agency throw up."[24] Rather than thinking of all human persons losing themselves and their individuality in acceding to the eternal, individuals are instead drawn—story and all—into the kingdom of God.

Fifth, Taylor indicates that the vision of our religious ethics should itself be incarnate—that is, it should suit embodied life. For the idealist in Plato's vein, "we reach our highest state in a condition beyond the body; being incarnate is a hindrance."[25] Many Christian ethics that Stassen is working against carry something of this idea in them as they press on toward a lofty, unattainable, excarnate telos. And in Taylor's analysis, "When the firm identification with a present or past order is consolidated, faith can too easily become defined in terms of certain codes and loyalties (or these codes and loyalties are boosted by their consecration in religion), and those who fall outside these tend to appear more easily as renegades than fellow Christians from whom one may have something to learn."[26] An ethic

---

20. Ibid., 94.
21. Ibid., 277.
22. Ibid.
23. Ibid.
24. Ibid.
25. Ibid., 275–76.
26. Ibid., 766.

that centers on communion in personal relationships with God and others may always be vulnerable to ideological cooptation, not least as the language and concepts of sacrifice and submission are abstracted and made serviceable to categorical societies. The incarnation disrupts our traditional ways of knowing, our traditional bases of identity security, and in its light, Jesus tells us who we are, shows us who our neighbors are. And as we move forward, such an identity cannot be deemed "solid" on the basis of its "haveability"; identification with Christ can only ever be secured in a relationship of grace with the one who came, who died, and who was raised again to new life. The goal in a life of following-after the living, biblical, historical Jesus is not merely instantiating an idealist ethic but living a with-God life.

An Incarnational Theology of Identity?

While Stassen is arguing in his own terms developed over a long career and drawing from different sources, his work runs parallel to much of what Taylor describes as a perennial, *incarnational* move. Reviewing the material from Taylor not only affirms "incarnational" as a viable identifier for an ethic that resists depersonalized social orders and excarnate idealisms; Taylor's particular emphases also add some new conceptuality and language for deliberation as we consider how to build from Stassen's work. In the face of emerging excarnate idealisms and heteronomous, categorical societies over time, Taylor tells us, Christians emphasizing Jesus' humanity have dignified the holistic, embodied nature of human life and increasingly extended the bounds of gracious and liberating community. And Stassen sees incarnational discipleship as identifying an ethic that is fundamentally embodied and resists idealisms in their various forms, all the way back to Plato and up through (we might say more explicitly here) "whiteness," especially as tied to its manifestations in Christian churches. This ethic entails a commitment to: (1) a thick (i.e., the living, biblical, and historical) Jesus who inhabits particularity in ways that liberate and disrupt; (2) a faith that takes seriously how communion with God permeates all sectors of life; and (3) an openness to the Spirit who prompts repentance, promotes peacemaking, and guides us into deeper understanding—including of our own blind spots. The idea that we might be calling something like *this* loose ethic "incarnational discipleship" is semantically correct in that it focuses on Jesus' humanity and our following-after him in the fullness of our own enfleshed lives; and there is something here that describes my own project.

At this point, I would like to begin again at the theological sense of the incarnation we get in Stassen's chapters on sin and the cross, especially his view of Jesus as entering empathetically into our situation to restore communion. What I develop below proceeds from the baptist vision and its conviction that the risen Jesus enters into the lives of would-be contemporary followers in much the same way he did with the first disciples. This interaction entails Jesus disturbing disciples' stable bases of identity certainty and calling them to follow-after him in a disruptive, restorative, reorienting practice of identifying with others. Jesus calls twenty-first-century Christians to wake up to how we and others have been ascribed social power on the basis of race, gender, class, sexual orientation, citizenship, and other categories and to where that social power is being transfigured into *theopolitical* power—such that those who already enjoy social power (e.g., straight, white American evangelicals) also become de facto authorities on Jesus' identity, God's will, and so on. Some of this may ring true of certain sources, certain heroes, in Stassen's project, and I think he would welcome the confrontation and ensuing conversation that could sharpen his analysis and use of such sources. In any case, our approach to identity security and the levers of power must be refigured to fit a new reality, a new life after death to self by a thousand cuts (i.e., to the ways, certainties, and powers of old selves).

All social identities and power axes are drawn into the disciple's following-after Jesus, such that they become obstacles in their impenitence or instruments of the kingdom by way of their inversion—being turned inside out for the good of others. Jesus encounters all people with a certain love and affection; and seeing each person as a person exactly where they are in their particularity and contingency, his good news is fit for their need at the time and at every time. For those whose daily experience is often very near to death, who assert their dignity in the face of those who would deny it, Jesus affirms their dignity by joining them in solidarity (as in his own incarnation and death) and offers restoration: God is with you, in it, working on your behalf to redeem the mess and honor your dignity. For those whose daily experience, whose disposition and affect, are ostensibly enriched at the expense of these others, Jesus meets them with resistance, disrupting their comfortable patterns of knowing and transforming their social statuses into sites for kingdom work—humbling, even humiliating, the powerful who must turn their allegiances inside out. Jesus' call is always a real-time, concrete ask of humans. Without the promise of success in worldly terms, he invites his followers into an everyday faithfulness that results in myriad forms of both asserting dignity in the face of powers that operate only as the world does and using one's ascribed power inversively. The latter strategy entails not simply (and safely) wielding that power better to benefit "the least of these" but prioritizing one's holistic identification by and with Christ in full view of once-similar, socially powerful others, whose response may predictably include disownment and disavowal. And meeting us in our complexity, Jesus will undoubtedly deploy different moves or combinations of these moves over time.

Many Christians want to start with the assumption that they know who Jesus is and the thrust of his progressive, social justice message. On the basis of this purported knowledge, Christians may also identify the marginalized person and seek to be Jesus' hands and feet to them, condescending (in a way they imagine to be like Jesus in the hymn of Philippians 2) from a place of privilege to meet others' needs. Yet in Jesus' own words, the kingdom is already nearer to those who experience oppression in this world and, in fact, he himself is (in some way) freshly incarnate among such persons as made clear in Matthew 25. Problematizing the question "What Would Jesus Do?" Jennifer Harvey encourages her (privileged) white reader to test out different roles in biblical stories.[27] For instance, in the

---

27. Jennifer Harvey, "What Would Zacchaeus Do? The Case for Disidentifying with Jesus," in *Christology and Whiteness: What Would Jesus Do?* ed. George Yancey (New York: Routledge, 2012), 84–100.

story of Jesus' encounter with Zacchaeus, the latter acknowledges his sin and, to enter into community with Jesus and others, he repents and pays reparations. Harvey argues that white folks should more often be asking "What Would Zacchaeus Do?" Those who feel compelled to identify (with) Jesus for others must first hear the lament of the other as the voice of Jesus to them—identifying them and their place in the communion of persons. This voice, when recognized in its dignity, creates the occasion for responsibility, repentance, and restorative action.

Furthermore, no one can start out thinking they can rightly identify Jesus, however thick he may be. Firstly, we can encounter him as one who speaks truth, be identified by him, and then seek to learn what we can in relationship. Jesus' call makes the same claim on all people in a limited sense, but his claim on each person or community is quite particular. "Who do you say that I am?" he asks—not *how*, but *who*. We may identify (with) Jesus only as he shows/tells us here and now who he is, who we are, and who others are. We must see with whom he identifies and join in solidarity as called in the moments of life. This identification leads to continuous repentance according to the contingent nature of our lives and the accidental nature of our responsibility as we actually encounter others. For some, identifying (with) Jesus is more disruptive, for others more restorative. To repeat my claim: for some, the call to die is not so far from their lived reality—at the very least in terms of an identity configuration that secures their embodied life—and for others, the call comes at great expense, real pain in terms of embodied comfort and security. Those on the margins already cannot rely on their identities (Christian or otherwise) to secure them social power, to secure their place in the world. And those who can must renounce their false security, established in their identity certainty (e.g., their false sense of selfhood based on their whiteness, their privilege, etc.) must die to those things in order to live with the personal God.

The search for a more solid, more comprehensive ethic than the communion at the heart of the emerging thesis is tempting but risks premature epistemic closure in the form of another conceptual Jesus. There is an irony in trying to capture both how Jesus as a person interacts with each of us differently in our utterly contingent lives and the multipronged *pattern* we may discern in scripture and more contemporary lives for how Jesus interacts with individuals. (It is like Søren Kierkegaard systematizing the "leap into faith.") The reliability of our own structures (this is me, from my social location) for determining these patterns is deeply suspect—given our own tendencies to misplace our confidence and mishandle our power in self-serving ways. We must resist abstracting Jesus into a thin principle or a predictable mechanism that doles out whatever judgment conforms to our thickest, most sanctified conscience. In the course of embodied human life, we cannot be helped much by projections from within the theological worlds of the confident "other" who wishes we would just take up his total worldview as our own. Rather, we need to be met in our thickness by others who are equally thick, whose inner constellation of selves may demonstrate for us more faithful patterns of living amid the principalities and powers that contend with each other to shape our lives; people who expose for us the ways in which our current self-configurations are concealing the infidelity of *convictional sins*. Put differently, we need to see and test how others navigate their many identities as they become sites for inner turmoil, ethical dilemmas, and genuine responsibility.

If there is something to this focus on the incarnation, then how can we do our best to identify (with) it? In contrast to whatever else we might want to call "identity," the solidity of a Christian identity is always in question. It is not found in assent to the idea of a Jesus who confronts, liberates, and saves; it is found in communion with the living, biblical, historical Jesus and in an expansive community that incarnates God's grace to us. Neither Jesus' identity nor our own identification with Jesus are "haveable" things we can seize and hold onto. An incarnational theology of identity, if we want to call it that, centers on an identity held in relationship with the living God in contrast to supposedly certain knowledge of good and evil and of God. At multiple points, Stassen speaks of human nature in terms of an "interactive self," and this conceptuality may well be the finest characterization of such selfhood. Human identity framed by the foundational reality of an interactive selfhood reckons more honestly with our embodied context and entails a mutually affirming, and (when necessary) confrontational, thickness. Such a theology reminds us that any sense of self—even a "Christian self"—centered in one's own self-understanding is ever on the brink of annihilation in an encounter with the Incarnate One.

THREE

Rejecting Stassen's Thick Jesus

Miguel A. De La Torre

My first professor of ethics was Glen Harold Stassen, whom I met while I was attending Southern Baptist Theological Seminary, which at the time was undergoing a fundamentalist takeover. When the seminary, under the leadership of its incoming president, Al Mohler, began purging what they considered to be liberals, theologically moderate professors needed either to retire or relocate to another institution. Stassen moved to Fuller Theological Seminary shortly after I graduated. Thanks to a powerful recommendation letter he wrote on my behalf, I was admitted into the doctoral program at Temple University. Graduating a few years later, I began a tenure-track position at Hope College.

Soon, Stassen and I reconnected when I joined the Society of Christian Ethics. In the summer of 2003, he honored me with an invitation to teach a course at Fuller. On one particularly sunny Pasadena day, he engaged me for hours in a spirited conversation, attempting to persuade me to accept and follow what he called a "thicker Jesus." He was concerned that ethicists had embraced a Jesus who was too thin and anemic. He argued for the embrace of a thickened Jesus, a process accomplished when the faithful make Jesus Lord over every aspect of their life rather than compartmentalize and relegate him to just religious rituals. He challenged me to accept a thickened Jesus and make him foundational to my own critical ethical thinking.

His argument would eventually become the thesis of his 2012 book: *A Thicker Jesus: Incarnational Discipleship in a Secular Age*. Stassen's evangelical zeal to convert me on the Fuller campus that day, and in the book he published almost a decade later, almost succeeded —for his sincerity was genuine, his commitment unwavering, his compassion heartfelt, and his persuasion powerful. In typical Baptist fashion, he ends his book with an altar call: "Now the one remaining question: Will you join in the apostolic witness to a thicker Jesus—in the tradition of incarnational discipleship?"[1] Stassen's good nature and sharp intellectual rigor were quite alluring; and had I been a Euro-American, I have no doubt I too would have walked down the proverbial sawdust aisle and given my heart to Stassen's thicker Jesus. But alas, I occupy a Latino body whose Jesús, like me, is immersed in my Latinx culture. As seductive as Stassen's altar call was, it nonetheless assumed that my Jesús was not thick compared to the Jesus that Stassen was trying to sell me.

My Jesús is already quite thick—thank you very much—as evident in my community's commitment to praxis that leads toward liberation. Jesús—with the accent mark placed over the letter "u"—is salvific for me; a non-accented Jesus is not. Privileging Jesús over and against Jesus literally attempts to do christology with a Latinx accent. The Gospel tells us of an encounter experienced by Pedro, who, incognito, sneaked into the courtyard of the high priest after the arrest of Jesús. While there, he was outed, not by his appearance, but by his Galilean accent. "Surely you are one of the followers of Jesús, your accent gives you away" (Matt 26:73, author's translation). I am consistently reminded that I speak "funny"; my accent always gives me away. In this chapter, I will boldly embrace my accented Jesús over and against Stassen's Jesus—no matter how thick he attempts to make his Jesus.

Although I reject Stassen's thicker Jesus, I nonetheless applaud his prophetic voice in seeking the conversion of his fellow skin-folk whom he believes follow a thin Jesus, even though those on the margins of whiteness recognized this Jesus not so much as thin, but, as

---

1. Glen Harold Stassen, *A Thicker Jesus: Incarnational Discipleship in a Secular Age* (Louisville, KY: Westminster John Knox Press, 2012), 221.

James Cone reminds us, satanic. Euro-Americans, who have accepted a nationalist Jesus who spiritualizes their complicity with white supremacy, desperately need the Jesús they have never known. However, when Stassen tried to convince me that my community is guilty of the same satanic christology his community embraced, I was left wondering if Stassen might be falling into the same Eurocentric trap of making his particular experience with Jesus normative for everyone. Stassen may write: "Trying to validate an ethic by an allegedly universal principle is no longer convincing";[2] nevertheless, he is guilty of the same universalization when he attempts to impose on my culture his thick Jesus void of any hermeneutical suspicion.

If the white Jesus is indeed satanic (as James Cone argued some fifty years ago), do we really want to make this Jesus thicker? Stassen did not live to see how the Jesus he hoped to thicken is beyond redemption. No greater proof is needed of how his white Jesus perverts Christianity than the 58 percent of Protestants, the 60 percent of white Catholics, the 61 percent of Mormons, and of course, the 81 percent of white evangelicals who voted for Trump in 2016. The majority of those who call themselves followers of this white Jesus voted for a person who promised them power and standing even though Trump's entire life has been a repudiation of everything Jesús modeled and taught. Maybe the task should not be to thicken this white Jesus, but to hasten his death and assist in digging the grave to bury him. The white Jesus is beyond reform; a new one, hailing from the margins of society, is needed if whites ever hope to achieve salvation. Whites can never be saved until they crucify their white Jesus!

My book, *The Politics of Jesús: A Hispanic Political Theology*,[3] was in part a response to Stassen's altar call, arguing that we Latinx ethicists neither ignore Jesús nor follow a thin Jesús. The book contends that all christologies are contextual. But not every context is liberating for Latinxs. Some contexts, specifically the Eurocentric context, have historically proven to be quite damning to those occupying Latinx

---

2. Ibid., 8.

3. Miguel A. De La Torre, *The Politics of Jesús: A Hispanic Political Theology* (Lanham, MD: Rowman & Littlefield, 2015).

bodies. The white Jesus has become the symbolic justifier of much global oppression, and, as such, is incapable of being redemptive for Latinxs. The crux of the problem is not that whites have a "thin" Jesus; rather, it is that their complicity with genocide, slavery, colonialism, neoconservatism, and neoliberalism demonstrate they have no Jesus whatsoever, and whatever they are calling Jesus is for the disenfranchised death-dealing masquerading as an angel of light. Through the reading of the Gospels, I demonstrate how deeply rooted are the ethics of Latinxs in the Jesús narrative, a narrative that resonates with the Latinx experience. The problem is that white scholars, like Stassen, failed to recognize the Jesús we Latinx follow. And while in my book, *The Politics of Jesús*, I focused on how, as a Latino, I read the scriptures from the Latinx margins, in this chapter, I will instead focus on Stassen's book, *A Thicker Jesus*, and why it is problematic for my community.

STASSEN'S THICK JESUS IS TOO WHITE

The problem with Jesus is not that he is too thin, but that he is too white, a whiteness that obscures the complicity with oppression of those whom Stassen believes were faithful in "historical times of testing." For example, Stassen argues that "the origin of democracy was not secularism; it was a Puritan movement, based on biblical understandings of covenant justice."[4] Whitewashed readings of history as expressed in statements such as this are exactly why Stassen's thick Jesus requires rejection by those on the margins of white interpretations of history. Puritans came to understand democracy in the United States through a Puritan worldview of white Christian supremacy based on an oppressive misunderstanding of both covenant and justice. For white nationalist Christianity, starting with the Puritans, all who fall short of the ideal of whiteness—even if Christian—reside outside of salvation history. Exclusion from the white Jesus and his salvation narrative has made the lives of the disenfranchised

---

4. Stassen, *A Thicker Jesus*, 59. Cf. Stanley Hauerwas and Romand Coles, *Christianity, Democracy and the Radical Ordinary* (Eugene, OR: Cascade, 2008).

living sacrifices to be offered up so God's frozen chosen can be assured an abundant life paid for with the blood of our crucifixion on the crosses of racism and ethnic discrimination.

What Stassen ignores is the flip side of so-called faithful democratic Puritans, who demonized the indigenous Other so that God-fearing whites could steal their winter provisions and slaughter them if they resisted. On May 26, 1637, a group of Puritan settlers from the Massachusetts Bay Colony raided and massacred the Pequot village at Missituck (modern-day Mystic, Connecticut). The economic and territorial competition between European settlers and indigenous people demonstrates how these Puritans read their Bible to exclude their Others from covenant justice. Puritan clergy justified genocide of the indigenous by pointing to alleged demonic and satanic beliefs held by "savages." According to Captain John Underhill's diary: "It may be demanded, Why should you be so furious (as some have said), should not Christians have more mercy and compassion? ... Sometimes the Scripture declareth women and children must perish with their parents. Sometimes the case alters, but we will not dispute it now. We had sufficient light from the Word of God for our proceedings."[5] The so-called God-centered devout and pious people to whom Stassen turns for their covenant of democratic justice justified starting the Pequot War and authorized the massacre of four to six hundred men, women, and children whom the Puritans defined as demon worshipers.

When Stassen looks to the Puritans as laying the foundation for the eventual constitutional democracy of the United States, he ignores that our Constitution had more to do with the Iroquois Confederacy that had existed since the sixteenth century than with whatever contributions the Puritans might have made. Before Puritans landed on Plymouth Rock, the Six Nations of the Iroquois Confederacy lived under a federalist constitution based on the three principles of peace, equity, and justice. Even Benjamin Franklin remarked that "if [the] six Nations of ignorant Savages [are] capable of forming a Scheme for such a Union" then surely those of European origin

---

5. Captain John Underhill, *Newes from America; Or, A New and Experimentall Discoverie of New England* (London: J. D. for Peter Cole, 1638), 40.

could do likewise.⁶ When we compare the U.S. Constitution to the Iroquois Confederacy, the similarities are striking; they have more in common than do the Constitution and the Mayflower Compact. Our democratic Constitution might have less to do with the Puritan's God or Bible and more to do with those whom Puritans perceived as demon worshipers.

A simplistic portrayal of those who were deemed faithful in historical times of testing also contributes to a romanticization of white people as liberators of the disenfranchised. We notice this in Stassen's treatment of Abraham Lincoln. He writes: "Lincoln was led to do what we now see was God's will by his commitment to the American tradition of human rights enumerated in the Declaration of Independence."⁷ Unfortunately, Lincoln's own writings make this statement false. Those familiar with the life and times of Lincoln know he was not an abolitionist, believing the solution for a divided nation should be for those of African descent to leave the Union for Africa or Central America, a notion he held as late as August 1862 while editing the Emancipation Proclamation. Furthermore, he rejected the idea that blacks should have the same rights as whites, as he said during the fourth Lincoln-Douglas Senate debate: "I will say then that I am not, nor ever have been, in favor of bringing about in any way the social and political equality of the white and black races."⁸ Even as late as April 11, 1865, in the last speech he ever gave, he argued for only imited black suffrage.

Stassen quotes Frederick Douglass's description of Lincoln as the "man of our redemption"⁹ to demonstrate blacks' adoration for white saviors, ignoring that Douglass's complimentary words, as

---

6. Lester C. Olson, *Benjamin Franklin's Vision of American Community: A Study in Rhetorical Iconology* (Columbia, SC: University of South Carolina Press, 2004), 18.

7. Stassen, *A Thicker Jesus*, 81.

8. Abraham Lincoln, "Never Have Had a Black Woman for Either a Slave or a Wife," *Lincoln on Democracy: His Own Words, with Essays by America's Foremost Civil War Historian*, ed. Mario M. Cuomo and Harold Holzer, rev. ed. (New York: Fordham University Press, 2004 [1858]), 129.

9. Stassen, *A Thicker Jesus*, 81.

well as those of other abolitionists, came only after Lincoln signed the Emancipation Proclamation—which freed no one because it still required a vote from Congress. All it did was free the slaves in the rebellious southern states over which he had no power; it did not free slaves in the Union or in the border states where he did have the power to act, making the misnomer "the Great Emancipator" somewhat problematic. I would agree that Lincoln was committed to the American tradition of human rights enumerated in the Declaration of Independence, human rights exclusively reserved for whites.

Most problematic is Stassen's turn to the pacifist John Howard Yoder as a model to emulate,[10] ignoring the violence he visited upon women since the mid-1970s. What is troubling is that by 1992, Yoder had been publicly confronted by the Prairie Street Mennonite Church in Elkhart, Indiana, with thirteen accusations of sexual abuse. Knowing this, Stassen nevertheless chose to include Yoder as an example in 2012 of one who was faithful in historical times of testing.[11] Ironically, Stassen dismisses Ayn Rand's thinking partly due to her "extramarital sexual relationship."[12] Do not misconstrue me; I believe that Rand's self-centered philosophy should be rejected for what she advocates, not for her lifestyle. However, if we are to pass judgment on her for her lifestyle, then the same gauge used to dismiss her must also be applied in judging Yoder. Further, by comparison, Yoder's acts were damning while Rand's were not, because her relationship was consensual while Yoder's actions were predatory. Stassen's incarnational discipleship saints must be measured with the same scrutiny. The inclusion of Yoder without teasing out his sexist abuses, even if he was a mentor and friend,[13] places Stassen in the awkward position of complicity with the ecclesiastical oppression of women.

One is left wondering if Stassen's romanticized examination of historical figures faithful to his understanding of incarnational

---

10. Ibid., 70–71.
11. Ibid., 14.
12. Ibid., 15.
13. Ibid., 70.

discipleship simply imposes his "thicker Jesus" upon the lives of historical figures (without their consent) to justify what Stassen hopes to contribute to the discourse. Unfortunately, relying on whiteness by ignoring the voices at the margins of whiteness works against any attempt to thicken the white Jesus. Instead, ironically, a thinning process is launched in spite of the best intentions of those committed to the thickening project. Rejecting Stassen's thick Jesus is necessary, for he presents a white historical perspective, ignoring the voices of those who have suffered because of it. This thick white Jesus is a house Stassen attempts to build on shifting sands.

Stassen's Thick Jesus Is Detrimental to Latinxs

Stassen's Jesus, thin or thick, is detrimental to Latinx well-being and mental health because the Jesus of Stassen's tradition and culture is simply not the Jesús of ours. To follow Stassen's Jesus would require an unbearable cut to our flesh and soul. Like some in the early church (cf. Acts 15:1–2), Stassen is asking me to self-circumcise so that I too can thicken my Jesús. Like the early Christian church that didn't know what to do with all those foreigners entering the faith, Stassen—with the best of intentions—is attempting to impose his cultural definition of Jesus upon me, an act that can be successful only if I self-circumcise. Fortunately, the debate no longer has to do with physically cutting off my foreskin. Instead, both women and men within our communities of color are being asked to cut off the foreskin of our identity, our culture, and the symbols by which we perceive the physical and metaphysical world.

To belong, the oppressed and repressed must first put on the Christian whiteface in order to be accepted. Accepting the white Jesus requires embracing the ritual of identity circumcision as our initiation to belonging—a death-causing cut deemed cheap and inconsequential by whites. To insist on my own Jesús only proves that—like the uncircumcised Gentiles of old—I *really* don't belong, and even if I am accepted, the inflicted cut of ethnic discrimination testifies that I will always be perceived as being somehow more primitive and uninformed, less scholarly, and somewhat backward regardless of how thick this white Jesus might become in my life.

STASSEN'S THICK JESUS NEEDS TO BE SAVED

Stassen wonders what it was "in Bonhoeffer's ethics [that] enabled him to see so truly while others failed."[14] The answer to Stassen's query is the Reverend Adam Clayton Powell Sr. Stassen asks the reader to look toward Dietrich Bonhoeffer as a model,[15] ignoring who Bonhoeffer looked toward. What Stassen misses is that Bonhoeffer's ethics were not due to a thicker Jesus, but to a black Jesus. Bonhoeffer's rejection of the white Jesus for the black Jesus is usually ignored because most white scholars who write about Bonhoeffer's six months at Abyssinian Baptist Church of Harlem focus on how black worship style influenced his ethical thinking. Attention is given to passionate black music or the emotional manifestations of worship. What few Euro-American scholars focus on are the intellectual contributions the black church—and particularly Adam Clayton Powell—made to Bonhoeffer's faith.[16]

According to Stassen, "the cross is God's entering into our shame with costly love." And while I may totally agree with Stassen on this point, we depart in what he considers to be "our shame." For Stassen, "our culture's worship of success leads us into shame when we fail or fear failure, and into shameful contempt for those who fail."[17] Echoing Reinhold Niebuhr's move to universalize pride as the root of all sins, Stassen imposes upon bodies of color shame as defined by how it resonates with white privilege. Shame for those falling short of whiteness is not the worship of success, but the

---

14. Ibid., 9.

15. Ibid., 43.

16. Some claim that Bonhoeffer, whom white scholars have associated with the term "cheap grace," learned this ethical principle during his student days at Union Theological Seminary from Powell. Ralph Garlin Clingan, *Against Cheap Grace in a World Come of Age: A Study in the Hermeneutics of Adam Clayton Powell, 1865–1953, in His Intellectual Context* (New York: Peter Lang, 2002), 4.

17. Stassen, *A Thicker Jesus*, 151.

shame colonized minds embrace for not occupying white skin. Not to be white becomes the shame induced. Thus, God entering our shame is God entering our skin, a radical act of solidarity with those crucified each day so whites can have life and life abundantly. Stassen's shame is so radically different from my shame because our contexts are so radically different. So, when he declares "they and we crucify him,"[18] I have to ask—who is the "we"? In the U.S. context, it is whiteness—and all the power, privilege, pride, and shame that whiteness signifies—that crucified Jesús, who now hangs on a cross alongside all those who also carry upon their flesh the stigma caused by white power, privilege, pride, and shame.

And while it could be argued Stassen was moving toward a more liberative understanding of the crucifixion with statements like: "[F]eminist and womanist theology in particular provide rich sources for understanding an incarnational atonement; God enters into human pain just as we are called to enter into the suffering of others, and also confronts injustice,"[19] he nevertheless still relies on the Eurocentric theological invention of personal atonement. I have no doubt that Stassen's heart was moving him to stand in solidarity with the crucified, but his universalization of the white Jesus continued to hamper his ability to move to radical solidarity.

Stassen's Thick Jesus Rests on the Illusion of Salvation History

A major component of Stassen's thinking is the concept of historical drama. He writes: "[H]istorical drama enacts time as events that participate in the next new event, time as continuous action in participative duration, not discrete moments that are separated from each other as one street is a block away from another."[20] Stassen uncritically accepts a progressive trajectory of time as the universal truth of

---

18. Ibid., 165.
19. Ibid., 171.
20. Ibid., 12.

the Logos. Salvation history—or any other form of progressive dialectical history—becomes crucial for Stassen (and many others) because it reinforces a stable and secure world that provides the privilege of ascertaining the movement of God's hand in the affairs of mere mortals. With Jesus' second coming, all of history will finally be comprehensible. But hope is provided in the messiness we call life. Rejecting the supposed determinism of the universe becomes an invitation to those accustomed to their stability and security to join the constant instability and insecurity that we who are relegated to their underside of time experience daily.

For Stassen, "the biblical expectation [is] of an order to history, since God is faithful.... God is working patiently and sometimes surprisingly through history to bring deliverance and community."[21] If indeed there is order to history, then, as Stassen suggests, "discerning the pattern required attention to the actual data of history."[22] Stassen makes the error many white Christian theologians and ethicists make: believing themselves to be historians, they impose a salvation history upon the passing of time. However, their embrace of salvation history is somewhat unsophisticated. Not explored in Stassen's thick Jesus is how the progressiveness of time becomes death-dealing to all who live in the shadows of salvation history where justice-based praxis is either absent or refashioned as some second act to Eurocentric universal theological concepts.

But what if, as I argue, there is no salvation history understood as a dialectical historical movement? What if Walter Benjamin and Michel Foucault are correct in their presentation of history as unrelated and unconnected events occurring in a nonlinear, disjointed, multidimensional passage of time? The past is not inferior to the future, for ages of ignorance can just as easily follow spans of enlightenment. Downward spirals are just as possible for our future as progressive upward treks. History exists neither as the salvation history of religious proponents like Stassen nor as the salvation history of secular thinkers like Hegel, Smith, or Marx. History is not

---

21. Ibid., 9.
22. Ibid.

an unfolding dialectic flow (metaphysical or materialist) moving linearly, uplifting human progress toward some logical teleological conclusion. Instead, history is non-evolutionary and disconnected, absent of linear successions and lacking a straightforward progressive narrative. It is fascinating that theologians and ethicists still insist on the concept of a linear history tied to some divine purpose, an idea rejected by historians during similar conversations from the 1860s to the close of the Second World War. If historians are correct and no such thing as universal linear progressive history exists, if history can best be understood as ateleological, then the hope Stassen holds onto is but an optimistic illusion.

I argue that the past is fluid, always evolving into new meanings, always changing in its significance, always being reconstructed by those connecting today's act to yesterday's unrelated events so as to justify their current actions. The past is whatever (dis)membered memories we choose to (re)member; and once we give this past meaning, we neatly place it in some artificial dialectical movement while labeling it some type of universal historical progress. We indulge in this illusion whenever we rely on the future to understand the present, predicting that the necessary acts taken today are to remain aligned with the harmony of the movement of history. My rejection of a religious salvation history, or a secular dialectical history, or any hybrid of the two, is an attempt to demystify the movement of time so praxis can be constructed and implemented based on what is occurring in the here-and-now. Simply stated: history's disjointedness has led Stassen to see patterns where none exists.

Stassen's Thick Jesus Condemns God

Stassen's God lacks complexity. For example, in his interpretation of the Cain and Abel story in Genesis, Stassen reads his theology into the tale by stating that "God seeks peacemaking,"[23] ignoring that the original cause of brotherly disharmony was the capriciousness of a God playing favorites, a pattern witnessed throughout the Hebrew

---

23. Ibid., 133.

Bible with devastating consequences. For Stassen, "God is sovereign through everything in creation."[24] With all my heart as a liberationist, I also want to proclaim: my God is the God of the oppressed who incarnates Godself among the least of these. But if God is indeed sovereign as Stassen claims, or the God of the oppressed as I want to claim, then God stands accused, for multiple examples abound concerning a God of liberation who fails to liberate. And to insist that God is in control, and that all things will work for good according to God's purposes, can sound hollow among disenfranchised Latinxs. The followers of Jesús ask that which Euro-Americans seeking to thicken their white Jesus have not yet dared to contemplate: Is God the God of the oppressor?

The God of the oppressor who rules has always been attested to by the biblical text, but our refusal to see was based on the imposition of the white Jesus who points to an all-good and all-powerful God. Whoever this God is whom the oppressed claim to follow, this is a God who slaughtered the firstborn of the Egyptians, an infanticidal act of unimaginable proportions that left behind wailing Egyptian nursing mothers (cf. Exod 11:4–6). This same God instructed God's chosen to steal the land of the indigenous people of Canaan and exterminate everything that breathed, including women and children (Jos 6:21; 10:40–41). This is a God delighting in dashing the heads of infants against rocks (Ps 137:9). This is a God who sends good and evil to the city (Isa 45:7; Amos 3:6); a God who sends evil spirits (Judges 9:23, I Sam 16:15ff., 18:10); a God who torments the righteous Job in order to win a bet; a God who, at times, appears more as a bastard than a redeemer.

How can this bloodthirsty God be the God of the oppressed? Are the inquisitors, conquistadores, colonizers, slaveholders, and today's neoliberals, who bow their knees to the Almighty, being more faithful to God's biblical ways than the oppressed who attempt to humbly wait for a deliverance which probably will never arrive in their lifetime? Once upon a time, God engaged in genocide (Canaan) for God's chosen. Does God still engage in genocide for God's new chosen who follow the white Jesus? Stassen's neat good-bad

---

24. Ibid., 92.

dichotomy when reading the text simplifies the complexity marginalized people face when forced to decide between the bad and the worse. The God that Stassen reads in scripture is a different God who raises different concerns from those of our Latinx community.

Stassen's Thick Jesus Stunts Liberative Methodologies

One should not be surprised that Stassen's white Jesus—like that of Yoder before him—leads to a nonviolent approach to oppression, especially when we consider Stassen's contribution of just peacemaking discourse. And while I agree with nonviolence as a methodology for liberation, the complexity of oppression makes clear dichotomies between violence and nonviolence somewhat naïve. Can nonviolence work when those victimized are not considered human? Imagine a Jew, at the dawn of World War II, going to the capital of Nazi Germany to reason with Hitler. Or an African American going to the deep South in the 1920s to reconcile with the Ku Klux Klan, or a Sioux warrior called to approach the U.S. cavalry on the eve of the Wounded Knee Massacre in the hope of arriving at some understanding. As noble as such peacemaking acts sound, the end result, more often than not, is subjugation or death for the messenger of hope because these are not meetings among equals attempting to seek justice. These are encounters with the powerful bent on maintaining their privilege by whatever means possible. Hence, just peacemaking means something different for those seeking Jesús as opposed to those advocating for the white Jesus.

I'm always concerned when white people living with the fruits generated by centuries of violence unleashed among communities of color—domestic and foreign—advocate nonviolence as the only methodological option available to us. Their complicity with oppressive structures responsible for institutional violence means they have lost all moral authority to dictate to marginalized communities how they can or cannot achieve their liberation. The only time whites can preach nonviolence is when in conversation with fellow whites complicit with white supremacy. The question for the followers of Jesús is not if Christians of color should participate in violence in their quest for liberation, but instead, do Christians of color have a right to defend themselves from the already existing institutional violence?

Stassen disavows violence as an ethical methodology, but for the marginalized communities, violence is already a reality, manifested whenever challenges are made to the dominant culture's grip on power. Such violence can be immediate or drawn out. Like César Chávez, "I am not a nonviolent man, I am a violent man trying to be nonviolent";[25] still, I must ask if there can be a biblically based principle for "just violence"? What would such a "just violence" look like as part of the quest for liberation in the face of the unjust violence required to maintain oppressive structures that benefit whites, like Stassen, who have not engaged in a critical race analysis? Violence, when employed by marginalized cultures to overcome their oppression, is self-defense and can never be confused with the continuing violence employed by those who are privileged by our current social structures.

Saying No to Stassen's Jesus

Writing this critique of Stassen's book has been a difficult task. He consistently demonstrated the best intentions for me and for humanity in general—oppressed and oppressors. Unlike so many white ethicists, he truly wrestled in seeking solidarity with the marginalized, a praxis that at times was costly for him. I liked Glen as a person and respected him as a scholar. And yet, as this critique of his work demonstrates, there exist major apprehensions concerning the Jesus he wishes to thicken. Out of friendship, do I remain silent about a christology I fear would be damning to Latinxs? Will my silence make me complicit with a train of thought I perceive harmful to my community? Because I was asked to participate in this project, I approach it with a certain degree of trepidation, taking great pains not to allow my love for the man to interfere with my assessment of his work.

---

25. Frederick John Dalton, *The Moral Vision of César Chávez* (Maryknoll, NY: Orbis Books, 2003), 143.

Reading about the Jesus Stassen hopes to thicken tells us more about the culture from which his Jesus narrative is constructed than anything specific about who historically or theologically Jesus was. If this is true, then all the Jesuses constructed serve the important function of uniting people into communities who share a similar quasi-religious political and economic worldview. Christian communities spanning different eras, occupying different geographical locations, and composed of different ethnic and/or racial groups all created a Jesus that gave meaning to their particularity while justifying their political actions, especially if those political actions ended up being oppressive. Stassen's Jesus tells me more about being white in the twentieth-century United States, just as my Jesús provides insight into living on the underside of that same whiteness.

Consequently, I must therefore respectfully conclude by saying: Jesus no—Jesús sí. As long as Latinxs bow their knees to a thickened white Jesus who looks and acts like the dominant culture, we will be worshiping the symbolic cause of our oppression. For our own salvation and liberation, marginalized communities must firmly say "¡NO!" to Stassen's white Jesus. Saying no to oppression and its symbol becomes our first step toward saying yes to the self, yes to liberation, and yes to the Latinx symbols of that liberation. Even Jesús must say no to this white Jesus, regardless of how thick he may be. For only Jesús can save Jesus from Jesus.

FOUR

My Jesus Is P-H-A-T: A Womanist Response

Stacey M. Floyd-Thomas

To those who might not know me, I am a Baptist and an ethicist. In light of those indelible truths of my existence, our dear departed colleague, Glen Stassen, was a permanent fixture in my understanding of the trappings of the Society of Christian Ethics annual meeting. As Baptists, we shared an investment in religious liberty that defends and extends God-given religious freedom for all, furthering the Baptist heritage of a *paideia* (democracy with a small "d") that champions the principle that religion must be freely exercised and congregationally empowered—without denominational hierarchies influencing or interrupting the community, or governments. And, of course, we felt the shared stronghold of our faith, which appealed to a notion that once one had truly experienced the salvation of God, it was virtually impossible to be loosened from the grip of that covenant and conviction.

Glen offered up his seniority and stature as a rock to which he often compelled me to hunker down and take hold as I navigated the often murky waters of a faith that had little appreciation for my intellectual formation and a formation within the academy that had even less regard for my faith. With his passing, the past few years have seemed hollow as I navigate the halls made hallowed by the appearance of hundreds of Christian ethicists descending upon a given hotel during what is for some of us the ongoing pageant of Christmas. Like self-proclaimed Magi, we leave the vestiges of our institutions, the ritual of our holidays, and the comfort of our homes, families, and friends to follow the signs that lead us to our annual meeting as if we were reenacting the mythical three wise men arriving at their epiphany. This was where Glen, as a proclaimed wise one among men, would invite even me as a womanist, a recognizable sister-outsider, to sojourn with him in what he called "an invitation to witness to a thicker Jesus in the true incarnation of discipleship." He did this without fail.

After numerous years, I came to expect it as I expect my Baptist pastor to extend the invitation to discipleship at the close of every service, with a fervent appeal that makes those of us who are already members feel ashamed for not going up again, just because the intention of his appeal is so enticing. Likewise, Glen came to expect and often chuckled at my extemporaneous reply, "Thick? No. My Jesus is PHAT."

I am fairly sure that Glen had no idea what I was talking about. He did not know that I was evoking my generational Ebonics to redeem something that might seem on the surface to be insulting and irredeemable. My answer perhaps struck him as wrongheaded or blasphemous. He had no idea that I was using a poignant yet playful term to call Jesus, who is ostensibly "thin" and Glen wants to be thicker, PHAT, creating some doubt over whether I meant fat (as in obese or overweight) or P-H-A-T, which stands for prophetic, human, advocate, and transgressive. Now, this homophonic wordplay is indicative of my identity as a Black woman as well as my embodiment as a womanist Christian disciple. Black women's bodies have been stigmatized, scandalized, and stereotyped as fat or obese, despite the ways those same bodies have been consumed or molested by others with the expectation of receiving comfort, care, and caress. In an American culture so obsessed with weight loss that this fuels a multibillion-dollar industry devoted to being thin and lean, being PHAT is a redemptive cultural critique. Fat, which normatively denotes the grotesque and enormously rejected, gets redeemed subversively by Black Generation Xers, millennials, and more recent generations, with the acronym PHAT, which connotes a thicker description of those bodies that are otherwise shunned when they are truly seen through an accurate gaze. As such, they are no longer viewed as simply fat but PHAT, that is, having "pretty hips and thighs" that are, in fact, "pretty hot and tempting" in a literal as well as colloquial sense. Black full-figured, faith-filled women's steps have been ordered not only by God but also by their foremothers who, as my good friend's grandmother would say, "walked through the world as if their footprints mattered and carried weight."

So, to Glen's invitation for me to take hold of his thick Jesus, I refused because I felt my Jesus to be vastly darker and a lot larger than the one that he reckoned. As Jacquelyn Grant, James Cone, Kelly Brown Douglas, and Delores Williams have reminded us, Black Christians and white Christians have never really worshiped the same God despite the shared Bibles they read and the similar stained glass that adorns their houses of worship.

As a womanist scholar who is also a faithful follower of Jesus Christ, I have fully figured out my faith enough to realize that there is an ever-stinging irony that I embody as one whose very *dasein* (being) and is-ness is both duly *and* dually bound to having African blood and being a Christian. As a woman who is both a descendant of enslaved Africans in America and a water- and fire-baptized Christian, I am one who is usually scorned, shunned, set aside, sentenced, or silenced when I seek any normative reflection of myself as well as my community in society and scripture.

In her novel, *The Color Purple*, Alice Walker offers a notable example of such irony in what I deem as a convergence of perspective, perception, and divine purpose found within suffering. This hermeneutic of suspicion and discovery espoused by Walker can be found in the epistles of her protagonist, Celie. Here, the reader can tell that Celie—the Black sharecropping, marital property of a cruel, unfaithful husband and survivor of incestuous sexual assault by a pedophilic predatory father—discloses that she is a "confused Christian who was taught to worship [and follow the lead] of a god that's a big, white, old, bearded, barefooted man with bluish-gray eyes." Celie has been thoroughly subjugated by the relentless abuses at the hands of her father and her husband in addition to the ensuing loneliness and shame of her sequestered torment. As the reader quickly learns,

Celie believes she can only speak of her interminable suffering to God who is both alien and alienating in essence. Due to her dissonance, she finds herself wanting more and ends up disavowing a god to whom she once bared her soul, submitted her will, and suffered her abuse in silence and shame. In a letter to her sister, Nettie, she writes:

> I don't write to God no more, I write to you.
> *What happen to God? ast Shug.*
> Who that? I say.
> *She look at me serious.*
> Big a devil as you is, I say, you not worried bout no God, surely.
> She say, "Wait a minute. Hold on just a minute here. Just because I don't harass it like some peoples us know don't mean I ain't *got religion.*"
> What God do for me? I ast.
> *She say, Celie! Like she shock. He gave you life, good health . . .*
> Yeah, I say, and he gave me a lynched daddy, a crazy mama, a lowdown dog of a step pa and a sister I probably won't ever see again. Anyhow, I say, the God I been praying and writing to is a man. And act just like all the other mens I know. Trifling, forgitful and lowdown.
> *She say. Miss Celie. You better hush. God might hear you.*
> Let 'im hear me, I say. If he ever listened to poor colored women the world would be a different place.[1]

The world of difference that exists between Celie and her perception of a Eurocentric, anthropomorphic, and sexist God is made all the more injurious because he is found to be not only alien but, more important, alienating by disposition. We know all too well how and why this alien and alienating God came into her consciousness to keep her inured to suffering while forever separating her from liberating salvation. This god she came to know was most probably

---

1. Alice Walker, *The Color Purple*, 10th ed. (New York: Houghton Mifflin Harcourt, 1992), 187.

manifested through an oppressive slave theology or a racist, misogynist, Bible-thumping, demonizing preacher, illustrated in the hard work of (often Baptist) preachers, patriarchs, and their pitiful female partners in crime who stand vigilantly silent in the face of death-dealing social oppression.

Within Celie's poignant depiction of the material suffering and soul murder dealt at the hands of a colonizing religion, there is a moment when, for the first time in her life, Celie (a U.S. poster child of suffering) is able to articulate her cognitive dissonance regarding her life-long relationship with God. During this intimate disclosure to her sister, Celie professes the abundant faith she has always demonstrated, the miserable return that has met her spiritual investment, and her realization that the world would be a better place if God could see it through her eyes.

Here, the voice of Celie represents a story that is well known but never told—the moral wisdom yet spiritual angst of those who have been rendered silent and invisible by the lack of ethics in proof-texting proselytizing or poor patriarchal biblical teaching and preaching. Preaching, as many know, is the major—if not the sole—vehicle through which many oppressed Black people and silenced women have come to imagine God—for those of us who are descendants of enslaved Africans, it was the spoken word that enslaved and liberated us. So, it is the spoken word today that still enslaves and/or liberates those like Celie who are triply cursed because of their race, gender, and class. It was with this in mind that I engaged the refrain of my close yet closed-off encounters with Glen. And yet, because I miss him dearly as that permanent and reliable rock in this sea-sickening tide of theological education and Christian social ethics, I wish he would make his appeal one more time so I could say, "Thick? No! My Jesus is PHAT, that is Prophetic, Human, Advocate, and Transgressive."

Prophetic

We find in Luke the following verse: "The Spirit of the Lord is upon me, because he has anointed me to bring good news to the poor. He has sent me to proclaim release to the captives and recovery of sight to the blind, to let the oppressed go free" (Luke 4:18). According to James Cone, it does not require pious talk or a seminary degree to interpret this passage. This is a message that resonates in the ghetto, in Vietnam, and amid all other injustices done in different contexts in the name of democracy and religion to further the social, political, and economic interests of the oppressor. This verse in Luke shows that Jesus Christ entered human affairs taking sides with the oppressed. Their suffering becomes his; their despair, divine despair. Through Jesus Christ, the poor are offered freedom and the tools to rebel against that which makes them other than human. For Cone, "It is ironic that America, with its history of injustice to the poor, especially the black man and the Indian, prides itself on being a Christian nation."[2] Is there really such an animal?

In the same vein, it is even more ironic that officials and theologians within "the body of Christ" (the church) have participated passively or actively in injustices. However, with Jesus, the impoverished were at the center of his mission: "So the last will be first, and the first will be last" (Matt 20:16). This verse explains why he was always kind to traitors, adulterers, and sinners, and why the Samaritan prevailed in parables. Hypocrisy dressed in sacramentality was an important theme in the Gospels, and it became evident when, speaking of the Pharisees, he said: "Truly I tell you, the tax collectors and the prostitutes are going into the kingdom of God ahead of you" (Matt 21:31).

Ethicist Ada María Isasi-Díaz concluded, in her *Mujerista* theology, that the kingdom offered by Jesus Christ would become the "kin-dom."[3] She skillfully argued that the gracious, salvific work of God is visible only through the prophetic presence of Jesus, through the love of the other as a neighbor, which entails solidarity characterized by interconnectivity (namely, commonality and mutuality). This understanding establishes a true dialogical relationship between oppressor and oppressed, as opposed to a charity which is "a one-sided

---

2. James H. Cone, *Black Theology, Black Power* (New York: Seabury Press, 1969), 35–36.

3. Ada Maria Isasi-Diaz, "Kin-dom of God: A Mujerista Proposal," in *In Our Own Voices: Latino/a Renditions of Theology* (Maryknoll, NY: Orbis Books, 2010).

giving, a donation, almost always, of what we have in abundance."[4] Yet, rather than describe solidarity as God's "kingdom," a term that Isasi-Díaz names as sexist and which is in the contemporary context "hierarchical and elitist," she instead uses the term "kin-dom" to emphasize that the eschatological community will be a family: "kin to each other." When Isaiah describes salvation as a meal—"The Lord of hosts will make for all peoples a feast" (Isa 25:6)—Isasi-Díaz thinks of her *abuelita* (grandmother), who always had a pot on the stove, ready to add another guest at her table. If the kingdom is like a feast, and if the Lord is the host of that heavenly meal, then God is like her *abuelita* with her *arroz con pollo*.[5] God is like my grandmother, waiting for another visitor to pull up a chair at her table. Her grandmother's table was a glimpse of "the kin-dom of God," as Isasi-Díaz puts it. In her book *En la Lucha*, she describes *la comunidad de fe* as *la familia de Dios*, the community of faith as the family of God, where we are all kin, part of God's "kin-dom."[6]

For a large group of Latinas "salvation refers to having a relationship with God, a relationship that does not exist if we do not love our neighbor."[7] For me, God's kin-dom looks like her grandmother's house and my Nana's—a house where there is always room around the kitchen table for another neighbor, another stranger, another guest, as God expands our vision for who are our kin, for who belongs in the household, for who can be served a bowl of *arroz con pollo* or a mess of pinto beans—and no one demands that you lose your birthright or place at the table in exchange for it. Salvation looks like my grandmother's table, where we learn how to belong to one another, where we learn how to love each other, where we can look around and catch "eschatological glimpses, part of the unfolding of the kin-dom," as Isasi-Díaz puts it. To be together as a church is the gift of salvation and to fellowship together is a glimpse of the

---

4. Ada María Isasi-Díaz, *Mujerista Theology* (Maryknoll, NY: Orbis Books, 1996), 224.

5. Ibid.

6. Ada María Isasi-Díaz, *En la Lucha/In the Struggle: Elaborating a Mujerista Theology* (Minneapolis: Fortress Press, 2009), 256.

7. Ibid.

kin-dom of God. To commune at the Lord's Table is to live into Isaiah's prophecy: "On this mountain the LORD of hosts will make for all peoples a feast of rich food, a feast of well-aged wines, of rich food filled with marrow, of well-aged wines strained clear" (Isa 25:6). Thus, salvation looks like a meal, an unending Communion feast, prepared by God for us, all of us.

Human

According to Stassen, "God was revealed not somewhere above history, but in actual history."[8] However, for him, this also means that history itself had become "a revelation of the dynamic will of God."[9] It seems that Stassen is projecting the trap that he is rejecting at the same time. Although he claims to be doing away with docetic delusions and hyper-spiritualized notions of Jesus, he still seems to give way to a transcendent Christ in his historical account rather than grappling with the historical Jesus and thereby giving primacy to the history, historical drama, and ultimately the humanity of Jesus. Therefore, Stassen, is at times one-dimensional in the celestial substance of Jesus and the passive piety of his followers as he gives preference to his Lordship or makes his humanity worthy of note only in terms of his sufferings.

Herein, Jesus becomes a trope in a literary tradition marked by the historical drama—like a Shakespearean trope wherein all conversations about romantic literature are invariably suffused by reference to the star-crossed lovers Romeo and Juliet, or when all questions of existential angst are marked by the melancholy Danish prince Hamlet's classic refrain "to be or not to be." However, what has been abundantly clear in the age of Trump is that there needs to be a bright and shining distinction between *being* a character—in Trump's case a grossly cartoonish one—and *having* character. So too, Jesus must in due course emerge from this historical drama that Stassen

---

8. Glen Harold Stassen, *A Thicker Jesus: Incarnational Discipleship in a Secular Age* (Louisville, KY: Westminster John Knox Press, 2012), 9.

9. Ibid.

invokes as more than a "Christ figure" because he was a divine figure and also an actual human being.

Moreover, it becomes evident, even as Stassen maps out incarnational discipleship, that many of the heroes of faith that he is lifting up as modern-day Magi are intentionally representing people who are marginal to the reality of their time. Further, he promotes a Jesus he describes as "sovereign," with power portrayed as "lordship" rather than liberation. Additionally, Stassen claims that incarnational discipleship consists of the foundational trinity of "(1) the holistic sovereignty of God and Lordship of Christ through all of life; (2) a thicker Jesus: God revealed incarnationally, embodied historically, realistically, in Jesus of Nazareth, thickly interpreted; and (3) a Holy Spirit independent from all powers and authorities, calling us to repentance from ideological entanglement."[10] But the best disciples to behold either in biblical antiquity or today are not imitators of Christ, but rather are everyday humans, most often women, who kept him grounded in humanity yet activated his divinity.

The "h" in Jesus' *phatness* is portrayed in those encounters led by women when they dialectically engaged Jesus as human and Christ as divine. Jesus Christ's mother, Mary, activated his divine abilities by shunning his refusal and compelling him to save her girlfriend's face and show the mutuality of hospitality by making him turn water into wine (John 2:1–10). Mary and Martha scolded him for his absence when they needed him most at the deathbed of their brother Lazarus (John 11:21). Then there was the Syrophoenician/Canaanite mother whom he likened to a dog yet who still implored him to heal her daughter who was vexed by the devil (Mark 7:24–30). We see also how the woman with fibroids for twelve years left the quarantine station of her condition to seek healing (Mark 5:25–34), and how the woman with the alabaster box crashed the house party at the house of Simon the leper and anointed Jesus with her expensive perfume as a foreshadowing of his impending end (Matt 26:6–13).

In honor of these womanish women, we recall how in the story of Mary Magdalene (Matt 28:1–10) the Gospel was entrusted to a woman to be carried out to the world. We reflect also on the way

---

10. Ibid., 223.

that Jesus scolded those who merely imitated him (his male disciples), pointing out their lack of humanity relative to that of the anointing woman, when he said, "Truly I tell you, wherever this good news is proclaimed in the whole world, what she has done will be told in remembrance of her" (Matt 26:13). These women show us that real discipleship is exacting in that it is taking Jesus *on*, not as an invincible and invulnerable Lord but trying him on to fit the size of our circumstances and crises. This fully human engagement of Jesus is the rock of my faith and the foundation of those who understand Jesus to throw his weight in the ring to fight their death-dealing adversaries.

In this sense, it is necessary to question if Stassen seeks to ground our ethics in such a way that it is embedded in the "thick" realities and struggles of earthly life, not in the "thin" representations of platonic idealism or sectarian perfectionism. We need to go beyond to see real encounters of Jesus (and not a pantheon of exemplarism or a pageantry of disciples), to see those who really tested Jesus Christ's ethics not in the "laboratory of history" to see who pass the test, but in the "living realities of herstory"—to notice those who put their faith to the test in ways that ignite and impress even Jesus. These women, who hoped against hope, displayed in their everydayness the divinity in their humanity. Their purpose was not an imitation of Christ but an invitation to Jesus. Thus, their practice of incarnational discipleship was literally *taking Jesus on* as a community—which is absent from Glen's account. These stories offer robust renderings of how to practice and live out a truer, fuller, more holistic and holy sense of the divinity-humanity continuum.

Advocate

The prophetic advocacy showed by Jesus in his ministry reveals his emphatic understanding of compelling pleas from the oppressed. John reminds us:

> In the beginning was the Word, and the Word was with God, and the Word was God.... All things came into being

through him, and without him not one thing came into being. What has come into being in him was life, and the life was the light of all people. The light shines in the darkness, and the darkness did not overcome it.... He came to what was his own, and his own people did not accept him. But to all who received him, who believed in his name, he gave power to become children of God. (John 1:1–5, 11–12)

In other words, God takes on flesh in faithful response to the cries of those in need of an advocate. Just as Jesus' death was the act of evil incarnate, so was Jesus coming into existence an act of incarnational advocacy wherein humans appropriate Jesus as inextricably linked to justice and Jesus responds as the advocate who takes on the flesh of justice. Therefore, we can conclude that Jesus' divine ethic is advocacy. Whether it is a modern-day Celie, or Job, who longed for an advocate to plead his case, they insist on an advocate who speaks on behalf of the downtrodden, to testify on behalf of those who have no rights.

In the same vein, historian of religion Charles H. Long has stated that "the West must realize that those who were formerly considered lesser or second-class human beings have always been fully human."[11] Long continues his argument on humanity stating:

> The community from which I come expressed another attitude, an attitude that confronted the reality of America, not as plastic and flexible, amenable to the will of the human being through hard work and moral fortitude, but a reality, impenetrable, definite, subtle, and other—a reality so agonizing that it forced us to give up our innocence while at the same time it sustained us in humor, joy, and promise. I am speaking of a quality of the American experience through which harsh discipline destroyed forever a naive innocence, revealing a god of creation—a god of our silent tears—a god of our weary years. This may be called "nitty-gritty" pragmatism. It is from this

---

11. Charles H. Long, *Significations: Signs, Symbols, and Images in the Interpretation of Religion* (Minneapolis: Fortress Press, 1986), 83.

kind of history and involvement with nature, humanity, and God that the dense richness germinates out of which profound religious awareness emerges.[12]

Thus, it is out of the particularity and the plight of the persecuted that immanence becomes transcendent and the narrow visions of our privileged perspectives become enlarged—the margins re-center us to what ultimately matters most. Ergo, our world is enlarged, our notion of humanity becomes more divine and our reality becomes *phat*.

Transgressive

The relationality and personified struggle of Jesus led him to be classified as a transgressor, and the Book of Isaiah shares the evidence (cf. Isa 53:12). Jesus himself was classified among the transgressors of his time. There were many compelling reasons for this. Jesus was numbered with the transgressors in order that they might feel their hearts drawn toward him. After all, who can be afraid of one who is written in the same list with us? His righteousness, his blood, and everything that he has he gives us as our inheritance and blessed assurance. Humanity's unison with him is tied to the ineffability of his divinity vis-à-vis his prominence among the transgressors.

Jesus Christ, despite possessing supernatural power and extraordinary potential, which could have served as a bulwark against oppression in his own personal experience, proved that we are truly saved and safe in our humanity because of his humanity manifestly numbered with those oppressed—like the womanish women who in their just claims for deliverance activate the God within his humanity so that they can claim, take hold of, and bear witness to a more abundant life. My interpretation of the call to leave everything, take up the cross, and follow Jesus (Mark 8:34–35) is as a challenge placed against the values of the Roman Empire, in which the cross represented the outcome of life for all those who were disloyal to the em-

---

12. Ibid., 151.

pire. The challenge launched by Jesus was and continues to be a political statement. This is about ultimate allegiance to God's kin-dom, which puts one on a collision course with the values and systems of empire structures.

Christian ethicist Gary Dorrien accurately describes how many womanist and feminist theologians have poignantly dissented on the glorification of the cross that Stassen problematizes but still gives primacy to as he privileges the historical drama and salvific value of the suffering of Jesus. For instance, womanist theologians Delores Williams and Kelly Brown Douglas, womanist ethicists Emilie Townes and Eboni Marshall Turman, and feminist theologians like Rita Nakashima Brock and Rebecca Parker protest against and reject the ransom theory (which makes Satan the problem) or the various satisfaction theories (in which Jesus rescued sinners from a wrathful God by suffering in their place). Stassen claims "the cross is the worst thing we could do,"[13] yet he upholds it. Stassen's critique of womanist/feminist approaches focuses much of its critical fire on moral influence theory, in which Jesus offered an exemplary religious ideal through his willingness to die for others, while he also rejects the surrogacy notions of atonement theory. Yet what Stassen offers pervades a great deal of white mainline theologies in terms of their glorification of the cross.

Atonement theology as a whole is problematic for perpetuating patriarchy, magical thinking, a vengeful deity, and an ethic of martyrdom. If Jesus exemplifies a religious ideal by suffering for others, the Gospel becomes a message of self-sacrifice and moral perfectionism. To this end, it is at best promoting the concept of a substitutionary faith or surrogate sacrifice that reifies rather than transgresses that stultifying status quo. Nevertheless, as Stassen accurately reminds us, the Sermon on the Mount was not about idealistic perfectionism,[14] but neither did it represent the concrete realism of peacemaking that he assumed. It was a transgressive act of overthrowing the tables that had been prepared by the privileged, creating clarity out of dissonance and community out of chaos by using dissonance and chaos as

---

13. Stassen, *A Thicker Jesus*, 166.
14. Ibid., 179–80.

the prime movers. By voluntarily and visibly aligning himself with the multitudes of human beings existing on the margins as indicated in the Sermon's articulated list of the Beatitudes, Jesus violates the intrinsic logic that the chief concern of the privileged and powerful is the preservation of their protected status in the world.

Moreover, Jesus never invited people into discipleship but, more often than not, sought to compel them through considerable degrees of conscientization. Likewise, Christian ethicists must join this transgressive act in the furthering not of the norm, which Stassen also refutes, but to compel us to take hold of an ethic of liberation. For womanist theologian Katie Cannon, "liberation ethics is debunking, unmasking and disentangling the ideologies, theologies and systems of value operative in a particular society." How is it done? It is done by analyzing the established power relationships that determine the cultural, political, and economic presuppositions and by evaluating the legitimating myths that sanction the enforcement of such values. Why is it worth doing? So that we may become responsible decision-makers who envision structural and systemic alternatives that embrace the well-being of us all.[15] Or consider the grave issues that are finally ethical, that challenge us to take more seriously human choice and action because our ethical concepts are not matched to our Anthropocene powers.[16] So this heavy work for Mother Earth is only one that following a PHAT Jesus can carry.

Conclusion

Going back to your question, old friend, *"Will I join you in the apostolic witness to a thicker Jesus—in the tradition of incarnational discipleship?"* My answer is, I hope you've already made it to the Upper Room and realize that a thick Jesus is still too thin and perhaps too slippery to grab hold of for dear life. I pray that a PHAT Jesus was the one who let you in. This, after all, is the Jesus Christ who has

---

15. Katie Cannon, "Wheels in the Middle of Wheels," *Journal of Feminist Studies in Religion* 8, no. 2 (1992): 128.

16. Cf. Larry Rasmussen's chapter 8 in this volume, p. 119.

shown to many women like his mother, Mary and Martha, the Syrophoenician mother, the woman with fibroids and ineffectual healthcare, and Mary Magdalene who refused to participate in the historical drama of the cross, how to lay claim to their divine power amid a depraved humanity marked by toxic masculinity and unmerited privilege.

These women were not star-studded exemplars but everyday women who as the very salt of the earth and light of the world were Jesus' life givers, life sustainers, and light bearers. They were the ones who stood in solidarity with him in the preparation for his resurrection, who as the true vessels and vines of his gospel were not just thick but PHAT as they made a way out of no way by "moving through the world as if their footsteps had not only weight but sway in the world they inhabited." The challenge for all of us—especially those of us who inhabit the margins of this world either by choice or by force—is to be one with Jesus in a way that fully invokes his presence, palpability, possibility, and purpose with a spirit of gratitude for the fact that many of us have rejected the thin application and thicker appeals to Jesus and fully figured out, based on our experiences, that ours is a PHAT Jesus, and that suits us just fine.

FIVE

Fidelity: A Sexual Ethic for Christians and Other Aliens in a Strange Land

George Hunsinger

The title of this chapter has been borrowed from William Stringfellow, who wrote the book *An Ethic for Christians and Other Aliens in a Strange Land*.[1] I follow him, here, not so much in content as in spirit. Stringfellow had a profound sense that Christian ethics is for Christians, not necessarily for anybody else, and that to be a Christian meant, in important respects, to live at variance with the ethos of the surrounding world. The motto for his thought might have been drawn from the well-known verse: "Do not be conformed to this world, but be transformed by the renewing of your minds, so that you may discern what is the will of God—what is good and acceptable and perfect" (Rom 12:2). How might this verse be applied in constructing a sexual ethic for Christians today?

Around 1975, I heard Stringfellow speak at Yale Divinity School, where he touched on this matter. At that time I think I knew that Stringfellow had been an outspoken critic of the Vietnam War; that he had harbored Father Daniel Berrigan, the Jesuit dissident, when Berrigan was a fugitive from justice for his civil disobedience actions against the war; and that Stringfellow and his partner, the poet Anthony Townsend, were living together as a gay couple in a remote res-

---

1. William Stringfellow, *An Ethic for Christians and Other Aliens in a Strange Land* (Waco, TX: Word, 1973).

idence on Block Island, off the coast of Rhode Island. I had also heard that Karl Barth regarded Stringfellow—a prominent lay theologian in the Episcopal Church—as the one American who had really understood him during his 1962 speaking tour of the United States, upon his retirement from the University of Basel.

The one thing I remember Stringfellow remarking on in his talk was that the place of homosexuals in the church could not be settled apart from a comprehensive sexual ethic.[2] I can recall him repeating that point, rather oracularly, more than once. Unfortunately, neither I nor apparently anyone else in the audience had the presence of mind to ask him to say more about what he meant. Nevertheless, I have found myself pondering his remark ever since. This essay is a belated attempt to take Stringfellow up on his proposition. What would a comprehensive sexual ethic look like that might help us to do justice to the place of gay and lesbian persons in the Christian church today?

Of course, answering this question is a tall order, and I can do no more here than scratch the surface. Many questions will need to be passed over in silence, such as birth control, abortion, and divorce. They would take us too far afield. What I will try to do is to think about gay and lesbian partnerships or same-sex unions from a center in heterosexual marriage as it might be understood in Christian ethics. Historically, of course, the church has paid far more attention to the ethics of heterosexual unions than to the ethics of same-sex unions. But the former provides a base of operations, so to speak, from which to think about the latter, in the hopes of outlining a comprehensive sexual ethic for all Christians, regardless of their sexual orientation. I will suggest a way of thinking about heterosexual marriage in the church from which extended lines of consistency can be drawn in order to extrapolate a proposal for how to think about same-sex unions in the church today. Finally, in an afterword, I will consider how this approach, which is mainly exegetical

---

2. Stringfellow, speaking in the 1970s, used the terms "homosexuals" and "homosexuality." Throughout this chapter, I will either use those terms or simply "gay and lesbian," rather than more complex newer variations ("LGBTQIA") to focus attention tightly on the sexual ethics of same-sex sexual relationships, rather than broader concerns that might be addressed.

and hermeneutical, might be related to the recent proposal by Glen Stassen about pursuing Christian ethics from the standpoint of "incarnational discipleship."

In considering same-sex unions from a methodological center in heterosexual marriage, I want to suggest at least three standards that need to be met: the standard of fairness, the standard of fidelity and chastity, and the standard of biblical integrity. No comprehensive sexual ethic for Christians can be valid, as far as I can see, if it fails to do justice to these standards. Nevertheless, doing justice to all three at once will perhaps prove to be impossible. In any case, it is bound to be controversial. In the end. I fear that I may not have the prowess to resolve this ethical Rubik's Cube, and the reader may not be convinced. Given the difficulty of the task, I do not necessarily ask for your agreement, but only for your charity. We are all trying to think these complex matters through to the honor of Christ and the gospel.

The Standard of Fairness

By the standard of fairness, I mean something like the Golden Rule. "Do to others as you would have them do to you" (Luke 6:31). I begin with this point not only because I consider it to be essential, but also because I am convinced that historically, the church has yet to meet this standard in thinking about same-sex unions. It has therefore failed to deal equitably with gay and lesbian persons in the church and in society. The level of ignorance about homosexuality that might have been excusable in times past is no longer excusable today. It is simply not the case, as was often supposed, that all persons come into the world as heterosexuals, so that having a homosexual orientation could be attributed simply to the operation of free choice. Homosexuality is a matter of deep-seated dispositions which, as a rule, are neither casually acquired nor easily discarded. Homoerotic desires are, for gays and lesbians, no more a matter of deliberate choice, as a rule, than heteroerotic desires are for heterosexuals. There is simply nothing shameful about having sexual desires, regardless of whether they are homoerotic or heteroerotic. No sexual desires in themselves, regardless of their orientation, should be taken as a cause for shame.

And yet an intolerable burden of shame has been laid upon homosexuals simply because of their dispositions. They have been subjected to painful feelings of humiliation and distress merely for being what they are. Deep feelings of unworthiness have been instilled in them—by their families, their churches, and their societies—not because of wrong or foolish behavior—I have not yet come to the question of behavior—but simply because of their deep-seated dispositions and sexual attractions, matters they can really do nothing about. How many conscientious young Christians and others—racked with shame—have striven to shed themselves of these desires without success? How many have been driven to despair because of not being able to remove the unremovable? How many have been stricken with self-loathing, leading to self-harm, and finally even to suicide? The church's failure on this has been a failure of empathy. It has been a deficit of fellow-feeling, a terrible failure to put oneself in the other person's shoes.

The Golden Rule cannot really function without empathy. A moral imagination cannot exist if it is not informed by compassion. It is necessary—morally necessary—to think about the plight of others as if it were one's own plight. It is necessary for us as Christians to feel our way into the situation of others, especially the marginalized person. We must treat others in their distress as we would like to be treated ourselves if we were in such distress. An empathetic imagination is morally necessary for the equitable treatment of others, especially when they are in need. A church that wishes to live in accord with the Golden Rule, as taught by our Lord, must repent not only of its culpable ignorance regarding homosexuals, but also of its lack of empathy toward them. Our homosexual neighbors and fellow-Christians have been historically afflicted with an intolerable burden of shame. They cannot be treated fairly, according to the measure of the Golden Rule, until heterosexuals, and especially heterosexual Christians, begin to regard them with an informed fellow-feeling.

The Standard of Fidelity and Chastity

Christian sexual ethics is distinctive because it refuses to separate sexuality from spirituality. It considers any sexuality that tries to disregard spirituality as dehumanizing and potentially demonic. It believes not only that human beings are essentially spiritual in their embodiment, but also that they are created for the sake of fellowship with God, and through God with one another. Indeed, all human relationships are not only grounded in our relationship to God, but also and primarily in God's prior relationship to us as enacted and revealed in Jesus Christ. Christian sexual ethics is therefore ultimately determined by Christ. Loyalty to Christ, correspondence to Christ, and fulfillment in Christ set the terms. All Christian ethics, in general, and Christian sexual ethics, in particular, need to be developed from a center in Christ.

God's fellowship with us in Jesus Christ is defined by a particular kind of love. It is love in the form of *agape*. Love in this form is also what defines all our relationships with one another when they are authentic. Agape does not necessarily mean self-sacrifice or self-denial, though it may include them, but it primarily means self-giving to others in appropriate, life-giving, and God-affirming ways. Agape means self-giving to God and one another as God has given himself to us in Jesus Christ.

Unfortunately, agape is sometimes defined as if it stood in contradiction to *eros*. When that happens, agape may be understood simply as self-denying, while eros is regarded merely as self-seeking. But this way of thinking distorts both terms. Agape, on the one hand, seeks the good of other persons in their concrete particularity apart from any special merit or attractiveness they may have in themselves. It seeks the good of others whether or not they have earned it or deserve it. Eros, on the other hand, seeks to unite with and possess that which is beautiful, attractive, and desirable. It can be self-seeking, and actually will be self-seeking, if it is allowed to proceed without restraint. But there is nothing inappropriate in itself about desiring and affirming anything that is beautiful with a chastened measure of eros.

In Christ, eros is redeemed by agape. It is bent from mere self-seeking into self-giving. In Christian marriage, and in the sexual union that takes place in Christian marriage, eros becomes a matter of mutual self-giving to one another in love. In Christian marriage, love finds its primary expression in the form of agape. It is an agape that includes eros, but that also orders eros and sanctifies it. In Christian marriage, the agape received from God and returned to God finds its counterpart in an agape received from one another and returned to one another. Because it includes sexual union, in mutual and self-giving love, Christian marriage promotes the reconciliation of agape and eros in Christ.

Two passages illustrate the biblical view of marriage as it pertains not only to the relationship between agape and eros, but also, more specifically, to that between spirituality and sexuality. The first passage reads as follows: "Therefore a man shall leave his father and his mother and cleave to his wife, and the two shall become one flesh" (Gen 2:24). As Walter Trobisch has noted, this passage contains three elements: leaving, cleaving, and becoming one flesh. I consider his analysis to be simple but profound.[3]

First, Christian marriage involves "leaving." One's family of origin is left behind and a new household is begun. The emphasis in this verse falls on the man. It is not only the woman who leaves to join the man, but also the man who leaves to join the woman. "The unheard-of and revolutionary message," writes Trobisch, "was that the man also had to leave his family." Undue influence from the family of origin can place great strain upon a marriage. Leaving is a precondition for establishing a stable marriage relationship. Without it, the marriage can be in jeopardy. The first loyalty of the couple needs to be to one another.

Trobisch associates "leaving" with having a formal wedding in the sense of a public event and a legal contract. However, as he does not observe, historically, it has not always been the case, not even in the church, that a couple could not validly live together without first having a wedding. Prior to the sixteenth century, in premodern

---

3. Walter Trobisch, *I Married You* (New York: Harper & Row, 1971).

Europe, Christian marriages did not necessarily have to begin with a wedding, though they did eventually have to be ratified by a wedding. They could begin with two things: first, a transfer of primary loyalty away from the family of origin to the beloved; and second, a vow of mutual commitment to one another in love and faithfulness. These two—making a break and making a vow, leaving and espousal, starting a household and pledging fidelity—were sufficient. They were enough for living together in marriage and for sexual union within it. Living together was common on this basis. The wedding came later.[4]

Second, marriage involves "cleaving." If leaving indicates the more public side of marriage, cleaving points to its more private dimension. "The literal sense of the Hebrew word for 'to cleave,'" writes Trobisch, "is to stick to, to paste, to be glued to a person. Husband and wife are glued together like two pieces of paper. If you try to separate two pieces of paper that are glued together, you tear them both. If you try to separate husband and wife who cleave together, both are hurt—and in case they have children, the children as well." Cleaving means forming a bond with each other that surpasses every other social bond. The couple are "closest to each other, closer than to anything else and to anyone else in the world." Cleaving, therefore, means love in the context of life-long fidelity. Agape between two marriage partners, as modeled on God's self-giving love to us, means life-long fidelity. It means love that is committed and mature, a "love that has decided to remain faithful—faithful to one person—and to share with this one person one's whole life," body and soul. In Christian marriage, the cleaving or self-giving in agape is total, committed, and exclusive.

Finally, marriage involves "becoming one flesh." This expression points to the physical side of the union, but not to the physical in isolation from the spiritual. The sexual union of the couple is also spiritual at the same time. It involves them as whole persons—heart, mind, and soul. In a deeply mysterious way—a way that can perhaps

---

4. See Todd A. Salzman and Michael G. Lawler, *Sexual Ethics: A Theological Introduction* (Washington, DC: Georgetown University Press, 2012), 130–32.

be experienced more than it can be grasped by the mind—their sexual union is uniquely expressive of their whole being as persons, both separately and together. To become one flesh means more than just their physical union:

> It means that two persons share everything they have, not only their bodies, not only their material possessions, but also their thinking and their feeling, their joy and their suffering, their hopes and their fears, their successes and their failures. "To become one flesh" means that two persons become completely one with body, soul and spirit and yet they remain two different persons. This is the innermost mystery of marriage.[5]

Becoming one flesh is a physical union with a spiritual dimension. It reflects the mystery of God's union with the church in Jesus Christ, and through the church with the world.

Therefore, from this point of view, a biblical understanding of marriage involves at least three elements: leaving, cleaving, and becoming one flesh. The social, the personal, and the sexual are all bound up with one another. They are distinct but not separate, in a mysterious and spiritual way. Cleaving, however, is the heart of the matter. It is what makes the leaving necessary, while it is also what consecrates the mystery of becoming one flesh, so that both are undertaken in a wholesome and life-giving way. In Christian marriage, cleaving—or mutual, life-long fidelity—sets the terms for both leaving and becoming one flesh.

Let us now consider briefly another passage. It is a much more complicated passage and one that is harder to interpret. I will not be able to dig into all of its important aspects. I will simply pinpoint some of its essentials. At the beginning of chapter 5 in the Letter to the Ephesians, we read: "Therefore be imitators of God, as beloved children, and live in love, as Christ loved us and gave himself up for us, a fragrant offering and sacrifice to God" (Eph 5:1–2). Then later

---

5. Trobisch, *I Married You*, 18.

on, just before we arrive at the detailed instructions given to husbands and wives, we read: "Be subject to one another out of reverence for Christ" (Eph 5:21).

The instructions given to husbands and wives in Ephesians 5 are not easy to interpret. They seem to combine two different logics: a logic of hierarchy and a logic of mutuality. It is difficult to see how these two logics fit together or how they can be disentangled. The logic of hierarchy refers to patriarchal social structures that the author, whom we assume was Paul, seems to presuppose without question, while the logic of mutuality pertains to some of the verbs that he uses not only in introducing his instructions but also in spelling them out. Putting many sticky questions to one side, I want to concentrate on three elements from this passage: the motivation in marriage, the pattern in marriage, and, again, the mystery in marriage.

More than in the passage about "leaving, cleaving and becoming one flesh," we now get a direct statement about the motivation for Christian behavior. The great motivation is "reverence for Christ." The Greek word translated as "reverence" is *phobos*, which can also be translated as "fear." Paul is clearly talking about a holy fear, not a servile fear. He is talking about a heartfelt reverence for God as revealed in Christ. He is thinking about the surpassing worth of God's grace as revealed on Good Friday. He is calling us to love and fear God above all else. "True piety," wrote Calvin, "dreads to offend God more than to die." It dreads this, not because offending God might end in punishment, but because it would mean ingratitude to God for so great a gift of self-giving in agape. "Even if there were no hell," Calvin explained, "the pious mind would still shudder at offending God alone."[6] For Paul, as also for Calvin, we should not wish to offend God under any circumstances, because God has proven himself to be worthy of our highest devotion and love. Reverence for Christ, according to Paul, is what finally motivates the love and life-long fidelity that rightly belong to husbands and wives. Reverence for Christ is the highest spiritual motivation for fidelity in marriage.

---

6. John Calvin, *Institutes of the Christian Religion*, I.2.2 (Philadelphia: Westminster, 1960), 43. This quote has been slightly revised.

The ethical pattern follows from this motivation. It is a pattern of mutual submission in self-giving love. "Live in love, as Christ loved us and gave himself up for us, a fragrant offering and sacrifice to God" (Eph 5:1–2). The exhortation to live in love is a way of commending agape. Both partners—the husband as well as the wife—are to give themselves to one another completely, and to submit to one another in love. That is the pattern of mutuality in marriage as motivated by reverence for Christ. Recall once again how the passage began: "Be subject to one another out of reverence for Christ" (Eph 5:21). The more detailed instructions that follow cannot rightly be detached from this requirement. In Christian marriage, husbands and wives cannot love Christ without also loving one another in the form of mutual submission. If they fail to submit to their partner in love—with all the difficult negotiation and patience and forgiveness that may be involved—they are not only falling short, they are failing to revere Christ, the supreme object of their devotion. As Christ has given himself to the world, and therefore to us, so we are to give ourselves to him. And so also are husbands and wives to give themselves in mutual submission to one another in correspondence to Christ.[7]

Finally, the motivation and the pattern—the reverence and the mutual submission—point beyond themselves to a great mystery. Or perhaps, rather, to a great twofold mystery. The passage from Genesis 2:24 that we considered earlier is quoted again in Ephesians 5:31. Leaving, cleaving and becoming one flesh are, Paul declares, already a great mystery in themselves (cf. Eph 5:32). But this mystery points beyond itself to another, even greater mystery. For it evokes the ineffable

---

7. Despite the direct wording of the text about submitting to one another in love (Eph 5:21)—which I take to be authoritative and equally binding for both partners—it should be noted that cultural conditioning may work against it. When it comes to "mutual submission," the pressures may fall more heavily on the woman than on the man. The text can be read, however, as placing a strong obligation on the man. He is to love his wife in the way that Christ gave himself up for the church (5:25). He is to love her as he does his own body (5:28). "For no one ever hated his own flesh, but nourishes and cherishes it, just as Christ does the church" (5:29). "He who loves his wife loves himself" (5:28). "Let each one of you love his wife as himself" (5:33). Whatever else may be present in the text, it places the man under a strong obligation to submit to his wife in love, just as the wife is called to submit in love to him.

union of Christ with the church. Whatever the mystery of Christ in union with the church may involve here, it can be understood to mean at least this: that Christ is the source of agape, that he provides the model for submitting to another in love, and that he validates life-long fidelity in marriage. In heterosexual marriage, therefore, agape, mutual submission in love, and life-long fidelity are the norms and practices that arise from the mystery of Christ.

Let's pause at this point and take stock. I suggest that key elements for a comprehensive sexual ethic have now been uncovered for all Christians, regardless of their sexual orientation. In fact, nothing stated so far about husbands and wives could not be applied equally well to same-sex unions in the church. Same-sex unions, too, would be marked in their own way by leaving, cleaving, and becoming one flesh. They, too, would be defined by self-giving to one another in love. They, too, would enact eros in the context of agape. They, too, would involve sexual self-giving that was uniquely expressive of each partner's whole being. They, too, would be grounded in the same Christ-given ethic of exclusive and life-long commitment in love. They, too, would affirm this ethic as establishing the only authentic context for total sexual expression. They, too, would acknowledge the spiritual aspect of all sexuality. They, too, would live out their union in reverence to Christ. They, too, would correspond in their own way to the mystery of Christ's love for the church.

What prevents the church from embracing such a vision of same-sex unions within its ranks? It seems that the prime obstacle that remains rests mainly in the third standard that was set forth earlier. We have already looked at the standard of fairness, and we have touched on the standard of fidelity and chastity. The standard of biblical integrity, however, still needs to be examined.

The Standard of Biblical Integrity

Although the Bible has very little to say about homosexuality, the little that it does say has been read as condemning all homosexual acts. Let me divide the question into two parts. First, does the Bible actually condemn all expressions of same-sex intercourse or only some expressions? And second, is there something intrinsically immoral about such intercourse in itself? These are complex and disputed questions. Essentially, we are looking for a way of validating committed same-sex unions within the church, and one that can meet the standard of biblical integrity.

It seems that nowhere in the Bible do committed same-sex unions come under consideration as such. The idea of same-sex Christian couples committing themselves to life-long partnerships that were analogous to heterosexual marriages was virtually unknown. Perhaps such partnerships would not have been condoned, but that is a moot point. What seems to have been denounced about same-sex sexual activity fell elsewhere. It was condemned, first, when entangled in sexual promiscuity (especially as associated with unbridled lust); second, in intercourse between adults and children; and finally, in abusive or violent acts of sexual behavior (such as rape). These debased types of behavior, however, would be blameworthy if engaged in by any Christian (or any person), regardless of their sexuality. There is nothing exclusively homosexual about them.

The question centers on whether homosexual intercourse is intrinsically immoral. The main biblical text used to support this idea is Romans 1:26–27. Here, homosexual activity is described as "contrary to nature" (*para phusin*) (Rom 1:26). However, this cryptic phrase is difficult to interpret, because it gives us so little to go on. Nevertheless, let us take the traditional Roman Catholic view that all homosexual acts are intrinsically disordered. A number of reasons are given, but perhaps the central one is grounded in human biology. Homosexual activity is thought to violate the natural use for which God intended human sexual organs. Their abuse in same-sex intercourse violates nature as grounded in the divine intention. In that sense, homosexual acts are condemned as "contrary to nature."

It would take a long treatise to sort these matters out. Let me cut the Gordian knot by making a preemptive suggestion. I want to propose that natural law arguments cannot be decisive, even if there should be some truth to them. I am making a hypothetical move, but I hope not an unimportant one. The natural law argument cannot settle the matter, because even at its best it cannot satisfy the principle of fairness, the standard with which I began. As far as I can see, the standard of fairness, as grounded in the Golden Rule, trumps the argument against homosexual activity based on "natural law." Given that a homosexual disposition, like a heterosexual disposition, is neither casually acquired nor easily discarded, the Golden Rule is greater than the so-called natural law (as traditionally conceived)—or so I would propose.

We need to ask an important practical question: If all homosexual activity is prohibited as immoral, then what possibilities do homosexuals actually face for living their lives?

Two primary options have been put forward: either sexual reorientation or else life-long celibacy. Let's take reorientation first. Although favored by many American evangelicals, among others, so-called conversion therapy is a bogus option. It claims to be able to convert people away from being homosexuals into being "born-again" heterosexuals in their sexual make-up. Exodus International, however, a leading proponent of conversion therapy, founded in 1976, shut its doors for good in 2013. Alan Chambers, the organization's final president, explained why. "The majority of people that I have met—and I would say the majority, meaning 99.9% of them—have not experienced a change in their orientation." He apologized for the previous Exodus slogan "Change Is Possible."[8] This type of therapy has not only been notoriously unsuccessful; it has often been deeply traumatic. No one should ever be pressured into it.

The second option proposed for homosexuals is a life of celibacy. But this is also a bogus option. Over against the Roman Catholic Church, the Reformation broke with requiring celibacy of its ordained ministers. It traced the notorious sexual immorality rampant among the priesthood in part to this blanket requirement—a demand that Luther labeled as "contrary to nature." As commended by Jesus and Paul, celibacy was to be highly honored, but only for those who were given the special charism or grace for it. Trying to impose it on those without the charism, whether heterosexual or homosexual, could only lead to disaster. "It is better," as Paul famously said, "to marry than to burn" (1 Cor 7:9). It was absurd to suppose that all

---

8. Chambers made this admission in a 2012 panel discussion at the Gay Christian Network. https://www.wthrockmorton.com/2012/01/09/alan-chambers-99-9-have-not-experienced-a-change-in-their-orientation/.

those who were called to the ministry were automatically endowed with the charism for celibacy. They were not. Likewise, it would be just as absurd today to suppose that all gay and lesbian people are automatically endowed with a charism for celibacy just by virtue of their sexual orientation. Let's face it. They are not.

Again, it is better to marry than to burn. If the church does not wish to consign homosexual Christians without a charism for celibacy to a life of perpetual vexation, failure, and shame, if it does not wish to abandon them to promiscuity as their only de facto remaining outlet, despite all good intentions, then it will have no choice but to promote life-long same-sex unions as the only true solution. It will commend same-sex unions of fidelity and agape. It will honor committed same-sex partnerships with essentially the same blessing as it honors heterosexual marriage. That is the church's only humane option, as far as I can see, and dare I say it, the only truly evangelical one. It is the option that was lived out by William Stringfellow.

Afterword

In this chapter, we have reflected on some biblical materials related to sexual ethics by considering three standards: the standard of fairness, the standard of fidelity and chastity, and the standard of biblical integrity. How might this approach be related to Glen Stassen's proposal about pursuing Christian ethics with an eye toward "incarnational discipleship"? It all depends, for it makes a difference whether one is talking about *incarnational* discipleship or incarnational *discipleship*. The first takes its bearings from the incarnation and does ethical reflection from there; the latter reads the adjective as roughly synonymous with "radical" or "faithful" so that the stress falls more on discipleship than on the Lord. In this chapter, we have taken the first approach.

If one adopts a high view of the incarnation, as do most of the ecumenical churches, then the second approach seems problematic. "Discipleship" is set forth as the substantive term, while "incarnational" is little more than an adjective that describes it. It is not clear how "thick" the idea of Jesus can be, however, if he is not regarded from the very outset in his uniqueness as the incarnate Lord, whom we are summoned to obey in life and in death, and as the world's Savior worthy of our supreme thanks and praise. Is "incarnational" really no more than a generic term that can cover a range of ethical cases? Does the term even make any sense?

In the other approach, by contrast, "incarnation" serves as the substantive term while "discipleship" is determined by it. Here, the incarnation is regarded as a unique and unrepeatable event. Jesus Christ as the eternal Word of God made flesh is a unique person who accomplishes a unique work. No one else will ever be God's self-revelation in person, no one else will ever save the world from sin and death, and no one else will ever be the proper object of Christian worship. No one else, in short, will ever be God incarnate.

Following Jesus, therefore, means following at a distance. It respects the uniqueness of Jesus Christ while bearing witness to him in word and deed. Witness involves being conformed to him in various ways without putting him on the same level as his disciples. Discipleship to Christ means adopting a *similar* pattern of life amid an infinitely greater *dissimilarity*. The incarnation is beyond all imitation in one way, while still being paradigmatic in another.

The ethics of "incarnational discipleship" intends to help Christians be better disciples. From my experience, two factors can generally bring people to a greater fidelity to Jesus Christ in their social attitudes, beliefs, and practices. The first factor is a personal devotion that raises Jesus Christ above all other earthly values and commitments. As Lord and Savior, he necessarily relativizes all our received cultural notions about matters such as wealth, power, status, nation, and personal well-being. He commands us to repent of our existing attitudes and beliefs when they are in conflict with our devotion to him. Although this repentance can be painful, in the end, it will always be salutary.

The second factor is a significant encounter with other human beings in their neediness and distress. When devoted Christians confront at firsthand the ravages of war, racism, sexism, and other grave social evils, they are moved from the heart. They become dismayed at their previous level of indifference, complacency, callousness, or obtuseness. They feel challenged to undertake a significant and sometimes painful form of self-examination. They understand, in a new way, that they cannot be faithful to Jesus without a deeper level of compassion toward others. They are called to depart from mediocre Christian niceness, for example, to a more serious level of commitment. Regarding our topic, it can actually help to have some Christian friends who are living lives of fidelity and chastity in committed same-sex partnerships (though I should add that there are no panaceas).

In one way or another, this form of repentance will be incumbent upon us all. We are all continually summoned to be better disciples relative to our personal or cultural assumptions and practices. In the famous words of the Barmen Declaration, we are all called to live in accord with Jesus Christ as "the one Word of God who is attested for us in Holy Scripture, and whom we are to trust and obey in life and in death."

SIX

Covenant as a Historical Drama for Incarnational Discipleship

Hak Joon Lee

Despite the differences in our theological vision, Glen and I shared our passion for Jesus, justice, and the renewal of the churches. It was in one class—"Faith and Politics"—that he and I taught together at Fuller Theological Seminary that Glen finalized the title of his ultimate book, *A Thicker Jesus*, after taking a student survey from the class in a typical Glen-like manner of democratic enthusiasm.

This book summarizes Glen's life-long scholarship and its foundational spirit. Glen's ethics of incarnational discipleship is more than an academic theory or a speculative moral philosophy. It speaks of who Glen was, what he believed, and how he lived out his faith. In addition to his academic achievement (as the culmination of his career as a Baptist ethicist), Glen's fidelity to Jesus as a Christian underlies the book's authority. He was a person who labored to embody "incarnational discipleship" in his own life. It is the product of his life-long commitment to justice and peacemaking as a follower of Jesus.

I was privileged to witness the depth of his discipleship in his treatment of colleagues, strangers, and students; his affection and care for international students was a special emulation of Jesus' example. Hence, my engagement with Glen's ethics in this chapter is a brothers' quarrel, as "iron sharpens iron" (Prov 27:17).

The Argument

Glen's idea of incarnational discipleship has three dimensions patterned after the Trinity; it is built on a thicker Jesus, which is "God revealed incarnationally, embodied historically, realistically in Jesus of Nazareth"; the "holistic sovereignty of God"; and the Holy Spirit's call for "repentance from all ideological entanglements."[1] Glen uses two methods to validate his ethics: first, by examining "great Christians" who embodied incarnational discipleship and passed the test of actual history,[2] and second, by evaluating incarnational discipleship as a plausible "research program" of a theological ethics using Nancey Murphy's framework.[3] His ultimate goal is to prove that "incarnational discipleship suggest(s) some answers for the challenges presented by secularism,"[4] as elaborated by Charles Taylor's *A Secular Age*.[5]

Thesis

In this chapter, we engage Glen's idea of incarnational discipleship from a covenantal perspective. Glen makes numerous references to covenant in his book, especially regarding Puritans and their contribution to the rise of democracy, human rights, and science (chapters 5 and 6, in particular). In fact, Glen's response to a secular age heavily relies on the Puritan heritage of covenant. Interestingly, despite his numerous references to the Puritan covenant, Glen does not extensively engage with the idea of covenant in the Bible—importantly, what covenant means for Jesus, his Sermon on the Mount,

---

1. Glen H. Stassen, *A Thicker Jesus: Incarnational Discipleship in a Secular Age* (Louisville, KY: Westminster John Knox Press, 2012), 17.

2. Ibid., 15.

3. Ibid., 49.

4. Ibid., 51.

5. Charles Taylor, *A Secular Age* (Cambridge, MA: Harvard University Press, 2007).

and incarnational discipleship. In other words, Glen studies covenant almost exclusively for a historical test of his incarnational discipleship without exegetically examining the significance and implication of the biblical drama of covenant for incarnational discipleship.

Here we will show that Glen's core biblical claims, notably Jesus' ministry and the Sermon on the Mount, are covenant-based. Furthermore, to identify and rework the covenantal ground of incarnational discipleship not only strengthens Glen's thesis, but also better serves Glen's purposes for church renewal and social peacemaking, as it offers a plausible social imagination for Christians to navigate a secular age with renewed commitment and relevance.

In testing this thesis of a covenantal basis of incarnational discipleship, I will use the same criteria Glen employed in testing his incarnational discipleship model: Nancey Murphy's research program. According to Murphy, a good research program first has "a coherent series of theories that preserve the unrefuted content of their predecessors and guide further research";[6] second, a competent research program helps to resolve some internal tensions and conflicts within a theological tradition, and "generates new content, predicting some novel, hitherto unexpected discoveries";[7] and third, a good research program is able to "demonstrate that some of the predicted discoveries are corroborated by others."[8] In presenting covenant as a research program, I will thus seek to demonstrate:

1. how covenant is a coherent historical drama of the Bible that offers the overarching narrative framework for Jesus' ministry, the Sermon on the Mount, and incarnational discipleship;

2. how a covenantal approach better accounts for and warrants some key ethical categories of incarnational discipleship; how it addresses some internal theological tensions and limitations within Glen's ethics, such as christology; and

---

6. Stassen, *A Thicker Jesus*, 50.
7. Ibid., 51.
8. Ibid.

3. how covenant guides further research in social justice; in particular, eco-justice, economic justice, and global justice.

In proposing covenant as a research program, I am certainly aware of the abuse of covenant in history, especially by Puritan colonizers in North America and Dutch colonizers in South Africa. However, I claim that these grievous errors are not due to an intrinsic fallacy of the biblical idea of covenant itself, but rather are the result of bad hermeneutics regarding the Exodus story and misuse of the covenant for racial and ethnocentric agendas and economic greed.

COVENANT AS A HISTORICAL DRAMA OF THE BIBLE

As mentioned earlier, one of Glen's objectives in *A Thicker Jesus* is to establish incarnational discipleship as an ethics that passes the test of actual history. Consequently, he develops a broad methodological framework that discerns and nurtures incarnational discipleship by introducing the concept of "historical drama" (chapter 1). The idea of historical drama enables Glen not only to interpret Jesus in a thick, historical, and realistic way, but also to establish solid ground for Christian identity and ministry by which Christians can navigate a secular age.

Glen claims that "'historical drama' is a more accurate understanding of a biblically influenced way of thinking"[9] than narrative or story. His preference is based on the idea that historical drama avoids the fictional ("mythopoetic") feeling that a story or a narrative usually connotes, and offers a continuity of meaning in interpreting historical events and peoples' lives and communities in light of their sacred text. In historical drama, people sense themselves as active, responsible participants—not passive objects—in a true unfolding drama—not merely fiction. Through historical drama, people experience time and history as "continuous action in participative duration."[10]

---

9. Ibid., 13.
10. Ibid., 12.

Enacting the drama requires fidelity to the written texts (the Bible); the response to the dramas cannot be arbitrary or subjective. People need to interpret the written text respectfully and responsibly without bending the text to their own tastes and self-interest. It does not gloss over the unfaithful parts of people in history, as a narrative often does in the defense of self-interest; it deals with the "real history of sinful people,"[11] a history that includes actual power relations, struggles, sufferings, and temptations.

Historical drama is performative. "It is not only read like a novel, but enacted, embodied, incarnated, as in a drama performed in community. For Christians, it is originally enacted by Israel and by Jesus and the disciples, and then read or performed in community with shared response, and meant to be enacted, embodied, by the drama's 'audience'—communities of disciples in their own ways of living."[12]

Historical drama is contextual; it respects historical realities and contingencies and emphasizes the creative responsibility of each generation in interpreting the written text and the signs of their time and performing the drama. It allows the hermeneutical freedom for different moral agents and communities to "interpret the text in differing ways according to their understanding of the meaning of the text for the community's context."[13] Character is formed and fruits are produced when people faithfully live out the demands of the texts in their own contexts. By introducing the idea of historical drama, Glen claims that actual history is the place where Christian witness happens and faithfulness (discipleship) is tested.

Glen's idea of historical drama is compelling in making a case for incarnational discipleship. He takes discipleship beyond individual piety, ecclesiastical politics, and the academic bickering of theologians and turns it into a matter of simple witness.

In my view, Glen's idea of historical drama is better accounted for when it is specified as the covenantal drama of the Bible: the central historical drama in the Bible is God's covenant.[14] As the plot of

---

11. Ibid.

12. Ibid., 11.

13. Ibid., 12.

14. Glen himself makes a passing reference to covenant when he says that historical drama is about "interactions and relationships, the struggle for and

scripture, covenant renders a coherent structure and meaning to a Christian worldview. It informs and underlies the key doctrines of the Christian faith such as creation, sin, Israel, redemption, church, and eschaton, rendering the Christian worldview coherent. If salvation means entering into a covenant relationship with God and others, sin is understood as its breach, reconciliation as its restoration, and the eschaton as its final fulfillment.

Kevin Vanhoozer is a theologian who has studied this performative, dramatic dimension of covenant and applied it to develop his theory of doctrine.[15] He notes: "The covenantal shape of the biblical *mythos* is arguably the architectonic scheme of the entire theodrama, not simply one biblical or theological theme among others. The God/world distinction and relation alike is ultimately a matter of covenantal drama."[16]

The stories of Israel, Jesus, and the church would not make much sense outside the covenantal plot. Covenant holds the key to the question of the identity and distinctiveness of Israel and church. The term "covenant" was consciously applied by the Israelites to their relationship with Yahweh from the earliest times, and this theological orientation was passed down to Jesus and early Christians. Additionally, covenant smoothly links the Old Testament and the New Testament. Covenant is found in every critical moment of God's dispensation and all major turning points in biblical history, such as creation, Noah's flood, Abraham, Exodus, David, Exile, and Jesus.

In the Bible, covenant is central to God's reign. The Bible is the drama of God's reign, and covenant has a unique status in offering a clue to the understanding of God's kingship and interaction with the world. God's reign and covenant go hand in hand. Covenant is a particular method or form of exercising God's authority and power in pursuing God's goal and actualizing God's reign. God's reign reflects covenantal values of love, justice, trust, truthfulness, reciprocity, and

---

against faithfully fulfilling covenants with one another" (see Stassen, *A Thicker Jesus*, 12), but he fails to elaborate this claim in any further detail.

15. Kevin Vanhoozer, *The Drama of Doctrine: A Canonical Linguistic Approach to Christian Theology* (Louisville, KY: Westminster John Knox Press, 2005).

16. Kevin Vanhoozer, *Remythologizing Theology: Divine Action, Passion, and Authorship* (New York: Cambridge University Press, 2012), 68.

solidarity. God's reign is based on giving, serving, and sharing in *koinonia*, not domination and exploitation.

Covenant displays major features of historical drama. Covenant is performative, and covenantal parties are expected to enact and perform in response to new and changing contexts. Covenant deals with the "real history of sinful people,"[17] and life in the covenant shapes people's lives and selfhood. Covenant norms test Israel's fidelity to God, themselves, and others in the actual unfolding of historical events and their opportunities and challenges. In a sense, the history of Israel (described in the Old Testament) is a biography that portrays the mixed ups and downs of Israel's covenantal relationship with God and others; it is written in an utterly realistic sense, addressing the dimensions of power struggles in a community.

Covenant is contextual; it is not a fixed event of the past, but rather the ongoing enactment of a community in response to its unfolding history. The Israelites were required by God to live out their covenant faithfully in every social context and every historical moment by loving God and loving their neighbors. In other words, they were required to be faithful not only to the text but also to new social contexts. Faithfulness is a key virtue of the people who live in a covenantal relationship with God and others; they are held accountable to their fidelity. However, this fidelity is not wooden but creative, requiring the exercise of a theological and moral imagination.

There are different forms of covenants in scripture (divine-human, human-human, divine-other creatures). The divine-human covenant is typically based on God's initiating grace, preceding an act of deliverance or promise of extraordinary blessings (royal grant). Established through the communicative exchange of promises, the covenant is based on the trust and free response of humans to God's gracious acts. It is maintained through ongoing fellowship and communication and ultimately aims at the communion and love of the two parties. The declaration "I will be your God and you will be my people" (Jer 7:23), which rings throughout scripture, sums up this intimate and reciprocal relationship that God intends

---

17. Stassen, *A Thicker Jesus*, 12.

for humanity. Although covenant does not exhaust all moral ideas and motifs of scripture, its status as a historical drama of the Bible is distinctive.

JESUS AND THE NEW EXODUS

As the historical drama of the Bible, covenant offers a thick description of Jesus' ministry and that of the early church. For Jews in Jesus' time, the covenant was a prevalent thought-pattern forming their religious worldview and practices.[18] Jesus and his disciples stood in the rich, dynamic, and long covenantal tradition of Israel reinterpreted through strong eschatological sentiments of the second temple period.[19] Jesus' contemporaries, living under harsh and brutal Roman rule, felt that they were still in exile while they inhabited their own land. They earnestly longed for the restoration of Israel, a return from exile, and they prayed that God would intervene in history and liberate his people. There was a high eschatological anticipation that Israel's God would soon redeem his people from exile and become their king again, and history would reach its consummation.[20]

Such collective longing and interpretation of their historical situation was deeply influenced by the Exodus tradition.[21] The central confession of the Exodus event is God as the liberator king who delivered his people from the oppression of Pharaoh. Following the pattern of the Exodus, Jews understood the return from the exile as a

---

18. "The covenant structure of biblical history was already clearly seen in Judaism prior to the dawn of the Christian era." Scott Hahn, "Covenant in the Old and New Testaments: Some Current Research (1994–2004)," *Currents in Research* 3, no. 2 (2005): 278. The Qumran and early Christian communities believed that they were participating in the "new covenant" that Jeremiah and Ezekiel had promised.

19. Paul Hanson, *The People Called: The Growth of Community in the Bible* (Louisville, KY: Westminster John Knox Press, 1986), 396.

20. N. T. Wright notes that there was "the anguished longing of Israel for her covenant god to come in his power and rule the world in the way he had always intended" (N. T. Wright, *Jesus and the Victory of God* [Minneapolis: Fortress Press], 203).

21. Wright, *Jesus and the Victory of God*, 155.

new exodus that entails God's reconstituting of God's people, which happens through the renewal of covenant including creeds and moral standards. The return from exile is inseparable from the narrative of covenant: in Israel's imagination, just as the exile is the result of breaking the covenant (sin and disobedience), so does the return indicate its restoration and renewal.

Jesus stood within the Exodus tradition and preached God's reign in this cultural and theological milieu. His followers, including the writers of the synoptic Gospels, compared God's deliverance in Jesus to the Exodus event; just as God had defeated the power of Pharaoh and drowned his army, Jesus was defeating the power of Satan. Jesus' salvation was a new Exodus event. By proclaiming God's reign, calling for people's repentance from idolatry and sin, and forming a new community, Jesus was engaging in a covenantal renewal of Israel by reworking the Exodus event in his own context.

Metaphors and performative actions associated with the Exodus story were unmistakable in Jewish people's imagination, religious behavior, and literature. This was equally found in the gospel stories, for example: Jesus' calling of twelve disciples signifies the gathering of God's people; Jesus' forty days and nights in the wilderness recalls the sojourning of Israelites in the wilderness; and Jesus' feeding of thousands in the wilderness is reminiscent of God's faithful provision for Israelites in the wilderness.

The idea of covenantal renewal is useful for understanding the contextual nature of covenant as the historical drama of the Bible as well as of Jesus' ministry. Covenantal renewal means the reworking or recontextualizing of the Sinai Covenant in a radically new and/or changing context; such revisions are not unusual in Israel's history, as we see the renewal of the Mosaic covenant in Deuteronomy, Joshua, Nehemiah, Jeremiah, Isaiah, Ezekiel, and finally Jesus. Covenantal renewal means retelling and re-appropriating the past event of God's deliverance in contemporary contexts; the revision of some rules and rituals happens together with the rededication of people to God and each other. This imaginative reworking of the Exodus story continued throughout Israel's history, finally reaching to Jesus.

A COVENANTAL GROUND OF THE SERMON ON THE MOUNT

The covenantal basis of Jesus's ministry becomes clearer when we examine Jesus' Sermon on the Mount—a central text for Glen's ethics. Even though the covenant is not explicitly mentioned in the Sermon on the Mount, the theological premises of a covenant are manifestly present.

Biblical scholars, notably Richard Horsley, have noticed a close affinity between the story of the Mosaic covenant (Exodus 20, Deuteronomy 5) and the Sermon on the Mount (Matthew 5—7), and agree that Matthew is introducing Jesus as a new Moses in the Sermon on the Mount. Consider the following examples:

> Jesus' act described in the opening two verses of Matthew 5 ("He went up the mountain; and after he sat down, his disciples came to him. Then he began to speak, and taught them") reminds us of Moses ascending Mt. Sinai, receiving the law from God, and giving it to the Israelites.

> Each beatitude is structured in a promise-fulfillment pattern, linked by a motivational device "for" (*hoti* in Greek), which frequently appears in covenantal documents of the Old Testament. The kingdom of heaven is promised to those who are willing and eager to live in the way of Jesus.

> In an echo of the Sinai covenant, the covenantal logic of divine-human reciprocity (gift-task) is found in various teachings of the Sermon on the Mount.[22]

---

22. This covenantal pattern of reciprocity appears in several places in the Sermon on the Mount (Matt 5:44–48; 6:4, 6, 18, 25–33). Consider especially: "Love your enemies and pray for those who persecute you, so that you may be children of your Father in heaven; for he makes his sun rise on the evil and on the good, and sends rain on the righteous and on the unrighteous. For if you love those who love you, what reward do you have? Do not even the tax collectors do the same? And if you greet only your brothers and sisters, what more are you doing than others? Do not even the Gentiles do the same? Be perfect, therefore, as your heavenly Father is perfect" (5:44–48).

As covenant typically includes the clause of blessing and curse, the Sermon on the Mount, despite its different structure and format, has references to both; it begins with blessings as we see in the Beatitudes, but it also includes curses (cf. Matthew 7).

The norms and values that Jesus emphasizes in the Sermon on the Mount, such as loyalty to God ("no one can serve two masters") and trust in God ("do not worry") are covenantal in nature.

As Moses did in the Book of Exodus, Jesus, in his sermon, teaches on the topics of murder, adultery, divorce, almsgiving, oaths, revenge, forgiveness, prayer, and fasting.

Matthew's report that Jesus speaks as the "one having authority" again reminds of Moses' authority in the Old Testament.

The ending of the Sermon on the Mount is also similar to Exodus 34:29; there was healing for the people after Jesus and Moses came down from the mountain.[23]

As the Ten Commandments were given to those who were liberated from slavery, the Sermon on the Mount presupposes the grace of God working through Jesus. Before Jesus preached, there was already the presence of God defeating the power of Satan as we see Jesus' healing of people (cf. Matt. 4:23–5:2). This means that "all the demands which follow presuppose that God's salvation is already in advance as absolutely free gift" and "the liberating and salvific reality of the reign of God is in principle a presupposition of all [his] demands."[24]

---

23. Dale Allison, *The Sermon on the Mount: Inspiring the Moral Imagination* (New York: Crossroad Publishing, 1999), 17.

24. Gerhard Lohfink, *Jesus and Community* (Minneapolis: Fortress Press, 1984), 59.

In short, Matthew introduces Jesus as a new Moses.[25] As Moses gave the law to the liberated people, Jesus is giving a new teaching to the people freed from the shackles of Satan. The connection of the Sermon on the Mount with the Sinai Covenant implies that the Sermon on the Mount is a covenantal renewal speech in light of the inaugurating kingdom of God. This covenantal renewal is found in Jesus' reinterpretation of the Torah. In particular, the six antitheses (two triadic sets) in the Sermon on the Mount (Matt 5:21–48) that begin with "you have heard that.... But I say to you that" redefine Mosaic laws in a new and far more radical and intense form. With their focus on the transformation of human desires and heart, Jesus' moral demands in the Sermon on the Mount go beyond those of Moses.[26]

Not only Jesus' preaching, but also his practices were covenantal. In fact, Jesus was a covenantal man *par excellence*. His life and ministry embodied the spirit and ethos of God's covenant. He concretely showed his followers how to live in covenant with God and others by practicing a life of love, justice, righteousness, and nonviolence. The cross was the climax of Jesus' fidelity to God and others.

Evaluating Glen's "Incarnational Discipleship"

So far, we have studied covenant as the historical drama of the Bible and examined Jesus' ministry and the Sermon on the Mount in its light. What does this study mean for Glen's project?

---

25. The Exodus typology is pervasive in the Gospel of Matthew. For instance, Matthew 2 shows a close association between Herod's killing of all male infants born in Bethlehem (2:16ff) and Pharaoh's edict to slaughter male Hebrew babies in the Book of Exodus.

26. Glen's ten transformative initiatives of the Sermon on the Mount can be explained by the idea of covenantal renewal; Jesus' covenantal renewal, theologically speaking, was not an ordinary renewal but the final, climactic renewal. Blasting all moral complacency, spiritual pretension, and listless ritualism (cf. Allison, *Sermon on the Mount*, 13), Jesus elaborates on what the real heart and true spirit of the Torah are.

The idea of covenant clarifies some conceptual uncertainties, tensions, and insufficiencies within Glen's ethics. Jesus' moral teachings become far clearer and more sensible when interpreted through the lens of covenant; such is also the case for the relationship of justification and sanctification.

First, a covenant interpretation of the Sermon on the Mount addresses a traditional criticism or reservation about the Sermon on the Mount: that it is too idealistic or impractical, even counterintuitive; as feminist theologians charge, the Sermon unintentionally inculcates passivity and servility that undermines women's agency and self-love. To counter this criticism, Glen introduced the idea of delivering and "participative grace."[27]

Covenant explains Glen's idea of delivering and participative grace more coherently than his concept of incarnational discipleship. In a covenantal relationship, Christian moral life is first indicative before imperative; as mentioned above, the covenant presupposes God's initiating grace in the form of either deliverance or royal grant (promise of blessings). Christian moral actions flow from our loving relationship with God, empowered by God's grace.

Second, covenant makes incarnational discipleship more explicitly relational and communal. Covenantal interpretation of the Sermon on the Mount fully captures the relational, solidaristic nature of Jesus' ministry and of discipleship. Despite his emphasis on community,[28] Glen's incarnational discipleship does not offer a concrete mechanism for building a community; actually, his historical examples mostly have to do with individuals. However, in this time of fluidity, mobilization, and fragmentation, one cannot simply presume the existence of a moral community; building such a community is a challenge and a task.

Covenant is the paradigm of God's community-organizing in the Bible. We should remember that Jesus preached God's sovereign reign, exercised prophetic criticism against idolatry and injustices, and

---

27. David P. Gushee and Glen H. Stassen, *Kingdom Ethics: Following Jesus in Contemporary Context*, 2nd ed. (Grand Rapids, MI: Eerdmans, 2016), 24–26.

28. Glen's character ethics presupposes a moral community and its practices for Christian character formation.

called for ongoing repentance; but he also formed a new community around his body, the Eucharist, a covenantal meal for Christians. Covenant aspires to shalom community, and it builds friendship interpersonally on the basis of freedom, mutual trust, accountability, reciprocity, and generosity inspired by God's grace. Without this relational ground of covenant, incarnational discipleship could be misconstrued as a form of moral heroism, especially in the current milieu of spiritual individualism.

Third, the proposal of covenant as the historical drama of the Bible renders not only coherence but also better comprehensive attention to the biblical data and doctrines—christology in particular, which Glen's ethics very rarely addresses. For example, Glen's reference to the Old Testament is quite limited; he connects Jesus primarily to the prophet Isaiah. By doing so, he makes Jesus' connection with the Torah and other books in the Old Testament tenuous or ambiguous. Similarly, Glen's view of Jesus is still very Gospel-oriented; Glen sees Jesus primarily through the synoptic Gospels. It is also unclear what the relationship of the Jesus of the synoptic Gospels is to the Jesus of the fourth Gospel and other New Testament literature. That is, his christological focus is more on the humanity than the divinity of Jesus, although the divinity of Jesus has moral implications, as Larry Rasmussen's essay in this volume brilliantly testifies in his discussion of incarnation. Similarly, Glen's christology focuses more on the prophetic and kingly offices than on the priestly office of Jesus, which is important for the formation and nurturing of moral agency and the empowerment of people.

Importantly, covenant bridges a christology from below and above. It attends to all three offices of Jesus, including the priestly one. Jesus proclaimed not only the reign of God's love and justice (in the anticipation of the New Exodus), but also built a new community around himself. He gave himself as the covenantal sacrifice and bond between God and humanity. He is the locus of divine-human, human-creaturely communication. Jesus fulfilled the covenant and has become the new covenant itself.[29] His New Covenant is eternally

---

29. Glen claims that "the central dramatic thrust is Jesus' embodiment of the reign of God as fulfillment of the Old Testament and his confronting the powers

celebrated as the key ritual of Christianity; his flesh and blood has atoning power, as the Letter to the Hebrews attests. A new, inclusive, and egalitarian community was formed around his body as the new covenant: the church.

Having examined covenant's contribution to resolving some internal tensions of incarnational discipleship, we now move to the next criterion: how it "generates new content, predicting some novel, hitherto unexpected discoveries."

Covenant and Ecology

Moving beyond an anthropocentric approach to social justice, covenant enables Christians to embrace the ecological dimension of social justice and incarnational discipleship. It expands the horizon of Christian witness and fidelity from human-to-human relationships to God-creation and human-creation relationships. Covenant helps Christians to embrace the entire biosphere as a domain of Christian witness and discipleship.

Covenant is God's cosmology that describes the interdependent, organic, unceasing communication among God's creatures. In the biblical idea of covenant, soteriology is cosmic in its scope; it locates human salvation in the cosmic redemption, and human economy in the planetary economy. It takes all of God's creatures and the natural world itself as rightful members and therefore stakeholders of God's moral community. By attending to the claims and rights of other species, it frees social justice from being enslaved by anthropocentrism.

Covenant and Global Justice

A novel, generative power of covenant is found in its moral relevance to building global institutions and global civil society. Just as the Pu-

---

and authorities" (*A Thicker Jesus*, 12). From a covenantal perspective, however, to proclaim that Jesus is the New Covenant, or the fulfillment of all covenants, is another way of saying that Jesus is the culmination of the biblical drama of God's redemption.

ritans discovered the idea of covenant as an inclusive theological framework for coping with the challenges of early modern society in the New World, key covenantal insights and principles (God's sovereignty, checks and balances, communicative reasoning, recognition of the depravity of human nature, the critical function of reason in knowing truth and morality, and the constitutive power of covenant) are still valid today in dealing with institutional and ethical challenges of a globalizing society.[30] These include fighting against neoliberal corporatocracy and devising global laws, institutions, and organizations that we desperately need in this era of climate change, human trafficking, and ethnic cleansing. A covenantal approach will empower the United Nations and other international organizations, which is consonant with Glen's eighth practice of just peacemaking.[31] A covenantal social imagination helps to conceptualize coherently the complex relationships of nations—affirming the autonomy of each in mutual coordination and checks and balances.

Misuse/Abuse of Covenant

In recent history, covenant theology has been extensively criticized for its misuse/abuse for its use of racist politics and association with colonial projects: Puritan genocide of Native Americans, American Anglo-Saxon nationalism, the South African apartheid system, and so on. Despite these troubling historical problems, there is no necessarily causal relationship between covenant theology and colonialism/racism; rather, the use of covenant for racist practices has to do with a narrow, distorted ethnocentric understanding of the Exodus narrative, especially the misappropriation of the conquest narrative. In fact, in the West, as an integral part of the Exodus story (liberation from Egypt-covenant-wilderness-the promised land), covenant has offered a democratic social imagination in constituting a new, just, and egalitarian society based on the consent of the people under

---

30. Daniel Elazar, *Constitutionalizing Globalization: The Postmodern Revival of Confederal Arrangements* (Lanham, MD: Rowman & Littlefield Publishers, 1998).

31. Glen Stassen,ed., *Just Peacemaking: Ten Practices for Abolishing War*, 2nd ed. (Cleveland: Pilgrim Press, 1998), 156–65.

God. That is to say, the Bible presents a covenantal community (Israel and Church) unequivocally as an alternative to oppressive systems and ideologies of existing societies. This transformative insight is still relevant today in building an ecological civilization that applies covenantal fidelity and commitment to the entire planet and other creatures beyond a human community.

To correct the Reformed misuse of covenant, we emphasize two things. First, the Exodus story should be qualified in light of Jesus' New Covenant. Ethno-racial exclusivism happens, as in the case of Puritans, when Christians borrow their ethics selectively from the Mosaic law rather than from the Sermon on the Mount. The Exodus story is the beginning story of the people of God, but not the final story of God's covenant. Jesus is the New Covenant; the covenant is fulfilled in Jesus Christ. Fulfilling God's promise to Abraham, the New Covenant expands membership (the boundary of a moral community) to the whole of humanity, with equality among the members and the entire creation.

A reconstruction of covenant on the basis of the New Covenant of Jesus provides a way to correct a racist interpretation of the covenant. It counters theocratic, authoritarian, or hegemonic tendencies, such as the Puritan "rage for order," and it severs the mistaken and dangerous tie of covenant with the story of conquest in the Old Testament. Jesus' story brings in the inclusive, nonviolent, and egalitarian nature and eschatological and cosmic scope of God's covenant, proclaiming God's promise of freedom for all humans. In addition, we need to uphold and teach the earthly Jesus as a concrete model of the covenantal life in the way Glen does in his book.[32]

Second, to overcome the dangerous misuse and abuse of covenant, we should emphasize God's solidarity with the poor and the weak (including other creatures) as the core component of God's liberation and covenant. This would undermine any attempt to hijack covenant for power and privilege. When properly interpreted in light of the great synthesis of the Exodus (liberation

---

32. Glen also notes that the early authoritarian tendency of Puritans was partly corrected with the more Christocentric voice of the radical wing of the Reformation: Baptists, Anabaptists, and Quakers (Stassen, *A Thicker Jesus*, 66).

motif) and the Jesus movement (nonviolence, eschatological inclusiveness), covenant evokes and releases the impulses of the radical politics of God's kingdom which is grassroots-oriented (not elitist), bottom-up (not top-down), organic/dynamic, and democratic (not bureaucratic) in nature.

The correction of the abuse/misuse of covenant was exemplified by Martin Luther King Jr. during the Civil Rights Movement; the African American church tradition embodies the best of both the Exodus and the Sermon on the Mount. With his emphasis on nonviolence and solidarity with the poor, King liberated a racialized covenant of whites with his idea of the beloved community—the inclusive covenant community of God.

Conclusion

This chapter argues that covenant has an explanatory power for key ideas and motifs of incarnational discipleship. When located in an explicit covenantal framework, Glen's ethics of incarnational discipleship obtains more problem-solving power and expansiveness. By taking covenant as its theological matrix, incarnational discipleship receives internal coherence, an encompassing social outlook, and broad social relevance. A covenantal interpretation of Jesus' ministry, life, death, and resurrection brings out a broader social and cosmic dimension and deeper ethical meanings of God's reign revealed and practiced in Jesus Christ. Furthermore, the fertility of covenant continues today as it offers new insights and directives for our moral life in a globalizing world threatened by ecological crisis and neoliberal domination.

However, this does not mean that covenant replaces Jesus-centered ethics. As the historical drama of the Bible, covenant is the framework (ground) and scaffold of incarnational discipleship that offers a deeper, relational, theological ground for incarnational discipleship. In fact, covenant delineates the moral ecology, theological mooring, and rich soil where incarnational discipleship is sown and grows.

Furthermore, in testing the historical fruits of incarnational discipleship, we need to pay close attention to a moral community or an environment where Christian heroes/heroines are shaped and nurtured. Generally, this moral community takes the character of covenant, with the qualities of mutual trust, care, commitment to justice and the common good (public interest), trust in God's sovereignty, sense of responsibility, affirmation of the universal dignity of every person, protest against injustices, and willingness to suffer.[33] We need to nurture a covenantal community among us that forms and sustains many incarnational disciples. Without this rich covenantal soil, such discipleship will not only be rare, but could be misconstrued as something possible only for extraordinarily spiritual persons. A thicker Jesus is our prime model to follow; however, we need many other models of Christians around us.

---

33. We see such examples of covenantal community in King's intimate relationship and support of friends, family, and communities, and Bonhoeffer's underground seminary in Finkenwalde.

SEVEN

America's Cultural Ethos of White Supremacy

Peter J. Paris

With a broad brush, so to speak, the purpose of this chapter is to discuss a particular form of idolatry that has been dominant in the western world for many centuries. It takes the form of a cultural ethos more commonly known as white supremacy, a subject that has been receiving considerable attention in recent years both in academic studies and public discourse.

When the American public first learned about the medical experiment on six hundred African American men without their knowledge or consent that had been undertaken for forty years (1932–72) by the United States Public Health Service at Tuskegee, countless numbers of people were greatly shocked. On May 16, 1997, President Clinton issued his apology to the eight surviving men and their families (five of whom were present for the occasion) in the East Room of the White House. The apology included the provision of initial funds to found, though not sustain, the Bioethics Center at Tuskegee University, which opened in 1999. Thus, the government's response to the tragedy was necessary but altogether insufficient.

In retrospect, we now know that we should not have been surprised by the news about the experiment. Many years ago, in an essay entitled "A Genealogy of Modern Racism," the renowned Professor Cornel West wrote:

> The notion that black people are human beings is a relatively new discovery in the modern west. The idea of black equality in beauty, culture, and intellectual capacity remains problematic and controversial within prestigious halls of learning and sophisticated intellectual circles.[1]

In this chapter, we will attempt to ground West's reference to modern racism in this cultural ethos of *white supremacy* in the western world. Ethos is the transliteration of the Greek word *ethos*, which designates the spirit or character of either a group or a society and which, in one way or another, integrates all the beliefs, values, and practices of its individual members, associations, and institutions. In short, a cultural ethos constitutes the substratum that holds everything together and readily separates those who belong from those who do not.

Thus, unlike such terms as white racism, white power, white privilege or even racial prejudice, the cultural ethos of white supremacy transcends all of them by its inclusion of the rational, emotive, political, economic, and psychological domains of its adherents. Further, it includes all those various manifestations of racism mentioned above. Consequently, West's term, "modern racism," not only assumes many forms but is expressive of and grounded in the cultural ethos of white supremacy, which implies a coherent set of normative values, beliefs, and attitudes that constitute the culture's essence or character. In short, a cultural ethos designates that culture's way of life. It is the living spirit of the people.

The Greek philosopher Aristotle considered ethos and ethics to be closely related in that the former constitutes the subject matter of the latter. Since ethicists participate in the society they study and embrace many of its basic values, beliefs, and practices that have helped shape them as moral beings, one might rightly ask how they avoid ethnocentrism in their studies. The answer lies in their engagement with other scholars, including ethicists from differing cultural contexts, by listening to their criticisms and demonstrating a willingness to respond to them in a collegial way.

---

1. Cornel West, *Prophesy Deliverance: An Afro-American Revolutionary Christianity* (Philadelphia: Westminster, 1982), 47.

We should note, however, that all who embrace their cultural ethos do so with their whole being, which includes both their reasoning and emotional capacities. It should also be noted that we are all born into a cultural ethos and are largely shaped by it morally, though not all in the same way. Now, despite their place of birth, both long-time racial minorities and recent immigrants are usually viewed by the dominant group as outsiders who will adapt gradually and according to the ethos they have inherited, with people of color being inferior under the aegis of white supremacy.

The cultural ethos of white supremacy did not just originate on European soil; it provided the motivation for Europe's many historical practices of oppressing indigenous peoples of color including: (a) the conquest of the Americas between the sixteenth and eighteenth centuries; (b) the transatlantic African slave trade between the sixteenth and nineteenth centuries; (c) European colonialism throughout the southern hemisphere between the eighteenth and twentieth centuries; (d) the American systems of domestic chattel slavery, racial segregation, discrimination, disenfranchisement, and disproportionate impoverishment of African peoples within its borders (seventeenth to twenty-first centuries); (e) South Africa's system of apartheid (twentieth century); (f) the oppression of indigenous people in Australia and New Zealand (eighteenth century) and the annexation of the Philippines (1898); (g) the genocide of Jews in Nazi Germany (twentieth century). Though the Jews were not people of color, their religion was considered alien to the European cultural ethos that for centuries had identified itself with Christian antisemitism based on the view that the Jews had killed Christ.

The cultural ethos of white supremacy that justified such horrific practices as conquest and enslavement also formed the framework for both the eighteenth-century French and American Revolutions. Their revolutionary goals of liberty, justice, and equality were intended to be the inheritance of white European men only. Furthermore, the worldview that had justified all such global conquests by Europeans also formed the framework for the writers of the American constitution who, because they were not able to resolve the problem of the African slave trade at that time, deliberately chose to forgo doing so for another twenty years.

Yet, after that terrible trade in human beings was abolished in England in 1807 and in the United States in 1808 the domestic system of chattel slavery was allowed to remain in place in the United States until the end of the Civil War in 1865. It is a curious fact, however, that in that same year, the Ku Klux Klan (KKK) was formed in Pulaski, Tennessee, as a paramilitary terrorist organization that lynched and intimidated blacks with impunity through the second half of the twentieth century. Further, and most important, full citizenship rights for formerly enslaved Africans were not protected by the constitution until the Fourteenth and Fifteenth Amendments were ratified, in 1868 and 1870 respectively.

After two-and-a-half centuries of chattel slavery the newly created institution of Jim Crow racism became the law of the land in the *Plessy v. Ferguson* Supreme Court decision of 1896. It remained in place until the 1954 *Brown v. Board of Education* decision, which became the impetus for the mid-twentieth-century civil rights movement. At that time, the United States of America was racially segregated throughout the entire South and largely so in the North. All of the above-mentioned racial proscriptions (and more) evidenced a profound discontent with all post–Civil War notions of equal citizenship rights for black and white Americans.[2]

While still grieving the assassination of President John F. Kennedy and bristling from the courageous leadership of Fannie Lou Hamer and the surprisingly powerful challenge of the Mississippi Freedom Democratic Party at the 1964 National Democratic Convention in Atlantic City, President Lyndon Baines Johnson astutely recognized that the time was ripe for the major legislative initiative that the late President John F. Kennedy had promised. Thus, he quickly pressed Congress to pass the Civil Rights Act of 1964, soon followed by the Voting Rights Act of 1965, both of which provided the structural framework for the most significant advances in racial justice since Reconstruction. Alas, the importance of those gains would soon appear to dissipate with the rising opposition to the war

---

2. See Henry Louis Gates Jr., *Stony the Road: Reconstruction, White Supremacy, and the Rise of Jim Crow* (New York: Random House, 2018) for a full study of the author's perceptive analysis of white supremacy during the Reconstruction era.

in Vietnam, the assassinations of Malcolm X (1965), Martin Luther King Jr. (April 1968) and Robert F. Kennedy (June 1968), numerous urban uprisings by oppressed blacks, and the 1968 election of Richard Nixon, who promised to return law and order to the nation's cities. All of those events combined in marking the continuing decline of racial justice initiatives for the next two decades. During that period, the nation launched a War on Drugs campaign that succeeded in incarcerating tens of thousands of young black men, with devastating effects on poor black families throughout urban America.[3]

Under President Obama's watch, a growing phenomenon of violence by the police against unarmed young black men reached an all-time high, with innocent victims like the seventeen-year-old Trayvon Martin, who was killed on February 26, 2012, in Sanford, Florida, by George Zimmerman (a watch coordinator for his gated community), and eighteen-year-old Michael Brown Jr., who was shot to death by a white police officer in Ferguson, Missouri, on August 8, 2014. The latter's body lay uncovered in the street on a hot summer's day for four hours, which was viewed by many as an act of disrespect. The deaths of these two young men soon became symbols of a rapidly emergent tragic reality. In their cases, and many others like them, the assailants were exonerated, much to the bewilderment and shock of the black community. Eventually, the Black Lives Matter Movement emerged in 2015. It comprised a new generation of interracial young people under the leadership of blacks militantly advocating for justice through disruptive public protests.

AMERICAN EXCEPTIONALISM

As an aside, let us note the ongoing importance of the popular doctrine of American exceptionalism which, to the quiet embarrassment of many blacks, President Barack Obama fully embraced. The doctrine is rooted in the ideology of the nation's uniqueness as established by its successful revolutionary victory over monarchical rule

---

3. See Michelle Alexander's award-winning book, *The New Jim Crow: Mass Incarceration in the Age of Colorblindness* (New York: The New Press, 2010).

and the founding of a nation based on the principles of liberty, egalitarianism, separation of church and state, personal liberty for its citizens, and laissez-faire economics. The combination of these values constitutes what is popularly known as American exceptionalism, which is an ideology that is affirmed by all patriotic Americans as a symbol of pride in one's nation, religion, and way of life. Both black and white politicians invariably evoke its symbolic power whenever they are campaigning for votes. For whites, it conveys an uncritical embrace of all the nation's basic beliefs and values as legitimated by the constitution. With the exception of Barack Obama, who heartily and regularly embraced the doctrine, most blacks are more apt to embrace it when addressing predominantly white audiences while side-stepping it when their audience is predominantly black because of a more critical and nuanced view of its meaningfulness.

The Eugenics Movement and Its Relation to the Experiment at Tuskegee

Though the cultural ethos of white supremacy was the primary cause of our government's medical experiment at Tuskegee, its ideological foundation was both strengthened and justified by the pseudo-scientific eugenics movement that began in the late-nineteenth century and reached its zenith in the United States in the 1930s when the experiment was being launched.

In the late-nineteenth and early-twentieth centuries, the so-called eugenics movement gained widespread prominence in the United States, Canada, the United Kingdom, and elsewhere in Western Europe. Its primary concern was to develop the ways and means to improve the quality of the "genetic stock" of the white population by prohibiting those carrying supposedly undesirable genetic traits from passing them on to future generations. By doing so, they sought to control the reproductive processes of all the so-called undesirables through programs that promised the elimination of all threats to *good* genetics; hence the term eugenics. All who were thought unfit to reproduce were forcibly prevented from doing so. Thus, those with low IQ's, the mentally deficient (then called the feebleminded), epileptics, the physically disabled, criminals, deviants, prostitutes, immigrants, unmarried mothers, and non-white racial groups were all candidates for the procedures. The vast majority of the non-white racial groups outside the United States were living at that time under the colonial rule of various European countries, not for altruistic reasons but for the economic advantage of the colonial powers.

In the 1930s, the eugenics movement became associated with the racial ideology of Nazi Germany. Tragically, Adolf Hitler was inspired by the leading proponent of eugenics, an American biologist named Charles Davenport, who was also a strong advocate for racial segregation and discrimination in the United States. Furthermore, the United States was also engaged at the time in its forced sterilization programs on poor black, Puerto Rican, and Native American women. Many of those procedures were undertaken in government hospitals immediately after women had given birth and without their informed consent. Others took place in prisons. Most occurred among women who were either illiterate or semi-literate and, hence, unable to understand enough to give their informed consent if they had been asked to do so.

Eugenics was not only taught and studied at most of our nation's prominent universities, but its research was funded by many of our leading philanthropic organizations like Kellogg, Carnegie, Russell Sage, and Rockefeller, to name only a few. Ironically, several of them were benefactors of the then Tuskegee Institute and had funded the construction of several buildings that now immortalize their names. The eugenics movement also enjoyed the support of many learned white Protestant and Catholic clergy. Most disturbing to this writer are signs of its influence on the iconic African American intellectual W. E. B. DuBois' understanding of his signature "Talented Tenth" doctrine.

During the early years of the twentieth century, medical doctors, legislatures, and social reformers with appreciation for the eugenics movement joined forces to put sterilization laws on the books, believing that reproductive surgery was a necessary public health intervention to protect society from deleterious genes that would certainly degenerate the majority race. In 1907, Indiana became the first state to legalize the practice of forced sterilization.

Some estimate that over sixty-four thousand Americans were forcibly sterilized and that more than twenty states have not yet removed laws like these from their books. Sadly, all of those so-called protective measures were practiced on such vulnerable populations as Mexicans and Asians on the West Coast, blacks in the South and Native Americans across the country. The slogan "Mississippi appendectomies" became a pseudonym throughout the South for unnecessary hysterectomies.

Interestingly, in 1973, the Southern Poverty Law Center filed a lawsuit (*Relf v. Weinberger*) on behalf of two mentally disabled sisters who were black—Mary Alice, age fourteen, and Minnie, age twelve. Their mother, who was illiterate, had signed a piece of paper with her "X" expecting that her daughters would have their tubes tied. Instead, they were surgically sterilized with full hysterectomies. The district court later found that between 100,000 and 150,000 poor people were sterilized annually under federally funded programs either without their informed consent or by threats to have their welfare payments terminated if they refused to consent to the procedure. The court case resulted in the judge ordering the government to cease payment for the sterilization of certain designated people and to ensure informed consent for all others.

In 1924, the State of Virginia enacted into law the Virginia Sterilization Act[4] which became the model for the nation after it survived the Supreme Court's review in *Buck v. Bell* (1927). The distinguished Chief Justice Oliver Wendell Holmes Jr. wrote the court's judgment that made the case for eugenics in our legal system. Seventy-five years later, however, on May 2, 2002, Governor Mark Warner apologized for the eugenics law and offered reparations to all who had been sterilized under it. Between 1924 and 1979, the State of Virginia had sterilized more than eight thousand people, which made it second only to California's twenty thousand sterilizations during the same time period. About thirty states, in total, authorized programs in support of the eugenics movement.

---

4. See "A Shameful History: Eugenics in Virginia," ACLU of Virginia, https://acluva.org/en/news/shameful-history-eugenics-virginia. See also *Buck v. Bell*, 274 US 200 (1927), https://www.law.cornell.edu/supremecourt/text/274/200.

Between 1929 and 1974 the State of North Carolina forcibly sterilized 7,600 people under its eugenics program. Though the state legislature voted to grant reparations to the living victims of the eugenics program, actual payment has been long delayed. The United States was not alone in these draconian practices. In 1999, the government of Alberta, Canada, apologized for the 2,800 mentally and physically disabled people it had sterilized, to whom it paid more than $140 million as reparations.[5]

The Enduring Power of the Ethos

The cultural ethos of white supremacy has continued to endure through the numerous struggles for racial integration in the military, public accommodations, access to polling booths, constant conflicts over gerrymandering of voting districts, access to jobs, even the receipt of a few academic awards by blacks. In fact, the ongoing power of the ethos seems to be as unshakable as the caste system in India or the notion that sexuality is solely binary.

Unfortunately, whenever and wherever individuals and groups are denied membership in the human species or granted only partial inclusion therein, they have no claim to unalienable rights whatsoever, and thus become vulnerable subjects to incredible abuse by perpetrators who have no conscience in the matter. In all such instances, the intellectual, spiritual, and moral resources support what we now know as abuse because the value of non-humans or those considered to be sub-humans has always been determined solely by their usefulness to those who exercise control over them.

The Collaborative Activities of White Supremacists

Recently, two scholars—Kathleen Belew, a historian at the University of Chicago, and author J. M. Berger at the Brookings Institution

---

5. See the Alberta Eugenics Board archives, http://eugenicsarchive.ca/discover/tree/5233c4865c2ec5000000008b.

—have gained national publicity for publishing books respectively entitled, *Bring the War Home: The White Power Movement and Paramilitary America*, and *Extremism*.⁶ As scholars of the phenomenon of white racism, which they claim has now morphed into a white supremacist movement, both of them conclude that that movement is bent on fomenting an unprecedented number of seemingly disconnected violent mass killings in both the United States and various European countries as preparatory for a race war that will eradicate peoples of color everywhere and thereby establish white supremacist rule throughout the world. The authors go to great lengths in demonstrating the seriousness of this movement, which they contend deftly utilizes modern information technologies to communicate with members in various types of code around the world. Moreover, they insist that the so-called "lone wolf" terrorist is a misnomer. Rather, they describe significant connections among such terrorist acts as Anders Behring Bievik's killing of seventy-seven people in Oslo, Norway (July 22, 2001); Dylan Roof's killing of nine people in the Emmanuel African Methodist Episcopal Church, in Charleston, SC (June 17, 2015); Omar Mateen's killing of forty-nine people at the Pulse Nightclub in Orlando (June 12, 2016); the white nationalist march at the University of Virginia (August 11, 2017) where three were killed; Robert Bowers's killing of eleven people at the Tree of Life Synagogue, Pittsburgh (November 5, 2018); Brenton Harrison Tarrant's killing of fifty people and wounding of fifty others at two mosques in Christchurch, New Zealand (March 19, 2019), while claiming inspiration from Donald Trump and streaming the horrible event online. Belew and Berger view all of these assailants and others as terrorist actors who enjoy wide support around the world. The movement also applauds the increasing tilt of governments in Europe toward the right, and its members feel energized by the 2016 election of Donald Trump as President of the United States.

---

6. Kathleen Belew, *Bring the War Home: The White Power Movement and Paramilitary America* (Cambridge, MA: Harvard University Press, 2018); J. M. Berger, *Extremism* (Cambridge, MA: MIT Press, 2018).

How to Eradicate a Cultural Ethos

We know how to stop or diminish various types of offensive activities by instituting and enforcing laws and by initiating new educational reform, therapeutic, and rehabilitative programs, but, like various types of cancers and other diseases, we do not know how to cure the ethos of white supremacy that denies others their humanity by declaring them to be inferior to whites. Thus, we currently face a spiritual and moral problem of the first order. Though templates for eradicating a cultural ethos are not readily at hand, might it be that some clues could be derived from the various societal changes that have occurred during the past half century, such as the general acknowledgement of the rights of women, African Americans and other racial/ethnic minorities, the disabled, and the LBGTQIA community? Some might also see evidence of cultural advances in such public practices as wearing seat belts, compliance with recycling programs, and the growing societal recognition of the value of diversity in schools, colleges, universities, and workplaces.

Since a cultural ethos is a powerful force for unifying a population, its embrace or rejection has consequences for the actions, attitudes, and emotions of all concerned. Clearly, the most effective way to do either is to focus attention on the various practices that the ethos inspires. Correspondingly, opponents of that ethos must diligently seek ways to make selected practices visible for public scrutiny, hoping to evoke feelings of abhorrence and shame on the one hand, along with the impulse to eradicate them from our society on the other.

The task of ridding our society of undesirable practices certainly requires use of the law as well as formal and informal education aimed at achieving the desired moral and spiritual development of the citizenry. The creation and support of creative programs aimed at quieting the voices of naysayers is a necessary asset in the quest for such change. For example, the steady public support for the Special Olympics program has done much over the years to change the public's attitude toward children with physical and mental disabilities who were once thought to be incapable of contributing any value to the larger society. Similarly, Gay Pride Parades (now inclusive of an expanded LGBTQIA community), coupled with various other endeavors to promote and actualize their rights as citizens, have resulted in LGBTQIA persons gaining considerable acceptance in the society, as is evident in such areas as the gradual legalization of same-sex marriage; election to political office and inclusion in national defense, industry, and the various professions, to name a few. All of these demonstrate that traditional social views and exclusionary policies can be changed.

Further still, we should mention another significant change in social outlook. The original program of Negro History Week was begun by blacks in 1926 for blacks in racially segregated schools to celebrate their many accomplishments and contributions to the larger society and thus help instill a sense of racial pride in each new generation. By 1970, black students and educators at Kent State University and elsewhere began calling for a month-long celebration of black history. During the 1976 bicentennial, President Gerald Ford recognized it as a fitting annual national event that was later adopted by the governments in Canada, the United Kingdom, and Sweden. All such celebratory events have contributed to the process of possibly weakening though certainly not destroying the cultural ethos of white supremacy.

Similarly, the proposal for a holiday to celebrate the birthday of Martin Luther King Jr., first launched in 1968, eventually became law in 1986 with the clear aim to weaken the ethos of white supremacy. Unfortunately, the nation soon lost sight of that mission, as it gradually though effectively turned the holiday into a national day of service, in which the nation annually turns its attention away from the cultural ethos of white supremacy to that of providing temporary help to people in need.

Memorials in Pursuit of Racial Justice

On August 21, 2011, the Martin Luther King Jr. Memorial was unveiled along the Tidal Basin on the National Mall in Washington, DC, and on September 24, 2016, the National Museum of African

American History and Culture was opened by President Barack Obama on the National Mall as a Smithsonian Institution museum.

On April 26, 2016, under the inspiration and tireless work of Bryan Stevenson, an African American attorney and founder of the Equal Justice Initiative, the National Memorial for Peace and Justice was unveiled in Montgomery, Alabama, along with The Legacy Museum: From Enslavement to Mass Incarceration on the same site. This is the first such memorial dedicated to the memory of more than 4,500 documented people who were lynched in over eight hundred counties (mostly but not all in the South) between the years 1877 and 1950. Those memorials are located across the street from the Southern Poverty Law Center where the Civil Rights Memorial honors the memory of forty-one persons who were killed during the Civil Rights Movement (1955–1968). Both are around the corner from the Dexter Avenue Baptist Church where Dr. Martin Luther King Jr. was pastor when the Montgomery Bus Boycott began in 1955. Unfortunately, the Civil Rights Memorial omits the names of many whose deaths were not verifiable at the time as having been connected directly with the civil rights struggle.

Reparations

In recent years, a steady refrain has been heard from various parts of our society calling for reparations for the centuries of pain and suffering inflicted on people of African descent by the ethos of white supremacy; people in all walks of life continue to suffer from the after-effects of the trauma caused by the ethos of white supremacy that can rightly be diagnosed as Post-Traumatic Stress Disorder (PTSD) and which, in varying ways, affects all African Americans.

Unlike the actions of some states vis-à-vis the practices of the eugenics movement, this nation has never officially apologized for its leading role in the transatlantic slave trade. Recent investigative endeavors undertaken by various universities into the ways they themselves have benefited from the profits of that trade have revealed much useful data in the service of developing a satisfactory argument for reparations which, undoubtedly, would take a long while to complete. Yet, the complexity of the task should not imply the need to abandon it, any more than the difficulties in finding a cure for cancer should lead to a similar decision. Regrettably, thus far, the cultural ethos of white supremacy has proven itself capable of surviving all the above societal changes. Thus, we are still left with the haunting question: Is it possible to eradicate a cultural ethos? If so, where is the evidence in support of such a claim?

Finally, if the embrace of a cultural ethos is an act of worship, as I contend white supremacy is, then readers might be helped by a story told by Professor Nimi Wariboko, the Walter Muelder Professor of Social Ethics at the Boston University School of Theology. In his recent book, *Ethics and Society in Nigeria: Identity, History and Political Theory*, he writes that on September 17, 1857, the people in his native village of Izon in the Niger Delta of Nigeria killed one of their gods (Owu Akpana, the Shark-god) because that deity's demands had become too harsh for the people to endure.[7] Their act of deicide was undertaken by withdrawing their worship and thereby freeing themselves from captivity. Such an act appears to be a most effective and possibly the only means to the desired goal of eradicating a cultural ethos that has become idolatrous. In the face of any such idolatry there can be no reform measures that are curative. There can only be eradication, which can be accomplished only by its worshipers withdrawing their worship. No counteracting external force can be effective.

Thus, in the spirit of Glen Stassen's peacemaking mission that was inspired by Jesus' Sermon on the Mount and Paul's conversion experience of turning away from persecuting God's people to that of embracing the vocation of Christian discipleship, all who read this broad historical overview of the ethos of white supremacy can only pray for sufficient grace to turn away from its grasp and inculcate within themselves Jesus' spirit of love, justice, and peace as explicated so well in his last book, *A Thicker Jesus: Incarnational Discipleship in a Secular Age*.[8]

---

7. Nimi Wariboko, *Ethics and Society in Nigeria* (Rochester: University of Rochester Press, 2019).

8. Glen Harold Stassen, *A Thicker Jesus: Incarnational Discipleship in a Secular Age* (Louisville, KY: Westminster John Knox Press, 2012).

EIGHT

Friendly Amendments

Larry L. Rasmussen

This is the conversation Glen and I never had. We had many.

The first ones we could only surmise, and chuckle about. The Stassens lived in South St. Paul, Minnesota, on what I recall was a circular drive. The Petersons—my aunt, uncle, and four cousins—lived across the circle, and cousins Gary and Loren were playmates with Glen, his sister, the Kellys, and other kids on the drive. Since I joined them when my family visited the Petersons, Glen and I likely were part of the fracas in the circle. But neither of us remembered the other from those times of tag, hide and seek, or catch. If we discussed Christian ethics, it was probably whether all's fair in love and war and hide and seek. What I remember, besides playtime, is my aunt and uncle's admiration of Glen's father, Governor Harold Stassen, and the honor of their family friendship. It is touching to read of Glen's esteem for his father, reflected in the dedication of *A Thicker Jesus*.

We held most of our conversations as Christian ethicists shaped by the 1960s and Union Theological Seminary in New York. Civil rights and race relations, the draft, the war in Vietnam, resistance to it, nukes and the Cold War, peace studies—these engaged us.

In our conversations, Dietrich Bonhoeffer was a meeting ground. "Bonhoeffer is my hero,"[1] Glen writes, and I was not surprised to find Bonhoeffer present throughout *A Thicker Jesus*.

---

1. Glen Harold Stassen, *A Thicker Jesus: Incarnational Discipleship in a Secular Age* (Louisville, KY: Westminster John Knox Press, 2012), 188.

Bonhoeffer's story was existential for Glen. Most vivid to me were our many conversations during a sabbatical year from Southern Baptist Theological Seminary that he spent at Union while I was teaching there. He audited my History of Christian Ethics class and after class we invariably "talked shop" in the Pit. While anything in the *New York Times* was fair game, usually at some point Bonhoeffer made an appearance. The reason stemmed in part from Glen's work on the Sermon on the Mount. His conviction was that of the two resistance movements engaging Bonhoeffer, the *Kirchenkampf* (church struggle) of the Confessing Church and the military-political conspiracy, Bonhoeffer's immersion in the former, driven by his exegesis of the Sermon on the Mount, was underrated and understated in Bonhoeffer studies. Glen saw it as a key to Bonhoeffer's life and thought in the critical years of the 1930s.

That conviction was driven by Glen's own struggle. As Professor of Christian Ethics from 1976 on at Southern, he found himself on the wrong side in nearly every battle with conservatives, whether on the subordination of women, abortion, race privilege, or biblical exegesis. Much of the Union sabbatical year was Glen's awake-at-night "*kampf*" over whether to return to Southern. And, without pretense, he often came back to Bonhoeffer's own decision during his stay at Union in summer 1939 about where he (Bonhoeffer) must, in good conscience, be. "Stay or go" was America or Germany for Bonhoeffer. "Stay or go" was Southern or somewhere else for Glen. I was elated when Fuller Theological Seminary called him as a senior professor of Christian ethics in 1996, a short while after his Union sabbatical. It was the finest possible setting for who he was and a gift for those he would teach.

Glen's immersion in Bonhoeffer studies continued after he moved to Fuller. Indeed, it probably intensified there because he directed PhD dissertations. I know this in part because, now and again, he asked me to join a dissertation committee as the outside reader. The superb quality of work, now available in books by Christine Schliesser and Reggie Williams, for example, is testimony both to their acumen and to Glen's.[2] That he was also a close friend to his

---

2. Reggie L. Williams, *Bonhoeffer's Black Jesus: Harlem Renaissance Theology and an Ethic of Resistance* (Waco, TX: Baylor University Press, 2014); Christine

students and their families simply reflected who he was. If a parallel with Bonhoeffer be risked, it is that what is most apparent for both Dietrich Bonhoeffer and Glen Stassen is the integrity of a principled life. The gap between words and deeds for these two "theologians and activists"[3] was precious small.

Given all this, I will use Bonhoeffer's own question for the conversation Glen and I never had. I do so principally because "Who is Jesus Christ for us today?" was also Glen's question. For Bonhoeffer, it bridged the entire twelve to fifteen years of his mature theological thought. Glen's answer is *A Thicker Jesus* but with much prior attention (e.g., *Kingdom Ethics*, with David Gushee).[4] Both Bonhoeffer and Stassen were self-consciously contextual and Christocentric, with the Sermon on the Mount as a center. "Who Jesus Christ is for us today" goes to the heart of their work.

For my part, I imagine a conversation on the specific meaning of incarnational discipleship. It is necessarily imaginative because my context in 2019 is not Glen's in 2012. Yes, that difference is but a wrinkle in time, but, for our interpretation of *"us today,"* a dramatic seven years.

Where might our conversation have gone? Since we often found ourselves aligned, I would likely have joined Glen in his responses to Donald Trump, Black Lives Matter and police killings, together with entrenched white supremacy and the constitutional crises of a flagging democracy, had his death not preceded these. So, if we differ, it is likely elsewhere, and likely related to a profoundly altered macro-context. A hugely changed context "for us today" might have provoked different responses.

What is today's profoundly altered context, and who are "we" as part of it? Here is a summary from Earth System sciences. (1) Nature is changing course. All systems across the entire biophysical world are in flux. (2) The planet-altering changes are so deep, widespread,

---

Schliesser, *Everyone Who Acts Responsibly Becomes Guilty: Bonhoeffer's Concept of Accepting Guilt* (Louisville/London: Westminster John Knox Press, 2008).

3. The title of the obituaries for Glen Stassen in the *New York Times* and the *Los Angeles Times* was "Theologian and Activist."

4. Glen H. Stassen and David P. Gushee, *Kingdom Ethics: Following Jesus in Contemporary Context* (Downers Grove, IL: Intervarsity Press, 2003).

and rapid that they are *not only historical*, they are *geological*. (3) For this geological lurch, "anthropogenic" change is decisive. Collective, cumulative human impact renders *Homo sapiens* a *geological* force for the first time in human history and Earth's history. (4) This human impact creates a unique moment for both humanity *and* Earth. The International Geosphere-Biosphere Program says that "evidence from several millennia shows that the magnitude and rates of human-driven changes to the global environment are in many cases unprecedented. There is no previous analogue for the current operation of the Earth System."[5] "No previous analogue" means that Earth's past operating systems have never matched present ones. This is in line with all geological change in that every geological epoch is unique, a one off. I know President Trump reassures us that, if, just perhaps, the climate *is* changing, we are not to worry, for "it will change back." No, it will not. Not for millennia and then not back to what it was. Climate system change is baked in and there is no dialing it back. We've broken out of the cycles the president assumes will return. "The planet *will* get warmer. The ice caps *will* melt. The seas *will* rise. The fossil-fueled, consumer capitalist civilization we live in *will* come to an end."[6] "Change back" the planet will not do. (5) Scientists thus announce a new epoch in geological history, "the Anthropocene"—"the Age of the Human." It succeeds the "late Holocene"—the "wholly recent" epoch. Or, in Bonhoeffer's prescient words, an age of unprecedented human knowledge and power has arrived in which "in the end it all comes down to the human being."[7] (6) All the grave questions and issues in this context are thus finally *ethical*—they all turn on human choice and action. Yet, *pace* Bonhoeffer, this age also strains our working ethical concepts to the breaking point and mandates rethinking and reinterpreting the basepoints of Christian faith itself—Who is God, and who is Jesus, Bonhoeffer asks, and what do "creation, fall, reconciliation, re-

---

5. W. I. Steffen et al., *Global Change and the Earth System* (Berlin and New York: Springer, 2004), 81.

6. Roy Scranton, *We're Doomed. Now What?* (New York: Soho Press, 2018), 68.

7. Dietrich Bonhoeffer, "Outline for a Book," in *Dietrich Bonhoeffer Works* (Minneapolis: Fortress Press, 2009), 8:500.

pentance, faith, *vita nova* [new life], last things" mean in this newborn epoch?[8]

This summary may be stark enough, but it doesn't begin to reveal how entrenched in the late Holocene is our perception and thinking, even imagination. Even less does it show that Anthropocene citizens who continue Holocene ways doom their children. Permit a supplement, breezy as it must be.

The supplement is that our Anthropocene powers are altering the core surface processes of Earth itself. "Unsustainability" was the initial recognition that post-1950 growth in the human economy could not be sustained without profoundly and negatively altering the economy it was part of and dependent upon—that of nature. So it turned out that "unsustainability" was a bland term for the late Holocene's dead end, the dead end for the geological epoch that has hosted all human civilizations, bar none, the geological epoch that has seen the writing of all the world's scriptures, indeed all writing of any kind, and, with its rare trademark of climate stability, the geological epoch that has made possible the surviving, even thriving, of human and other life. In fact, the Goldilocks range of temperatures—2 degrees Celsius—bracketed the most essential chapter of *Homo sapiens* life.[9]

We are now leaving that behind, though for what we do not know. It is certainly not "sustainability/unsustainability," since those terms assume some equilibrium, some normal to which we adapt, some frame for ordering our lives, some natural cycles we can rely upon and live with. But nature's mutiny and the defiant Earth of the Anthropocene does not give us a new normal. Rather than a different equilibrium, it yields *a new abnormal* that continues as far as we can see, and beyond. We really have no idea what the end of even this century will look like in Lagos or Miami, Anchorage or Cape Town, Vladivostok, New York, or Santiago.

Yet our default thinking is so rooted in Holocene stability that we try to adjust to changes that are real with conceptions that are

---

8. Ibid., 502.

9. David Wallace-Wells, The *Uninhabitable Earth: A Story of the Future* (New York: Penguin Books, 2019), 43.

not. This is the opening paragraph of David Wallace-Wells's *The Uninhabitable Earth*; our default positions are delusory:

> It is worse, much worse, than you think. The slowness of climate change is a fairy tale, perhaps as pernicious as the one that says it isn't happening at all, and comes to us bundled with several others in an anthology of comforting delusions: that global warming is an Arctic saga, unfolding remotely; that it is strictly a matter of sea level and coastlines, not an enveloping crisis sparing no place and leaving no life undeformed; that it is a crisis of the "natural" world, not the human one; that those two are distinct, and that we live today somehow outside or beyond or at the very least defended against nature, not inescapably within and literally overwhelmed by it; that wealth can be a shield against the ravages of warming; that the burning of fossil fuels is the price of continued economic growth; that growth, and the technology it produces, will allow us to engineer our way out of environmental disaster; that there is any analogue to the scale or scope of this threat, in the long span of human history, that might give us confidence in staring it down.[10]

I only underscore that, in the long span of human history, there isn't any analogue "to the scale or scope of this threat that might give us confidence in staring it down." Which is to say that of the three tattoos of the Anthropocene—climate volatility, eco-social uncertainty, and mass extinction—ongoing uncertainty "is among the most momentous metanarratives that climate change will bring"[11] us. There is no new normal.

And we don't want to contemplate the single analogue that may possibly fit. Of Earth's five previous mass extinctions (we are in the sixth) the one we all know about is the extinction of the dinosaurs in the wake of a huge meteor strike in the Yucatan. None of the other mass extinctions were the work of such aliens, however. All were the home-

---

10. Ibid., 3.
11. Ibid., 43.

grown result of spikes in greenhouse gases. Moreover, none of those, including that of the Eocene, proceeded at the pace by which we are presently changing the chemistry of the atmosphere and the biochemistry of the oceans. We're outpacing previous mass extinctions.

I spare us any further video of the break between the Holocene and the "Age of the Human." My point is far less dramatic. It is this: assuming these Anthropocene powers and the context they have generated, is the Jesus Christ of *A Thicker Jesus* sufficiently "thick"? Does this Jesus address not only a different history but *a successor Earth*? What is incarnational discipleship "for us, today" in the face of realities that witness human powers affecting not only planetary systems in the present but powers that extend our presence into deep time—powers that determine the possibilities for life and death across the community of life for generations unseen? Are human "history" and the human historical drama really the right categories for incarnational discipleship in the face of such planet-shaping powers? Should it not be "planetary creation" and its drama? If "history" *is* to be used, is it not "Big History," where the human drama is a chapter in Earth's drama, even a chapter in the journey of the universe?

In other words, Glen's notion of "history" and the historical drama is Holocene "history." It assumes the stability of that geological epoch and our capacity to track historical changes in order to measure their good or bad fruit. For Glen, historical outcomes test faithful discipleship.

This gives *consequentialist ethics* pride of place as the measure of Christian ethics itself. But what happens to consequentialist ethics when our choices and actions travel so far down the future that we *cannot know* where they finally land? Does not this clear limit to what we can know about outcomes at least mute, if not eviscerate, our notions of what responsible action would be?

In short, how does incarnational discipleship spell out responsibility for large-scale, distant, non-linear consequences of collective, cumulative human powers in an unsettled, qualitatively new epoch? And if incarnational discipleship cannot spell out this responsibility, is that not a reason to bench it?

Before all these questions sound rhetorical, let me say that Glen was keenly aware of what was happening to planetary creation and that it called for repentance and transformation of our way of life. We talked about it, and he writes about it in *A Thicker Jesus*:

> The clearest message from scientists calling for repentance today is that the glaciers are melting, the seas are rising, large areas are suffering from the worst droughts in history, and storms are getting more destructive as carbon dioxide is increasing in the stratosphere. Millions of people are suffering, and even-larger numbers will suffer in the next generations. Furthermore, the earth has a finite quantity of oil, natural gas, and nonrenewable minerals. We are using them up at ever-increasing rates, so they will be mostly all depleted early in this century. They will not grow back. Because of our greed and ignorance, future generations will have almost no resources. We cannot find a nearby planet to migrate to. Mars will not do. Will the Big Bang end with the Big Chill?[12]

My distinction, then, of "creation" from "history" as the laboratory of faith may not, in the end, be meaningful for Glen. Evidently for him, "historical realism" encompasses the fate of planetary creation.

Or does it? Let's pursue the conversation by attending to his key terms, "incarnation" and "discipleship."

I was editor for the English language translation of volume 12 in the collected works of Dietrich Bonhoeffer. It includes Bonhoeffer's lectures on christology. The chief editorial task was to check the English translation for consistency of meaning and expression vis-à-vis Bonhoeffer's writings in previously published volumes. I made a few changes, the most important of them in the christology lectures. There I substituted God's "incarnation" for God "becoming human." The German editor strongly objected. *Nein! Nein! Nein!* bullied its way through the ether. He pointed out that Bonhoeffer uses two words—*Menschwerdung* [becoming human] and *Inkarnation* [incarnation]—and they are not simply interchangeable. Rather, *Menschwer-*

---

12. Stassen, *A Thicker Jesus*, 100.

dung is one instance of *Inkarnation*. Christians may regard God "becoming human" in Jesus as decisively revelatory for *human* being—that is certainly Bonhoeffer's position, and Glen's—but *Inkarnation* is far broader, more ranging. Its domain is creation, or cosmos, not human nature and human society only. *Inkarnation* includes the human story but its cosmic reach encompasses far more, and Bonhoeffer was deliberate in his choice of words.

In other words, when "incarnation" is used christologically, the proper reference is the Cosmic Christ, the one in whom "all things in heaven and on earth were created" and in whom "all things hold together," "the firstborn of all creation" and "the firstborn of the dead." In this one, all "the fullness of God was pleased to dwell," and "through him God was pleased to reconcile to himself all things, whether on earth or in heaven." (cf. Col 1:15–20). "All things"—*ta panta*—is a drumbeat in this Colossians hymn, repeated five times in five verses.

Consider, too, the Prologue to John's Gospel. The creating Word was with God, was God, and is the one through whom all things came into being and without whom "not one thing came into being." This same one also pitched a tent among us (cf. John 1:1–3, 14).

This has been termed christology from above. It starts in heaven with God as Word creating the world and then, with a downward arc, covenants with "all flesh" (Gen 9:16–17). This is YHWH, "the God of all flesh" (Jer 32:27) who "will pour out my spirit on all flesh" (Joel 2:28). This one, sometimes named *Sophia* (Wisdom), sometimes *Logos* (Word), also chooses to become *sarx* (flesh) as a person and dwell among people, "full of grace and truth."

By comparison, christology from below starts on Earth, in Galilee, with the life, teaching, ministry, and death of Jesus of Nazareth, and then "traces his resurrection into glory into heaven, so to speak, from where as Lord and Christ he sends the life-giving Spirit."[13] Here christology's arc is upward. The Gospel of Mark most vividly displays this, almost in staccato fashion, and I think it not coincidental that Glen chooses Mark and Bonhoeffer for his study in

---

13. Elizabeth A. Johnson, *Creation and the Cross: The Mercy of God for a Planet in Peril* (Maryknoll, NY: Orbis Books, 2018), 159–60.

christology, together with another christology from below, that of Matthew and the Sermon on the Mount.

Christology from below is, in Bonhoeffer's term (and true to Glen), *Menschwerdung*, God "becoming human." By way of contrast, but not opposition, christology from above is *Inkarnation*, the living presence of God in all that ever was or will be, from Alpha to Omega.

An Orthodox icon in poster form presents *Inkarnation* and christology from above in striking fashion.[14] The occasion was an Orthodox Summit on the Environment where the public ritual was a blessing of the waters in Baltimore harbor after extensive port renovations. The icon displays the familiar Orthodox images of roiling waters as the waters of life, the tree of life at the center (as it is in Eden), and the sacred mountain divided so as to become a wide opening to Paradise. The dome is home to golden rays of sunshine and plentiful refreshing rain, both streaming down from above. The calligraphy identifies this as: *The Incarnate God*.

Notably missing are human beings, indeed signs of any distinctly human presence whatsoever. No buildings, no cultivated fields, not even a well-traveled pathway. There is writing, however—Greek shorthand astride the tree of life. The full identification that draws on this shorthand reads as follows: "'Christ the Tree of Life,' by Father Andrew Tregubov, is an allegorical image of Paradise. Of the Kingdom of God, whose gates are open and whose waters of life stream from their source—the Tree of Life—that is Jesus Christ, the only begotten Son of God, the Savior of the world."[15]

"Christ the Tree of Life" and "the Savior of the world" is redemption theology. And true to Orthodox theology, redemption is cosmic in scope and focus. In contrast to Protestantism, the Eastern Church does not concentrate on sin but on the deliverance from death and its corruption into flourishing creation. Furthermore, this is good news for *all* creatures, not humankind only. Indeed, in the central sacrament of every Mass, the Eucharist, *all nature* is transfig-

---

14. An image of the icon is available at https://www.svspress.com/incarnate-god-the-set/. *The Incarnate God* is the title of a two volume set, *The Incarnate God* (Crestwood, NY: St. Vladimir's Press, 1995).

15. Cited from *The Incarnate God* and used with permission by St. Vladimir's Seminary Press, 575 Scarsdale Road, Crestwood, New York.

ured.[16] To cite Ambrose of Milan in the fourth century: "In Christ's resurrection the earth itself arose."[17]

Clearly, this is a different provenance for "incarnation" from Glen's historical realism and God become human in Jesus of Galilee. The laboratory of lived faith here is creation. If human history is included, there are no obvious signifiers of it. It certainly is not singled out, nor made the testing ground.

But for Glen, the full force of "incarnation" *is* God "becoming human." *Menschwerdung* and *Inkarnation* are synonyms. The question that follows is whether "becoming human" suffices for the scope and content of "incarnational discipleship." What happens to other-than-human and more-than-human creation crowned, along with 'd m/' d mâh as "very good" (Gen 1:31)? What is their place as the partners of God in the first and everlasting covenant, the covenant "between me [God] and you [Noah and his family] and *every creature of all flesh*"? (Gen 9:15; emphasis mine) What happens to the more than 13.6 billion years of the universe before humans appear?

Christology from above includes those 13.6 plus billion years. Glen's, however, is christology from below and the normativity of its Jesus. Oddly, for an ethicist so biblically grounded as Glen, this neglects the Pauline and Johannine christologies. Jesus seems thinner, rather than thicker.

I'm omitting Protestant parallels to Orthodox panentheism, specifically Luther's and Bonhoeffer's, and going straight to the question: If panentheism ("all in God and God in all") is the heart of incarnation, with the entire cosmos the heartbeat of God, does that make a difference for incarnational discipleship as Glen recommends it? What difference does it make if planetary creation comprehensively, rather than human history and its drama, is discipleship's terrain?

Perhaps none. A backstory that mattered to Glen was his training as a nuclear physicist. He pictured the universe interacting at every level, with indeterminacy and interaction even at the atomic and subatomic level.[18] The science chapter of *A Thicker Jesus* testifies to a

---

16. Johnson, *Creation and the Cross*, 190–91.

17. Cf. Johnson, *Creation and the Cross*, 190.

18. Stassen, *A Thicker Jesus*, 84.

God who continually renews a creation that is "alive."[19] The sovereignty of God "throughout all of life," one of the pillars of incarnational discipleship, thus includes cosmic reality.[20] All this leaves Glen, the scientist, a person given to cosmic wonder. The question is how this metaphysic and this wonder belong to the *methodology* of incarnational discipleship. They clearly belong to Glen's piety. Do they also belong to his ethical method? If so, how?

Another way to pursue our imagined conversation turns to "discipleship," there to ask about social justice and creation justice.

The long obedience of discipleship for Glen is about social justice. But what is its assumed context?

Its assumed context is human-to-human relationships across human society. Responsibility is conceived as human choice and action undertaken with a view to the consequences for society. But responsibility does not include responsibility in and for the ecosphere (planet) as a whole *even when* the global economy profoundly alters the generative elements of life itself—earth (soil), air, fire (energy), and water. In this moral world, soil, air, energy, and water must necessarily be attended to, but not because they make *moral claims* on us. People living this version of responsibility do not ask, as a matter of ethical method: What does water require of us? What does the river want, or the oceans? What sacrifice does the atmosphere ask of us for its life-essential work? What is our moral obligation to forests and mountains and their life? Rather, nature exists for human well-being, albeit for some humans far more than others.

Important exceptions to this understanding of moral responsibility exist. Many, perhaps most, indigenous peoples' traditions align human responsibility with the requirements of the ecosphere as that is present where they live. They understand what the industrial revolution sublimated: namely, that *because human well-being is always deriva-*

---

19. Ibid., 84.

20. Ibid., 86. While Stassen states this earlier, it is repeated here in the science chapter. Note should also be made that Nancey Murphy, a colleague specializing in the relationship of science and religion, is clearly appreciated by Glen. Her work is a source for him years after having left his time as a physicist behind. This is testimony to his ongoing attention to science as important for theological ethics.

tive, ecospheric well-being is always *primary*.[21] More recently, the Environmental Justice Movement of peoples of color has underscored a similar understanding of human bodies in their environments.[22]

A bounded notion of responsibility and justice as human-to-human blinded most to the impact of human choices and actions as spatially coterminous with the ecosphere itself. It also blinded most to consequences traveling into deep time, constraining what future generations will have for their diminished planet. By not taking responsibility for these choices and actions, we brought an end to the late Holocene and its climate stability, and created the climate volatility, eco-social uncertainty, and mass extinctions of the early Anthropocene.

The question for us is: How do we reconceive moral duty and discipleship when our powers are exercised "cumulatively across generational time, aggregately through ecological systems, and non-intentionally over evolutionary futures?"[23] Might contrasting social justice with creation justice suggest an answer?

There is no doubt about Glen's continuous passion for social justice, nor any doubt that *A Thicker Jesus* is a splendid work in Christian social ethics. But unless Glen's is an exception, most Protestant social justice campaigns, at least white Protestant ones, have focused on human society as a domain abstracted from the natural world. Harm that falls outside intra-human relationships is an "externality." Like an externality in the market economy, it is real and must be addressed. But it does not fold in the full and true costs. Likewise, (white) social justice did not fold in the following *as matters of justice*: disappearing species and shrinking habitat, eroding soils, altered gene pools, collapsing fisheries, souring seas, receding forests, melting glaciers, river delta dead zones, migrating pests and diseases, rising sea levels, biodiversity loss, changes in coastal zone structure, lost

---

21. A paraphrase of Thomas Berry's "Planetary health is primary; human well-being is derivative," in Thomas Berry, "Conditions for Entering the Ecozoic Era," *Ecozoic Reader* 2, no. 2 (Winter 2002):10.

22. See Melanie Harris, *EcoWomanism: African-American Women and Earth-Honoring Faiths* (Maryknoll, NY: Orbis Books, 2018).

23. Willis Jenkins, *The Future of Ethics: Sustainability, Social Justice, and Religious Creativity* (Washington: Georgetown University Press, 2013), 1.

wetlands and bleaching coral reefs, gyres of deadly plastic in the oceans, more greenhouse gases, rising surface temperatures, more intense storms and flooding, deeper drought, and climate volatility.

Of course, items on this miserable list were noted—many of them by Glen himself. But until their impact extended to potential or actual *human* harm, they were externalities that failed to capture attention as *justice* issues. Until they intersect human health, they don't fit the template.[24]

In other words, largely gone missing in Protestant social justice is the natural world as worthy of any reverence such that it makes moral claims upon us and is itself due justice. The quest for social justice, and the glory of its achievements, was to render the consequences of the industrial economy *fairer* in the lives of many of those determined by it. But this was justice captured by an economic cosmos tone deaf to the needs of the natural world. And precisely that economic cosmos, gone global, is, as we have noted, an economy on a collision course with the economy upon which it depends but which it neglects and degrades—that of the planet.[25]

Social justice as it emerged here assumes that the basic unit of human survival is human society. It is not. It is planetary creation comprehensively, with the primal elements—earth (soil), air, fire (energy), water—truly primary. The human common good is not possible without care for the goods of the planetary commons. "Creation," rather than human "history," is the key domain.

So let's propose "creation justice." The question then becomes: What would it take for social justice to become creation justice while at the same time not losing the fire of social justice? The fire of social justice must *not* be lost because Anthropocene climate change makes social justice both *more difficult and more urgent.* More difficult because injustice has a farther reach in space and time, with probably fewer resources relative to the scale of the problems; and more diffi-

---

24. There are exceptions, the exceptions noted earlier—the attention of most indigenous peoples and of many in the Environmental Justice Movement.

25. This discussion of social and creation justice draws upon my chapter, "Getting from Protestant Social Justice to Interfaith Creation Justice: What Does It Take?" in *Living Cosmology: Responses to Journey of the Universe,* ed. Mary Evelyn Tucker and John Grim (Maryknoll, NY: Orbis Books, 2016), 145–53.

cult because those who contribute least to climate injustice are those who suffer most from it. With climate injustice, "life [as] unfair" is on steroids.

For social justice to become creation justice, deep theological and moral transformation is required. We can still conceive of it as incarnational discipleship, and we should. But incarnation here is cosmic and asks for a cosmology that locates humankind as a chapter in the planet's story which is a chapter in the universe story. One might picture its grand frame as Carl Sagan once did. Using a calendar year as the timeline, the Big Bang occurs on January 1, our solar system is formed about September 1, life on Earth starts about September 25, and humans emerge at ten minutes before midnight on December 31.[26] In this cosmology, we might still consider ourselves "the true wonder of this world," as Maya Angelou does in *A Brave and Startling Truth*.[27] But incarnation as "becoming human" only, shrink-wrapped around one species only and arriving ten minutes before midnight on the last day of the year, is much too narrow a gauge for the uncontained God's presence. That we picture ourselves at the center of it is ludicrous.

Glen would have insisted upon initiatives that would follow from any revisions of his proposed method. Two policy initiatives, on economy and energy, can serve for illustrative purposes.

In keeping with the ancient Christian understanding of *oikos*, Greek for "household" and the root of ecology, economics, and ecumenics, economics and ecology merge to become "eco-nomics." Eco-nomics embeds all economic activity within the ecological limits of nature's economy and pursues the three-part agenda of production, relatively equitable distribution, and ecological regenerativity. Differently said, incarnational discipleship here would claim "the first law of economics [as] the preservation of the Earth economy"[28] both because human health is derivative of planetary health and because that holds for the rest of the community of life as well.

---

26. Cf. Johnson, *Creation and the Cross*, 207.

27. Maya Angelou, *A Brave and Startling Truth* (New York: Random House, 1995), last page, but no page number given.

28. Berry, *Ecozoic Reader*, 10.

Incarnational discipleship in pursuit of creation justice would also alter energy policy. Human Anthropocene energy use is changing planetary energy processes via global warming. Any consideration of that exposes the attention of social justice as largely misplaced. Almost all justice attention to energy is about energy resources and use: Do we have enough to grow the economy to meet human needs? Are we energy secure and independent? How will energy be distributed fairly? These discussions all go on without *first* asking what energy sources and uses are mandated by the *planet's* climate-energy system. They assume that human energy use is primary, then we'll deal with negative externalities. This is proceeding backwards. For creation justice, the first law of energy is preservation of the *planet's* climate-energy system *as conducive to life*; human energy use is *derivative of the planet's energy use* (above all, the planet's capacity to set the thermostat). This is the energy parallel to Thomas Berry's maxim that the first law of the human economy is the preservation of nature's economy.[29]

Other initiatives of creation justice as incarnational discipleship are in order: for cosmology, christology, and anthropology. They are reflected in the three friendly amendments with which I end:

That cosmic incarnation and Big History include but supplement "becoming human" as the uncontained God's presence amidst all that is.

That creation justice include but supplement social justice as the work of incarnational discipleship.

That the Cosmic Christ of Incarnation supplement the Jesus of God becoming human.

For the conversation we never had but I wish we had had, would Glen accept these friendly amendments to *A Thicker Jesus*?

---

29. Berry, *Ecozoic Reader*, 10.

NINE

A Thicker Jesus and Democracy

Ron Scott Sanders

A Thicker Jesus was Glen Stassen's last word in Christian ethics before he passed away in 2014. For Glen, this book was the occasion to bring together some of the defining features of his distinctive Christian ethic: his triadic interpretation of the grace-based transforming initiatives in the Sermon on the Mount (Matthew 5–7); his vision for how to fill the space between pacifism and the just war theory with the practices of just peacemaking; and his insistence that Jesus of Nazareth had something important and meaningful to say to our most pressing social problems—if only we could find the real Jesus hidden in the morass of competing ideologies and thinned-out cultural appropriations of him. This was probably Glen's greatest contribution to the field of Christian ethics: to find Jesus again as the orienting center of belief and practice for the church so that it can have a meaningful and positive bearing on the challenges of living in a pluralistic society.

To "thicken" Jesus, for Glen, was to locate him in continuity with the prophetic stream of Israel. His threefold emphasis of "incarnational discipleship" set out to do just that: (1) God's sovereignty over all of life meant that there was no realm of society where God might not have a say in how it should go; (2) the rich, textured, and concrete teachings of Jesus were necessary to guide the church into deeper discipleship and equip it to be a transformative presence in the world; and (3) the real company of the Holy Spirit was to spur the follower of Jesus and the church into a Matthew 7 kind of continuous self-reflection—at peace with God, but always repenting from the human propensity to bend the moral universe in one's own direction. Glen's hope was to show that incarnational discipleship resolves a crisis in the Christian faith and produces some unexpected resources to help society flourish.[1]

One of the crises that Glen identifies is the history of Christianity's authoritarian posture, conflated with national interests—an unholy overlap of church and state—that contributed to the secularizing trajectory of Western culture. Utilizing Charles Taylor's work in *A Secular Age*, Glen wants to "take up... the various causes of the secularism of our age" and to ask whether his idea of incarnational discipleship can "suggest some answers for the challenges presented by secularism."[2] Taylor defines secularism as "the shift from earlier ages when belief in God was so widely shared that it was almost automatic to 'a condition where we cannot help but be aware that there are a number of different construals, views which intelligent, reasonably undeluded people, of good will, can and do disagree on.'"[3] A secular age is one in which religious belief, a theological frame for viewing life, is just one of many equally valid options to gather the events of one's life into a meaningful whole. For Glen, Western democracy reflects that shift. He argues that democracy started within a Christian framework but gradually swung toward a more secular and liberalized trajectory. It becomes one line (along with science and rationality) on the promissory note of secularism: give democracy enough time and it will help to produce a society "in which political action conducted in the name of religious belief is treated as a ladder up which our ancestors climbed, but one that now should be thrown away."[4] Glen wants to counter this idea by infusing (or re-infusing) democracy with his notion of incarnational discipleship.

---

1. Glen Harold Stassen, *A Thicker Jesus: Incarnational Discipleship in a Secular Age* (Louisville, KY: Westminster John Knox Press, 2012), 51.

2. Ibid.

3. Ibid., 53.

4. Richard Rorty, "Religion in the Public Square: A Reconsideration," *Journal of Religious Ethics* 31 (2003): 143.

In chapter five, "Democracy: And the Tradition of Human Rights," he sets out to recover the historical roots of constitutional democracy and covenant-based human rights, a tradition with Puritan roots, buffered by the free-church emphasis on freedom of religion, and exemplified in Abraham Lincoln and Martin Luther King Jr. The end goal of this project is to forge an American identity that can motivate citizens to make their civic contribution in ways that address "racism, segregation, discrimination, and greed."[5] Glen maintains that his notion of incarnational discipleship supports democracy and mitigates an unbridled secularism that strips the public square of its sacred value.

For Glen, the three streams of incarnational discipleship converge in the Puritan origins of democracy and then are lost again as the democratic tradition drifted from these roots on a more secular trajectory.[6] He distinguishes liberal democracy from constitutional democracy and states that constitutional democracy and incarnational discipleship have a mutually beneficial relationship. The Free Church's emphasis on voluntary commitment to Christ and covenanting together to live out the life of faith was a model for constitutional democracy; the emphasis on communal discernment through the guidance of the Holy Spirit meant that each member participated in the decision-making process, undergirding the idea that each person has a say in determining the goods of society and how those goods get distributed justly.[7] And finally, the separation of church and state sprang from the emphasis on freedom of religion—to separate the power of the state from controlling religious practice. This kind of constitutional or covenantal democracy plays a significant role in Glen's lived theology. It was a consistent theme throughout his writings.

Glen loved democracy. He dedicated *A Thicker Jesus* to his father, Harold Stassen, the former governor of Minnesota, who ran for president nine times. He mentions his father several times in chapter five.

---

5. Stassen, *A Thicker Jesus*, 79.

6. Ibid., 70.

7. Michael Walzer, *Spheres of Justice: A Defense of Plurality and Equality* (New York: Basic Books, 1984).

His family was steeped in democratic politics and this carried over into Glen's own life: he marched in the Civil Rights Movement, and he saw democracy as a key practice in his theory of just peacemaking. In 1992, Glen published *Just Peacemaking: Transforming Initiatives for Justice and Peace*. He argued that we find in the Sermon on the Mount transforming initiatives that become peacemaking practices to be applied in international conflict. Of the seven steps toward peacemaking he outlines, the fourth is "to seek human rights and justice" because the deprivation of justice and the lack of human rights contribute to violence and conflict.[8] In 2008, Glen edited a collaborative project titled *Just Peacemaking: The New Paradigm for the Ethics of Peace and War*. In this volume, he set out to argue that his original idea of seven peacemaking steps derived from the Sermon on the Mount could be expanded to ten practices of peacemaking that had their basis in his original project but have proven to be successful without specific reference to the teachings of Jesus. If the teachings of Jesus are true and efficacious, then we should be able to find common ground with those outside of the Christian narrative—we just have to do it in a different language. In this edited volume, the various authors add a layer to Glen's step of seeking human rights and justice by arguing that the advance of democracy contributes to international peace. For the authors, democracy is important for two reasons: (1) democracies institutionalize the human rights tradition—they back the ideas of human rights with the coercive power of the state and allow citizens to argue for their rights in the public square; and (2) stable democracies rarely fight one another. The qualifier "stable" is important because democracies are rarely established peacefully. Most often, they follow some kind of revolution by the people to upset and overturn authoritarian regimes.[9] Glen went on to contribute to the 2011 book, *Interfaith Just Peacemaking: Jewish, Christian, and Muslim Perspectives on the New Paradigm of Peace and War*, and he also argues for democracy in his edited volume of John Howard Yoder's posthumous work: *The War of the*

---

8. Glen Stassen, *Just Peacemaking: Transforming Initiatives for Justice and Peace* (Louisville, KY: Westminster John Knox Press, 1992), 103.

9. Glen Stassen, *Just Peacemaking: The New Paradigm for the Ethics of Peace and War*, new edition (Cleveland: Pilgrim Press, 2008), 119–21.

Lamb: The Ethics of Nonviolence and Peacemaking. Democracy, the human rights tradition, and justice are central to Glen's articulation of a thicker Jesus in Christian ethics that points the church outward in a pluralistic culture.

Glen is an internal critic of the democratic tradition, bringing the best of the Christian tradition to bolster the weaknesses that he sees. The defining question to answer is whether his three pillars of incarnational discipleship strengthen democracy in the way that he intends—a covenantal and constitutional form of government that guarantees the involvement of its citizens, pays attention to the marginalized person, and hedges against abuses of authority. Furthermore, does his concept of incarnational discipleship answer the challenges of secularism? The answer is "yes and no." Yes, because the democratic tradition needs a complementary tradition to flourish and to keep it from devolving into Nietzschean power struggles. No, because as it stands, Glen's definition of incarnational discipleship does not carry the weight of a fully formed Christian political theology. We need Glen to fill in some gaps.

First, the notion that constitutional democracy is a product of the Puritan idea of a covenant is problematic. The Puritan idea of a covenant was extended too far and produced the very oppression that Glen opposes, which, in turn, contributed to the argument for secularism. Second, the very notion of democracy has inherent contradictions to the kind of incarnational discipleship that Glen is articulating. If Christianity is going to be a complement to democracy, then it has to have some "prophetic distance." Creating an American identity that has "specifically Christian roots, and...welcomes the support it receives from other religious traditions and from secular sources as well" seems ironically triumphalistic.[10] Finally, Glen's definition of incarnational discipleship is vague enough to be co-opted by ideologues in all directions—a result that he very much wants to avoid. Something more is needed in *A Thicker Jesus* to avoid these false ideologies that Glen warns against.

Let us take up these three concerns in turn. However, before we do, a note about Glen's background framework: Alasdair MacIntyre's

---

10. Stassen, *A Thicker Jesus*, 82.

definition of a "tradition" and "tradition constituted rationality," the subsequent critique of MacIntyre and the ensuing conversation about democracy as a tradition, and the colloquy partners that Glen chooses inside that conversation. The idea that democracy is a tradition on MacIntyre's terms means that it is a narrative extended through time that tells a historical story about the good, the true, and the beautiful and how to know these things.[11] A tradition starts contingently with a set of beliefs, sacred texts (sacred to the tradition) and authorities; it develops historically as it survives and thrives amid challenges. It becomes a mature tradition (more likely to be true) as it survives its internal and external challenges.

For Glen, incarnational discipleship is a sub-tradition within the larger tradition of ecumenical Christianity. And, as he states, it draws from the Free Church Puritans—especially in relationship to democracy. He affirms that there is a democratic tradition and contrasts two forms for his argument: (1) The kind based on covenant that borrows heavily from the Puritans—the kind that Michael Walzer articulates in his book, *Revolution of the Saints*. Glen argues that this form of the democratic tradition, buffered by the experience of the free churches being a minority to the magisterial form of Calvinism in Europe, lays the groundwork for some of the best attributes of democracy: religious and civil liberty, a focus on human rights—especially for those on the underside of the majority—and the invitation for all to participate. (2) The kind of democratic tradition anchored in the Enlightenment that borrows heavily from the pragmatists—the kind offered by Jeffrey Stout, Richard Rorty, Walt Whitman, John Dewey, and Ralph Waldo Emerson. Glen argues that this latter form of government developed out of a reaction to the convolution of the church and the state, abuses of power, and violence done in the name of religion (Christianity especially) to coerce citizens. For Glen, this liberal democratic tradition that sprang from the Enlightenment assumes a more positive view of human nature. It relies on the idea of social cooperation and the goodwill of individual citizens, it flips the idea of religious liberty (arguing that the state

---

11. Ron Sanders, *After the Election: Prophetic Politics in a Post-Secular Age* (Eugene, OR: Wipf and Stock, 2018), 15.

should be protected from the influence of the church), and it assumes that social consensus is the best way to access the good, the true, and the beautiful, thus privileging the majority.

The Puritan idea of a covenantal democracy was born out of the Puritans' frustration with their inability to gain ground on what they thought England could be. After several attempts to establish a state that reflected their vision, continually thwarted by successive monarchs, the Puritans left England for America—a new land with fertile soil for the kind of nation that they hoped to build. In contrast to what they had experienced in England, the national experiment in America was a creative project rather than a revolutionary one. There were no magistrates to convince, no monarchies to overturn, and no established traditions to counter. The Puritans were a persecuted minority who fled England for something new.[12] They borrowed Exodus imagery from the Hebrew Scriptures and saw England as Egypt, the Atlantic as the Red Sea, and America as the new "Promised Land." Michael Walzer argues that this imagery often captures the imagination of people who are in the minority and who experience oppression and suffering at the hands of a dominant culture.[13] Elsewhere, I have argued that this Puritan project was fundamentally flawed; because they borrowed the wrong metaphor from the Hebrew Scriptures to envision a new promised land, they believed they had the right to displace its current occupants.[14] The removal of indigenous peoples from their land was a consequence of the authoritarian perspective of the privileged—the "civilized," "educated," and "Christian" Europeans. It also paved the way for subsequent abuses of privilege and power over against Africans in the transatlantic slave trade and "negotiations" over the southern border between Mexico and the newly forming United States. It is often argued that racism was "America's original sin," but equating America with theocratic Israel was the precursor to paternalistic prejudices toward others who were deemed separate from those chosen to carry

---

12. Richard Hughes, *Myths America Lives By* (Champaign, IL: University of Illinois Press, 2004).

13. Michael Walzer, *Exodus and Revolution* (New York: Basic Books, 1986).

14. Sanders, *After the Election*, 27–44.

this manifest destiny forward.[15] For the Puritans, the center of Christian faith had moved from Israel to Europe, and now from Europe to America.[16] In contrast, for Africans and Native Americans the narrative was reversed—America became a land of slavery and oppression. This aspect of Puritanism should be fully abandoned.

Glen wants to hedge against these abuses by drawing from the experience of "Free Church Puritanism," a form of Puritanism born from the margins of the conflation of church and state in Europe. Because they were a persecuted minority, the Free Church Puritans carried with them the idea of freedom of religion as a basic human right. This is a reflection of the first characteristic of incarnational discipleship: "following a thicker Jesus rules out coercion and so contributes to religious liberty."[17] For Glen, eliminating religious coercion would satisfy one argument that contributed to the secularizing trajectory of the West—the church (religious reasons and religious language) needs to be removed from public discourse because every time you trot it out into the public square it causes conflict and violence. It is acceptable to hold religious beliefs as a personal, private matter, a psychological and emotional comfort, but religion should not have any efficacy in public matters where pluralism exists.[18] He cites Roger Williams and William Penn as models of this kind of Free Church Puritanism. Further, Glen argues that Richard Overton (as an example of a Free Church Puritan) first articulated a threefold model of human rights in England: the right to religious and civil liberty, the right to the basic necessities of life, and the right to participation in community. This was the basis for the American ideals of life, liberty, and the pursuit of happiness. Thus, for Glen, when democracy draws on the idea of human rights for all, it is borrowing a belief from the Free Church Puritans. As was the case with other aspects of covenantal democracy, Glen argues that this idea of human

---

15. Jim Wallis, *America's Original Sin: Racism, White Privilege, and the Bridge to a New America* (Grand Rapids: Brazos Press, 2017).

16. Willie Jennings, *The Christian Imagination: Theology and the Origins of Race* (New Haven: Yale University Press, 2011), 292.

17. Stassen, *A Thicker Jesus*, 66.

18. Richard Rorty, *Philosophy and Social Hope* (New York: Penguin Books, 2000), 170–71.

rights was also thinned out by the Enlightenment and lifted from its Christian origins. This is the space that the unique democratic experience in America occupies today.

There is a tension in making such a historical argument—history can easily slip into nostalgia where details get lost. Even if we give Christianity credit for the nascent stages of democracy, what resulted did not have the moral heft to sustain the pressures of pluralism and was quickly replaced by something more "neutral," "enlightened," and "modern." The Christian tradition was not designed to carry democracy forward.

This brings me to my second concern: Glen wants to create a space for Christianity to find its way back into the conversation over the future of the democratic tradition. He argues that the three characteristics of incarnational discipleship are the tools to create a public ethic that can help forge an American identity. The sovereignty of God over all creation means that there is no space that God does not care about. This implies that Christians must find a way to articulate the things that God cares about (the flourishing of human life as a broad generalization, *shalom* if we want to use Judeo-Christian language) in a secularized political space. To do this, he argues for the church to be multilingual—to be able to articulate its faith-based views for human flourishing in language that the culture understands (secular language). He also argues that the church can form tactical and creative alliances, "So when we communicate that Jesus is Lord to people in our culture, we may make tactical alliances with the kinds of language used in our culture, including relativism, liberation, the Enlightenment, or the Gandhian vision."[19] Following the Augustinian and Thomistic models, Christians can "communicate effectively by connecting with cultural themes of their time."[20]

I like the term "multilingual" because it represents something more than a sacred/secular split in language. It circles back to concerns about honoring the communal origins of rationality and morality that Glen finds attractive in MacIntyre, and the idea that secularism might be a tradition itself. Richard Rorty says as much when he

---

19. Stassen, *A Thicker Jesus*, 71.
20. Ibid., 72.

admits that secular language is not neutral—it has its "conversation stoppers" just like religious language.[21] This is an important point because it acknowledges that there is no "privileged perspective" in public conversations. Jeffrey Stout's argument that the exchange of reasons is a core practice of the democratic tradition (liberal or covenantal) remains true as long as we can avoid the "conversation stoppers" in the exchange. What Glen is hinting at here is the supererogatory duty for Christians to love their neighbors as themselves—when the Christian tradition and the democratic tradition intersect, one way that Christians can love their neighbors as themselves is to learn their language. This means the language of secularism, the language of Islam, the language of Judaism, and so on. This fits well within the definition of incarnational discipleship—taking the teachings of Jesus seriously. It also treats secular language for what it is, language from within a tradition.

Glen has tried to create room for religious reasons and motivations in the public square. This is an important project. His characterization of incarnational discipleship emphasizes the concrete teachings of Jesus, and with this he is trying to correct a common deficiency he finds in some Christian circles: to bypass the teachings of Jesus and rush to the passion and resurrection for personal salvation. Glen is very clear that he doesn't want to pass over the teachings of Jesus for Christian moral formation. But Glen's definition of incarnational discipleship is lacking here. There are relatively few teachings of Jesus in this chapter. The three characteristics he offers are broad theological categories that are vague enough that anyone can find themselves within their boundaries. A progressive Christian could argue for the evolution of culture by quoting Jesus, appealing to God's sovereignty over historical progress, and the independence of the Holy Spirit in repenting from our fixation on the Bible as the only authoritative source for life. A fundamentalist Christian could argue for the culture wars by appealing to the teachings of Jesus, trusting in God's sovereignty to overturn the "moral decline of American culture," and the independence of the Holy Spirit in repenting from our fixation on reason, science, and experience as the authoritative sources for life.

---

21. Rorty, "Religion in the Public Square," 143.

More is needed in order to add texture to Glen's political theology. Something like Jesus' answer to the Pharisees and Herodians in Mark would be a good place to start to strengthen his argument: "Give to the emperor the things that are the emperor's, and to God the things that are God's" (Mark 12:17); or his conversation with Pilate over the nature of authority: "You would have no power over me unless it was given you from above" (John 19:11a); or Jesus' interaction over the nature and use of power: "You know that among the Gentiles those whom they recognize as their rulers lord it over them.... But it is not so among you: but whoever wishes to become great among you must be your servant" (Mark 10:42–43).

Further, it seems important in a chapter on democracy and human rights to ferret out the implications of the teaching of Paul and the author of 1 Peter that speak directly about the early church's role and relationship to the government—especially as the Gospel spread throughout the Roman Empire (cf. Rom 13:1–7 and 1 Pet 2:13–17). This is not an attempt to bypass Glen's focus on thickening our understanding of the teachings of Jesus, but a look at how the church applied those teachings while it was under the ubiquity and authority of the Roman Empire. In neither of these passages is the author trying to argue that the church contribute to forging a unique Roman identity; the church is more concerned with survival, faithfulness to Jesus, and calling the government to contribute to the flourishing of all citizens by fulfilling its mandate to promote the "good" and punish the "evil."

A "thicker Jesus" might mean keeping democracy at a larger "prophetic" distance: a distance that is not directly tied to a specific American identity but is concerned with the welfare of the people. Glen has always maintained that Jesus should be understood in the prophetic tradition of Israel—especially the Book of Isaiah.[22] Here is another gap that he could bridge to fill in his political theology. Walzer argues that in ancient Israel's life as a nation, the prophets were a unique set of political characters in the monarchical life of Israel—they were flies in the ointment of the king's plans when those plans veered from faithfulness to YHWH. They played a critical role

---

22. Stassen, *A Thicker Jesus*, 42.

in Israel's national life: "The prophets were social critics, perhaps the first social critics in the recorded history of the West.... [They] became the representatives of God in the world, with no practical tasks except criticism."[23] And they paid special attention to those on the margins of society (Mic 6:8). Prophets stood in the courts of the king to remind the king of what faithfulness looked like. They also stood in the public square reminding the people that they had made a covenant with YHWH at Mount Sinai and that they needed to turn their attention to what that meant in their national life.

We find resonances with this kind of "social criticism" embedded and recorded in Jesus' life in the Gospels. He is concerned with the law (Matt 5:17–20) but chastises the Pharisees for using the law to exclude people from the kingdom of God and missing the most important aims of the law (Matt 23:23–24). He stands in opposition to the corrupting influences of "the world" but doesn't withdraw from it like the Essenes (John 17). When given the opportunity for a revolution in the face of injustice (such as with the Zealots), he heals a soldier's ear (Luke 22). And when faced with a test of his allegiance (to work with Rome or to join the revolution), he turns the test back on itself and reminds his interrogators of their ultimate allegiance (Mark 12:13–17). So Jesus does stand in the prophetic tradition of Israel.

It would be better and more in line with Glen's project to make the argument that the New Testament does not endorse any particular governmental structure (democracy included), but instead positions the church to be a prophetic presence within any form of government. This is not an argument against democracy per se, just a reminder that the church's mission in the world is larger than being a pillar for the covenantal democratic tradition and an identity marker in the development of an American civil religion that makes tactical alliances with "other religious traditions and secular sources as well."[24] The democratic tradition in any form has its inherent weaknesses—it is a thin tradition, even in a "covenantal" form, and it needs a complementary tradition to support it. Left to itself, it will

---

23. Ibid.
24. Ibid., 82.

devolve into assertions of power, it will marginalize the weak, and it has the potential to collapse in on itself. The Christian tradition is uniquely equipped to be a prophetic "fly in the ointment" to these tendencies of democracy—embedded in its social ethic is keeping those on the margins within our moral view, it is an ethic independent from social consensus, and it maintains the supererogatory virtue of loving one's neighbor in all circumstances.[25]

If we can create a prophetic distance—I think that this is Glen's intent, but he seems to flirt around the edges of that distance with the idea of the church's contribution to an American identity—the church can give prophetic affirmations when the government does good, and prophetic social criticism when it creates injustice. Here, Emilie Townes' six key "threads" of what a womanist prophetic voice entails might be utilized by the church when it considers how to play a prophetic role in society.[26] First, the church must do the hard work of discerning "the will of God in the midst of injustice and hopelessness." Second, it "exposes the oppressive nature of society," meaning that we stand for justice and work toward the transformation of unjust social structures. Third, it admonishes the culture for its "wrongdoing" and is a catalyst for involvement in change. Fourth, it must be confrontational—where the marginalized and the strong are considered equals and face injustice together. Fifth, "the prophetic voice seeks to create a community of faith, partnership, justice, and unity." This falls closely in line with Glen's argument that the church should be multilingual and work hard at making key tactical alliances. The church isn't the only prophetic presence, and it can recognize and affirm when other groups of people are working toward dismantling injustice. Finally, "self-critical inclusivity is mandatory." This is a form of self-reflection found in Matthew 7 that warns against the triumphalism that so often accompanies "speaking for God" in public spaces.[27] This is not everything it could mean to be

---

25. Sanders, *After the Election*, 45–60.

26. Emilie M. Townes, "Ethics as an Art of Doing the Work Our Souls Must Have," chapter 3 in *Womanist Theological Ethics: A Reader*, ed. Katie Geneva Cannon, Emilie M. Townes, and Angela D. Sims (Louisville, KY: Westminster John Knox Press, 2011).

27. Townes, "Ethics as an Art," 44–47.

prophetic, but it is a start to fill in what a thicker Jesus might mean in a political theology.

What we have argued here is threefold. First, if we take the idea of incarnational discipleship seriously, it needs more texture and definition. Of course, Glen is trying to answer a specific set of questions in the context of the development of Western Christianity and the challenges of secularism. But a thicker Jesus must be able to wander outside of those constraints and address a wider swath of questions. We also argued that his Free Church Puritanism that supports the ideals of a covenantal democracy is inadequate. The Puritan project (Magisterial or Free) had fundamental assumptions that need the prophetic words and life of Jesus to challenge it; the "historical drama" that Western democracy has produced is a mixed bag of moral progress and oppressive moral setbacks. Finally, if we take the idea of incarnational discipleship seriously, then we should recognize that the New Testament does not directly say much about governmental institutions but places the church in prophetic tension with them as it seeks to live out the Lordship of Christ over all of life. This prophetic role can affirm rough approximations of the good, challenge the evil, injustice, and oppression that these governments produce, and model to the world what life could be like if Jesus was Lord. Consequently, Glen's definition of incarnational discipleship needs more. I think that he knew this and would be happy with the project of this book.

TEN

Seeing Jesus:
The Muslim Refugee Crisis

Peter M. Sensenig

I work in a region of East Africa where the population is almost entirely Muslim. In that context my spouse Christy and I serve with a Mennonite mission organization in the areas of university education and healthcare, but also on the day-to-day tasks of building relationships across vast cultural, socioeconomic, and religious differences.

The devotion of our Muslim neighbors to their faith is evident everywhere and at all times. A neighbor of ours is the *muezzin* in the nearby mosque, and his voice calls the neighborhood to prayer five times a day. His wife is our dear friend, who prays faithfully and studies the Qur'an daily. In the course of our friendship, Christy asked if she might have interest in studying Holy Scriptures together, with special attention to the Prophet Issa (the Arabic name for Jesus). Her response was enthusiastic, but she wanted to clarify something from the outset: "What you really need to understand is that Jesus was *not* the son of God. People might say that he was, but he was not."

My intent here is not to address the vigorous theological and missiological debates surrounding the use of divine familial terms in Islamic contexts.[1] I relate this story only to highlight the complexity

---

1. For Islamic perspectives on Jesus and divine sonship, see Mahmoud Ayoub, *A Muslim View of Christianity: Essays on Dialogue*, ed. Irfan A. Omar

of using the concept of incarnation as a basis for witness, particularly among those for whom the idea of God taking on human form is offensive. Yet the Islamic objection to the theology of incarnation is helpful to Christians, as it forces us to clarify, along with Glen Stassen, the profound ethical meaning of incarnational discipleship. It is such encounters that drew my spouse and me to the majority-Muslim coast of East Africa. We want our discipleship to be centered on entering into the everyday joys and struggles of people who are very different from us. We live where we do because we believe that what we do with our bodies matters; as Willie James Jennings argues, seeing God at work in the world requires Christian bodies loving people concretely, participating in God's love.[2] We have also learned from Stassen to put words to this calling: participating in God's delivering grace, entering into the suffering of others; in other words, incarnational discipleship.

The reason many Christians experience interfaith dialogue and witness among Muslims as so difficult is that we are inclined to assume that the foremost undertaking of Christian mission is to help others to see Jesus rightly. Within that framework, the obstacles seem insurmountable: religious commitments, cultural misunderstandings, the betrayals of the Gospel not only in colonial mission endeavors but also in ostensibly Christian societies.

Arguably, Stassen's account of incarnational discipleship as concrete ethical obedience to Jesus of Nazareth helps us realize that we have these tasks reversed; rather than helping others to see Jesus, the first calling is for us to *see Jesus in the vulnerable other*.

The degree of our faithfulness to Jesus is the extent to which we are able to see Jesus in the stranger. First, we will reflect on Jesus' words and actions in Luke 13 and Matthew 25, showing how

---

(Maryknoll, NY: Orbis Books, 2007), 122–29. Ayoub argues that the division between Muslims and Christians is not over the figurative sonship of Christ, but over his divinity. The Qur'an favors the concepts of adoption or servanthood rather than of begetting, yet Ayoub claims that Muslim commentators have not sufficiently pondered God's role in Jesus' conception as the "Word of God" in Qur'an 3:45 and 4:171.

2. Willie James Jennings, *The Christian Imagination: Theology and the Origins of Race* (New Haven, CT: Yale University Press, 2010), 167.

Stassen's incarnational theory of the cross requires us to see Jesus as incarnated in the other. We can then apply the current Muslim refugee crisis as a "fruits test"—a favorite concept for Stassen—in order to measure the preparedness of Western Christians to practice incarnational discipleship. The challenge to Christians in the West is to turn the past-tense understanding that Jesus *was* a refugee into present-tense recognition that Jesus *is* the refugee.

THE QUESTION OF IDENTITY (LUKE 13)

Michael Frost names one of the challenges of incarnational discipleship as confusion about identity. Who do we claim to be when we formulate our ethics as putting flesh on the presence of Jesus in the world? What do we mean when we say that our discipleship is incarnational? Is there any other way to be but embodied? Or are we actually saying that God takes on flesh in us when we respond faithfully to Jesus (and not when we fail to do so)?

We rightly shy away from such a formulation of incarnational discipleship, sensing that, given our personal and collective record, a little modesty is in order. In short, incarnational discipleship leaves no space for us as heroes. Frost writes, "Pity, condescension, or paternalism misses the mark; only a compassion *that acts* is acceptable in incarnational ministry."[3] Faithfulness to the way of Jesus is grounded in the life of a community that produces witnesses, not heroes.[4] Frost therefore characterizes incarnational ministry as *exilic* in nature; it actively shares life in all its challenges, goes among people who are different, and communicates the Gospel by ordinary means of service and loving relationships.[5]

---

3. Michael Frost, *Exiles: Living Missionally in a Post-Christian Culture* (Peabody, MA: Hendrickson, 2006), 54–55.

4. Stanley Hauerwas, *A Better Hope: Resources for a Church Confronting Capitalism, Democracy, and Postmodernity* (Grand Rapids: Brazos, 2000), 130. Hauerwas notes that John Howard Yoder's goal in *The Politics of Jesus* (Grand Rapids, MI: Eerdmans, 1972) is to "serve those who are living better than he writes," as the imitation of Jesus does not make sense abstracted from the church.

5. Frost, *Exiles*, 55.

Echoing Frost, Emmanuel Katongole and Chris Rice frame incarnational discipleship in terms of lament: "When we draw near to those who are most sinned against, our call is not first to make a difference but to allow the pain of that encounter to disturb us." The spiritual practice of lament is a journey that transforms us as we unlearn three pervasive aspects of hero identity: speed, distance, and innocence.[6] We are tempted to seek quick solutions that can be imported from afar, require no sacrifice on our part, and do not demand any recognition that we might be a part of the problem.

In *A Thicker Jesus*, Stassen posits an incarnational theory of the cross that further sharpens the exile and lament criticism of the hero identity. First, one of the key dimensions of an incarnational discipleship tradition is Spirit-prompted repentance for ideological entanglements like racism, nationalism, and greed.[7] Repentance is not the language of classic heroes; it is the language of those who are forgiven and brought into a story not of their own making.

Furthermore, Stassen's account of the cross as Christ becoming present in our own lives, and our call to embody the cross in our own discipleship as a response,[8] moves us away from the deceptions of speed, distance, and innocence and into the Christ-like realm of lament. If entering into the presence of pain is the meaning of the cross,[9] then the deliverance that Christ promises, and that Christians have always attributed to the cross, cannot be divorced from the incarnational act itself. Stassen demonstrates that entering with compassion into the lives of those who were excluded, ill, and outcast was Jesus' direct challenge to the powers and authorities, which led directly to his crucifixion. We see such a direct challenge from Jesus:

> Now he was teaching in one of the synagogues on the Sabbath. And just then there appeared a woman with a spirit that

---

6. Emmanuel Katongole and Chris Rice, *Reconciling All Things: A Christian Vision for Justice, Peace and Healing* (Downers Grove, IL: Intervarsity Press, 2008), Kindle edition, Location 900.

7. Glen Harold Stassen, *A Thicker Jesus: Incarnational Discipleship in a Secular Age* (Louisville, KY: Westminster John Knox, 2012), 16–17.

8. Ibid., 152.

9. Ibid., 157.

had crippled her for eighteen years. She was bent over and was quite unable to stand up straight. When Jesus saw her, he called her over and said, "Woman, you are set free from your ailment." When he laid his hands on her, immediately she stood up straight and began praising God. But the leader of the synagogue, indignant because Jesus had cured on the Sabbath, kept saying to the crowd, "There are six days on which work ought to be done; come on those days and be cured, and not on the Sabbath day." But the Lord answered him and said, "You hypocrites! Does not each of you on the Sabbath untie his ox or his donkey from the manger, and lead it away to give it water? And ought not this woman, a daughter of Abraham whom Satan bound for eighteen long years, be set free from this bondage on the Sabbath day?" When he said this, all his opponents were put to shame; and the entire crowd was rejoicing at all the wonderful things that he was doing. (Luke 13:10–17)

Like the narratives Stassen identifies in Mark's Gospel, this story sets up a confrontation between compassion that enters into pain, on the one hand, and religious authority that seeks to preserve the status quo, on the other. As in Mark, as readers we are called to identify ourselves not as heroes but with other characters: perhaps with the woman in need of healing, so bent over that she can see only his feet; perhaps with the synagogue leader who is so caught up in religiosity and dogmatism that he fails to see the human dignity in others; perhaps with the disciples or the crowd who so often miss the profundity of the transformation Jesus offers.

It is helpful to ask what we might learn from each of these characters. What do we do with the deep wounds each of us brings, sometimes for eighteen years or longer? How do we as religious people and communities recognize the blind spots that cause us to place anything at all—including our most deeply held religious convictions—above the dignity and worth of the people in need around us?

These questions are good, but Stassen's model of incarnational discipleship draws us first into a necessary task that precedes even the compassionate action that discipleship requires, and that liberates us from the burden and the delusion of acting the part of the hero. This is the practice of *seeing Jesus* in the other.

Seeing Jesus as the First Task (Matthew 25)

Stassen embeds his incarnational theory of atonement in Bonhoeffer's christology of empathetic representative action, captured in the term *Stellvertretung*. To enter into another's place means to act representatively with and for that person. Bonhoeffer uses the term to mean that Christ in the incarnation represents all humanity, and in the crucifixion bears the guilt of all.[10]

The miracle of the incarnation is that this representative act cuts both ways. Christ both represents all humanity before God and is, at the same time, represented by all humanity. We can therefore say that Christ's incarnation means that he takes on flesh in every human being at the point of their need.

Nowhere is this more poignant in Jesus' teaching than in the famous judgment passage of Matthew 25:31–46, in which the Son of Man, seated on his throne at the end of time, identifies with the hungry in need of food, the naked needing to be clothed, the sick in need of healing, and the prisoner alone in a cell. If we read this passage strictly in terms of the actions that we should be doing—feeding the hungry, healing the sick, visiting the prisoner—we fall into the trap of making ourselves the heroes of the story. We then miss the striking fact that Jesus directly identifies *himself* as hungry, naked, poor, a prisoner. The first calling of the disciple, therefore, is to see Jesus in the vulnerable other. The transformation of vision, of seeing others as Jesus even as we recognize our own deep need for healing, is precisely how Jesus ministers to us through the hungry, the sick, and the prisoner.

In his commentary on Matthew's Gospel, Stanley Hauerwas notes, "The difference between followers of Jesus and those who do not know Jesus is that those who have seen Jesus no longer have any

---

10. Ibid., 152–53.

excuse to avoid 'the least of these.'"[11] We can take Hauerwas one step further in saying that the *only* way to see Jesus is first to see him in the "least of these." This is a crucial insight about Bonhoeffer's transformation that Stassen, following Reggie Williams, attributes to his experience among African American Christians in Harlem.[12] To see Jesus first in African American Baptists translated directly into seeing Jesus in European Jews. Out of this transformation emerges empathic resistance in the form of compassionate acts of deliverance.

Returning to the Sabbath healing in Luke 13, we notice what immediately follows. Jesus has confronted the criticism of the religious authority by showing the true meaning of God's law: the centrality of human value. In the ancient world, the ashamed silence with which he was met signified that he had essentially won the debate.[13] The audience was amazed and was rejoicing at what he was doing, and in this moment, Jesus had their full attention. What he chooses to say in such circumstances must be of crucial importance: the reign of God is like a mustard seed that grows into a home for birds, and like a tiny bit of yeast that changes the texture of a whole loaf of bread (cf. Luke 13:18–21).

What is the connection between a Sabbath healing and a mustard seed? Jesus is talking about transformation of the kind that starts with what is unseen, something so small one can barely detect it; that is, the way that we view ourselves and others. The unseen transformation has great power to change us and transform our lives and our society.

Miroslav Volf captures this transformation in his formulation of the "will to embrace" the other. Stassen rightly includes Volf's work as a particular theory of the cross, as Volf describes crucifixion with Christ as a de- and re-centering of the self, a truth that makes us free

---

11. Stanley Hauerwas, *Matthew*, Brazos Theological Commentary on the Bible (Grand Rapids, MI: Brazos, 2006), 211.

12. Reggie Williams, *Christ-Centered Empathic Resistance: The Influence of Harlem Renaissance Theology on the Incarnational Ethics of Dietrich Bonhoeffer* (PhD dissertation, Fuller Theological Seminary, 2011).

13. Craig S. Keener, *The IVP Bible Background Commentary: New Testament* (Downers Grove, IL: Intervarsity Press, 1993), 227.

in that it allows us to see from the other's point of view.[14] In a paper emerging from a Muslim-Christian dialogue in Turkey, Volf interrogates how the "thickness" of a relationship affects our will to embrace; should not we reserve our deepest loyalty and commitment to those who are closest to us? Volf's argument is that proximity matters; like Stassen, he is seeking not an Enlightenment universalist ethic but an ethic that enters into the lives of others with compassion.[15] This is how Volf, following Jürgen Moltmann, can make the claim that the meaning of the cross is a double-edged solidarity: Christ both identifies God's solidarity with the victims of violence and identifies "the victims with God, so that they are put under God's protection and with him are given the rights of which they have been deprived."[16]

Moltmann's and Volf's "identifying victims with God" in a way that enters into their pain is what it means to see Jesus in the other as a key dimension of incarnational discipleship. Volf's extensive treatment of the transformation of vision that makes it possible to see Jesus in the other also reveals why the practice of "inverting perspectives"[17] is so difficult for those with power and privilege:

> Inverting perspectives is second nature to the weak. In encounters with the strong, they always have to attend to how they and their actions are perceived by the strong. Their success and even survival depend on seeing themselves with the eyes of the other. The strong are not in the habit of taking into account what the weak think of them; they can do without inverting perspective.[18]

---

14. Miroslav Volf, *Exclusion and Embrace* (Nashville: Abingdon, 1996), 70, 272. Volf uses the term "double vision" to describe the practice of recognizing the other's sense of justice or injustice, experience, and point of view (215).

15. Miroslav Volf, "Living with the 'Other,'" in *Muslim and Christian Reflections on Peace: Divine and Human Dimensions*, ed. J. Dudley Woodberry, Osman Zümrüt, and Mustafa Köylü (Lanham, MD: University Press of America, 2005), 19–21.

16. Volf, *Exclusion and Embrace*, 22–23.

17. By "inverting perspectives" Volf means the exercise of seeing others through their own eyes and seeing ourselves through the eyes of others. Volf, "Living with the 'Other,'" 13–15.

18. Volf, "Living with the 'Other,'" 15.

Those who are most excluded develop out of necessity the ocular muscles required for inverting perspective. But the beautiful irony is that the same skills allow them to enter into the perspective of Jesus as divine co-sufferer. Jacquelyn Grant, M. Shawn Copeland, Nekeisha Alexis-Baker, and other womanist ethicists argue that the daily experiences of suffering by African Americans drew them to Jesus as a trusted companion.[19] In the practice of learning to identify God with victims and victims with God, of learning to see Jesus in the other, those who have been excluded and who have suffered the most are the teachers.

The slave trade continued off the eastern coast of Africa into the twentieth century, well after it had been abolished on the Atlantic. Around the time legal slavery was finally extinguished, British and African abolitionists between 1873 and 1879 built the first Anglican cathedral on Zanzibar, the island that served as the main portal for slave trade over the Indian Ocean into the Arab world. For the location of the church they chose the former slave market, and for the site of the altar they selected what had been the auction block. Today the table where bread is broken in memory of Christ's broken body is marked by a circle where the slave post stood. The juxtaposition is clear and intentional; the broken body of Christ is the broken body of the slave. This remarkable act of "translation," to use Jennings's term,[20] is the process of learning to feel pathos for those treated as nonhuman, and it serves as a poignant reminder that seeing Jesus as incarnated in the vulnerable other offers a profound challenge to colonialism of any kind.

THE MUSLIM REFUGEE CRISIS AS A FRUITS TEST

Let us now consider the refugee crisis—particularly the double challenge of Muslim refugees—that presents Christians in the United States with precisely the kind of historical test identified by Stassen. The same kinds of forces that pull Christians in the direction of scapegoating, hostility, and fear are in play here as they are in the

---

19. Stassen, *A Thicker Jesus*, 172–73.
20. Jennings, *The Christian Imagination*, 166.

examples often given by Stassen: the Third Reich, segregation, dictatorship. The same temptations of speed, distance, and innocence pull Christians away from lament and toward the dehumanizing thoughts that Jesus exposes in the synagogue leader we met in Luke 13. How are Christians in the United States faring in the face of such a historical test?

The crisis has been huge in proportion and has proved politically divisive in the United States. The wave of xenophobia that swept Donald Trump to power in 2016 has found political expression in restrictions on immigration, demands for funds for a border wall, and executive orders banning refugees from certain majority-Muslim countries. The latter move has served to place Muslim refugees in a category of their own, as doubly worthy of suspicion. This brand of politics has seduced certain evangelical leaders such as Robert Jeffress of First Baptist Church, Dallas, who has stated that border security is "God's idea," and Samaritan's Purse president Franklin Graham, who claims that the Bible has nothing relevant to say about a nation's immigration policy.[21]

The impact of these attitudes and policies has been a sharp drop in the number of Muslim refugees admitted to the United States. Over the past decade, two-thirds of refugees globally have come from Muslim-majority countries, and the civil war in Syria has greatly increased the number of Muslim refugees in recent years. But the number of Muslim refugees admitted to the United States in 2018 dropped sharply compared to other groups. Three of the top five countries of origin for refugees in the United States in 2017—Iraq, Syria, and Somalia—were no longer in the top five in 2018. In short, the United States, under the current administration, has engaged in a systematic targeting of Muslim refugees that has prompted Supreme Court arguments on the legality of imposing restrictions on religious grounds.[22]

---

21. D. David Lee, "Response to Proclaiming Resurrection," in *People Disrupted: Doing Mission Responsibly Among Refugees and Immigrants*, ed. Jinbong Kim, Dwight P. Baker, Jonathan J. Bonk, J. Nelson Jennings, and Jae Hoon Lee (Pasadena, CA: William Carey, 2018), 245.

22. Phillip Connor and Jens Manuel Krogstad, "The number of refugees admitted to the U.S. has fallen, especially among Muslims," *Pew Research Center*, May 3, 2018. Available at http://www.pewresearch.org.

A recent study found that white evangelicals hold the most conservative views on immigration of any religious group in the United States, followed closely by white mainline Protestants and white Catholics.[23] The best predictors of white attitudes toward immigration were negative attitudes toward President Obama, and as the survey was conducted in 2016, the contrast with candidate Trump was clear.[24]

Another study looked specifically at attitudes toward both immigrants and Muslims among religious groups, finding that sectarian Protestants, white Catholics, and biblical literalists hold more hostile views of immigrants and Muslims than do nonwhite Catholics, nonwhite Christians, and the unaffiliated. This study also found that Christian nationalism plays a role in structuring negative views of immigrants and Muslims and fuels preferences for restrictive immigration policies.[25]

Anti-refugee and anti-immigrant rhetoric does not paint the whole picture, even for religious conservatives. Indeed, the current administration's efforts to restrict refugees are met by opposition from religious groups, including evangelical organizations. But when conservative Christians are forced to decide between the president's views and those of his religious critics, most fall squarely in line with Trump. One explanation for this phenomenon is that they are taking their cues from religious figures appearing on Fox News.[26]

The evidence suggests, therefore, that many evangelical Christians and conservative Protestants and Catholics are failing the historical fruits test of compassionate identification with vulnerable refugees. These studies portray a strong correlation between whiteness and

---

23. Ruth M. Melkonian-Hoover and Lyman A. Kellstedt, *Evangelicals and Immigration: Fault Lines Among the Faithful* (London: Palgrave Macmillan, 2019), 113.

24. Ibid., 130.

25. Darren E. Sherkat and Derek Lehman, "Bad Samaritans: Religion and Anti-Immigrant and Anti-Muslim Sentiment in the United States," *Social Science Quarterly* 99, no. 5 (2018): 1791–1804.

26. Brian Newman, "In the fight over Republicans' attitudes towards refugees, President Trump and Fox News are beating religion," *American Politics and Policy* (July 9, 2018). Blog Entry.

hostility toward Muslim refugees. The pervasive sickness of white supremacy that infects the culture of the United States at all levels impacts this issue as well, to the extent that vulnerable women and children are perceived as a threat. Given the political and theological obstacles to seeing Jesus incarnated in the other, it is tempting to lose heart.

Nevertheless, when we look beyond the rhetoric there is hope. A more profound test than political views or even voting patterns is the way in which churches actually respond to refugees' needs. My research into two Mennonite congregations' reception of Somali refugee families indicates the impact of such a response, not only on the refugee but on the life of the congregation. In other words, receiving the vulnerable other in obedience to Jesus is transformative.

The nature of this transformation, while not surprising, is perhaps counterintuitive. In both cases, the language and worldview of the congregations' welcoming teams shifted over time from a paternalistic framework to one of mutuality. In theological terms, the shift in understanding could be described as moving away from "being the hands and feet of Jesus" toward experiencing the refugee as an agent of change.

For example, in conjunction with a refugee resettlement program, one congregation assisted a Somali family from the moment they arrived in the United States with housing, job training, education, transportation to appointments, and other practical needs. The demand on the church team was immense. As the Somali family acclimated, however, they became liaisons for other new arrivals in the community. They were better equipped than any of the original members of the church could ever be to help new immigrants find their way. In the process, they invited other immigrants to church, and now the worship, youth group, and ministries of the congregation are revitalized by the fresh diversity, much of it springing from the initial act of welcoming one refugee family.[27] The church expected to be Jesus to this family, but instead became the recipient of a powerful ministry.

---

27. Peter M. Sensenig, "Somali Refugees Received by Mennonite Congregations in Pennsylvania, US: Two Case Studies," in *People Disrupted*, 151–63.

Like many acts of faithfulness of the kind that Stassen calls incarnational discipleship, the fruit of welcoming Jesus the refugee takes time to come to bear. In some cases, the historical fruits test can be measured only many years—or even centuries—later. I was invited to participate in an interfaith dialogue in Uganda hosted by the chancellor of a major Islamic university. When it was my turn to address the gathering of Muslims and Christians, I stated that the most important point of connection we have as people of faith is what we do to welcome the stranger. Why is this so important? First, our holy books dwell intensely on how God pays special attention to displaced people, to refugees, orphans, people who have lost their homes and identities. But second, our major prophets are displaced and vulnerable people: Moses, the castaway in the face of genocide; Jesus, the refugee to Egypt; and Muhammad, the orphan.

I then told the story of when Muhammad sent eighty-three members of his community to find refuge from the Meccans in the Christian Ethiopian kingdom of Abyssinia. When the Meccans asked King Negus to turn the refugees over to them, he protected the Muslim immigrants.[28] His kindness is praised in several Qur'anic verses. I stated before the group, "This is an important example of mutual love between Muslims and Christians." Our Muslim host stood up after me and exclaimed, "Yes it is—and it will never be forgotten!"

The practical reality behind this exclamation is astounding; some seventh-century Christians extended hospitality to vulnerable Muslim neighbors, and the incident has been memorized and recited by Muslims around the world for fourteen centuries. Here we see the mustard seed logic that Jesus describes in Luke 13; the simple transformation of seeing the stranger as a human with dignity—as seeing Jesus in the vulnerable other—yields a deeper, more significant impact than we can imagine.

At a meeting of African peacebuilders, a Tanzanian woman related how her family received Rwandan refugees into their home. She recalls that the father of the refugee family, bearing the burden of moving his family in the face of trauma and violence, threw back

---

28. Karen Armstrong, *Muhammad: A Biography of the Prophet* (London: Phoenix, 1991), 122.

his head and sang with all his might the words of the classic hymn, "If ever I loved thee, my Jesus, 'tis now." How could he sing such words, unless he understood as never before the living presence of Jesus the refugee?

The move away from heroic paternalism and toward seeing Jesus in the other is only one part of the shift that must occur in the Christian response to Muslim refugees. The crises that produce the displacement and suffering of people demand sober reflection as well as the practice of lament that heals us from the deceptions of speed, distance, and innocence. Here also we find help from Stassen, who tirelessly advocated the practices of just peacemaking that lead us to repentance and toward concrete steps that actually work to make peace, based on the teachings of Jesus.[29] Christians in the United States should be the first to decry the role their nation has played in the destabilization of refugees' countries of origin, including Somalia, Iraq, and Syria. The next wave of Muslim refugees will likely come from Yemen, where the United States is actively supporting a Saudi war that has led to the greatest current humanitarian crisis in the world.

There is crucial advocacy, repentance, and peacemaking work to be done that addresses the primary causes of this suffering. But for those who already find themselves displaced by violent conflict, the needs are immediate and urgent. The question remains for Christians in the West: Will we experience the transformation that turns the focus of our response from ourselves to see the incarnated presence of Jesus the refugee in our Muslim neighbors in need?

---

29. Glen H. Stassen, *Just Peacemaking: Transforming Initiatives for Justice and Peace* (Louisville, KY: Westminster John Knox, 1992), 53.

ELEVEN

Race

Reggie L. Williams

One month after Glen told me that he had terminal cancer, I was sitting with him at his dining table in Pasadena, California, discussing an autobiography that he intended as his final book. Glen asked me, "What should I include in my autobiography?" I insisted that he finally write about race. I knew that the topic was important for him as one of the central concepts influencing the connection he made between the way of Jesus and justice within his overall project in theological ethics. Throughout his long and fruitful career that included active participation in the Civil Rights Movement, advocating for human rights, opposition to the death penalty, opposition to torture, advocacy for Palestinians, for the environment, and for just peacemaking, one could hear a latent response to racism. But it was subtle, and awkward. He wanted to talk about it to improve his understanding. I was sure that he should finally do so in his autobiography.

Glen had stories. During the Civil Rights Movement he was an activist, partnering with other activists who struggled for an end to Jim Crow segregation. His family was involved in that work as well, in a collective advocacy for a better society and in opposition to practices of authoritarianism and domination that target society's most vulnerable. Glen's activism stemmed from his formative childhood years in a Christian family that valued integrity and fairness and paid attention to social issues.

By the time Glen began his teaching career in the late 1960s, black intellectuals had, for years, been problematizing authoritarianism and domination at the intersection of race, politics, and religion. Scholars like W. E. B. Du Bois, Howard Thurman, James Cone, and Albert Cleage had already published major works interrogating the connection between a white Christ and white supremacy, and examining its destructive social impact. Their work was available to aid Glen in his quest for a Jesus ethic with norms to resist injustice.

It's not clear if Glen had any interaction with their work. It's most likely that he did not, since for decades he worked with the assumption that a non-specific resistance to domination and authoritarianism was broad enough to ultimately include, by association, racism. Glen's concern about injustice served as the location from which to see the way of Jesus as justice, and that focus set in motion the method he describes as incarnational discipleship, which stands on three legs:

1. Recognizing God's sovereignty throughout all of life in opposition to any body/soul split, or two-kingdoms, or body-soul dualisms;

2. Interpreting the teachings of Jesus "thickly" in a way that provides concrete norms for daily living, and not merely as high ideals or principles; and

3. Practicing continual repentance to resist the temptation to interpret the Gospel as justification for ideologies.

But I believe the model needs help to do the work he hoped for in light of a Christianity co-opted by whiteness. He underestimated the problem of racism.

When Glen was thinking about his autobiography in 2013, he was also hard at work planning the gathering of scholars to formally recognize his method of incarnational discipleship—the gathering that finally took place in 2019 in order to develop this book. At that time, we picked up with a discussion about race that began when I was his PhD student. Here, we will continue that dialogue with my dear late mentor, as an engagement with the way he addressed the problem of racism.

For Glen, racism was a matter of affect that could be corrected through loving confrontation and acceptance. Incarnational discipleship offers that possibility through concrete obedience to the social teaching of Jesus, which is a life ordered by justice. But while it is important to recognize the way of Jesus as justice, the problem of racism has little if anything to do with affect; the problem of racism is primarily one of anthropology, which is where we must begin to see the connection between Jesus and justice in a dialogue about incarnational discipleship. We must identify the weaknesses in Glen's approach to the problem in order to assist him in his efforts toward a method thick enough to address what he rightly identified as singular failures of Christianity in the United States.

The Problem with a Thin Jesus

In the classroom, Glen would often tie historical misrepresentations of Jesus to foundational problems with Christianity in the United States. He claimed that dominant streams of Christianity in the United States suffer from a problem that has beset the faith since the birth of the nation. It was at the beginnings of the United States when the way of Jesus was stripped down, turned into thin principles that transform commandments like "turn the other cheek" into high ideals and abstract universals, seeing the commandments as spiritual teachings rather than concrete claims on actual behavior. Thinning the way of Jesus to principles allowed a Christian mutation to slip into the cracks of powerful ideologies, changing the way of Jesus into a theological justification for social evil.

Glen described as harmful ideologies and hegemonic belief systems that are "invented in order to defend special privilege for an in-group and provide justification for excluding other groups while covering up what the belief system is doing."[1] Hence, chattel slavery was

---

1. Glen Harold Stassen, *A Thicker Jesus: Incarnational Ethics in a Secular Age* (Louisville, KY: Westminster John Knox Press, 2012), 18.

fueled by Christian ideological support. Christians empowered slavery in the United States with a thin Jesus, emaciated to such a degree that he could make slavery a Christian franchise by dwelling within the lucrative slaveocracy as theological justification. The thin Jesus is at home with social evil, and an adversary of social justice.

Thin Jesus was the religious object of the Christian slave owner's devotion, and of all subsequent Christian devotion that is not equipped to recognize and to resist that historically menacing spirit. Because the emaciated Christ is a fetish crafted as religious support for domination and exclusion, it is a rival to God's truth.[2] The prophets described rival truth as idolatry, and Jesus referred to it as hypocrisy.[3] Alternatively, the gospel of a thick Jesus is guided by concrete norms like justice, which, as Stassen indicates, is referred to in the Bible 1,060 times. Emptying Jesus of that substantial content leaves a void for Christian discipleship that is filled in by -isms and phobias that co-opt the way of Christ for evil. It is a Christianity guided by ideologies as norms: racism, classism, heterosexism, patriarchy, ableism, and greed become normative for a warped Christian life. Glen's Jesus-centered response to domination makes the claim that concrete faithfulness to Jesus' social commandments represents a commitment to social justice and is a corrective to these problems.

The Test of History

In *A Thicker Jesus*, Glen references a host of witnesses who represent a thick, Jesus-centered response to domination and thus passed the test in the laboratory of history where other Christians failed. He cites figures like Dietrich Bonhoeffer, Andre Trocmé, Clarence Jordan, Dorothy Day, Muriel Lester, and Martin Luther King Jr. Glen's witnesses demonstrate the effectiveness of taking Jesus' social teachings seriously for discerning a way through morally confusing times.

Furthermore, they all lived with a hermeneutic set within a community that operated according to the field of aesthetics. With the

---

2. Ibid.

3. Ibid.

exception of Martin Luther King Jr., Glen's witnesses are all white people in a post-Enlightenment Western world, where the field of aesthetics emerged alongside biological anthropology. It was informed by such figures as Immanuel Kant who, in his *Critique of Judgement*, claimed that "beauty is the symbol of morality."[4] White is the standard for beautiful in the world of Kantian aesthetics, and people who are white are seen as the aesthetic representation of ideal humanity. Accordingly, white men, half of Glen's witnesses, represent autonomy, self-determination, and innate morality. Not only are they better equipped for leadership; society is best served with them in charge, and community with them is what we should all want. White women have their place, as do black people, all in subordination to the autonomous white masculine sovereign who is the template for beauty and morality. In this world, only one of Glen's witnesses, King, was a fugitive subject of this racial order. He defied the rules and the religion. Yet all of Glen's witnesses share at least this in common; in the world of racial aesthetics, they all demonstrate a connection between Jesus and justice by resisting norms that set idealized humanity as the prevailing good. And as models of Glen's incarnational ethics they represent norms from Jesus within adherence to a tripartite mechanism of discernment. Yet there is something more operating here, something that has to do with aesthetics that Glen did not identify. Although Glen's witnesses freely chose a different politics, risking their lives as enemies of the racist and sexist polis, for the sake of a wildly different interpretation of the way of Jesus, they all shared in the task of navigating a society structured by a belief in God's template for ideal humanity.

THE THIN JESUS AND RACISM

For Glen, the way of Jesus that was the guide for faithful Christian discipleship worked from the command to "Love your neighbor as yourself" (Matt 22:39), which Glen took to mean a mutual understanding

---

4. Immanuel Kant, *Critique of Judgement* (New York: Oxford University Press, 2008), 178–82.

of the needs for justice in our neighbor's context as well as our own. This is the way that Jesus works in our lives: Jesus encounters us as we are in our most vulnerable selves to empower us toward participation in the way of Christ and love of neighbor. Glen asserts that understanding Jesus' concrete way in this manner addresses the core problem that sustains racism, which he believed was shame. Here, it is important to understand the distinction that Glen makes between shame and guilt. Guilt can be addressed by attention to a wrong committed by an offender. But shame is different. Shame is perceived as something that is wrong with the self. It is a negative self-assessment that we hide from others behind emotional walls. Because of shame, we practice evasion from others and from God, and we replace God with some other source rather than living in the presence of God and basing our social ethics on God's revealed word, doing justly and walking humbly with God.[5]

The discussion of shame in relationship to race, for Glen, is a combination of influences from sources like Reinhold Niebuhr, Thandeka, and Dietrich Bonhoeffer. Glen is influenced by Niebuhr's description of human nature as a contradiction between freedom and finitude. According to Niebuhr, human beings are capable of transcending ourselves for self-reflection, which gives the impression of limitlessness. Yet, as we see ourselves, we find ourselves to be naturally contingent and limited by our historical and physical state as creatures. We are finite, and to deny our finitude is to become prideful. We encounter finitude in our rational capacities, yet we pretend that we are not finite. Niebuhr claims that we assume we can gradually transcend the limitations of our finite minds until our mind becomes identical with the mind of God.[6] We also encounter our finitude in other aspects of the self, and the contrasting encounter between our transcendence and freedom is cause for tension, but not necessarily cause for sin. It is not inevitable that we will sin and become prideful or abdicate responsibility by simply acknowledging our human nature; nevertheless, we sin.

---

5. Stassen, *A Thicker Jesus*, 146–47.

6. Reinhold Niebuhr, *The Nature and Destiny of Man: A Christian Interpretation*, vol. 1. (Louisville: Westminster John Knox Press, 1996), 178–79.

For Glen, the tension that is felt in the contrasting encounter is shame. It is here, in the exposure to shame, that a problem arises. One response to shame is a refusal to accept finitude, which results in a prideful will-to-power that is a mask for insecurities. Another response is a sensual abandonment of responsibilities in a refusal to accept freedom.[7] The diagnosis of human nature that we see with Niebuhr indicates that the social struggle between groups of people begins with the internal self struggling with the self.

Niebuhr argues that a collective group mentality is more dangerous than an individual one because the individual has access to a moral conscience, but groups do not.[8] Groups are inherently self-serving. Glen agreed with Niebuhr's reading of human sinfulness, and Glen's claims about our harmful responses to shame further illustrate Niebuhr's influence. Consequently, Glen argued for the need for checks and balances against the danger of the concentration of sin within a collective mentality. When we take into account the influence of shame on the collective mindset—as in, for example, the national climate in Germany after World War I or the South after the Civil War—we get a graphic illustration of the dangerous deforming effect of shame on a community's sense of itself and of others. The presence of racism today, understood in this way, is a sinful, prideful reaction to a sense of communal inadequacies revealed in the history of whiteness. It is a reaction to shame that leads to abuses of power, the desire to dominate others, and authoritarianism. Racism misleads us. It directs its hosts to hide from God in defense and denial, even posturing as faithful Christian discipleship to give the appearance of moral legitimacy, while refusing to face failures and limitations. Glen's analysis, then, highlights the hidden yet crucial role of shame as a catalyst in collective racism. Unable to deal honestly and without defensiveness with their historical sins, white people react with a buried shame that only heightens expressions of racism.

In, *Learning to Be White: Money, Race, and God in America*, Thandeka describes the distinction between guilt and shame that Glen

---

7. Ibid.

8. Reinhold Niebuhr, *Moral Man and Immoral Society: A Study in Ethics and Politics* (Louisville: Westminster John Knox Press, 2001), 23–50.

values as she builds a description of white shame. Shame is the emotional product of an internal civil war. White shame is an internal conflict for whites that occurs as a result of membership in a racial community that one rejects on moral grounds. It is the catalyst for forming a white racial identity in response to the wounds of childhood, as the first victims of white supremacy are not people of color, ironically, but white children. Whiteness causes distress in the psyche of the developing white child that functions as a type of child abuse. The process of learning to be white occurs as a defensive response to traumas that produce shame about one's white racial identity. "Each defeat...when acknowledged, produces the disconcerted feeling that something about one's own white identity is not quite right." She continues, "This sense of misalignment with one's own identity could serve as a definition of shame."[9] In response to the misalignment, white children engage in a process of creation: "Rather than continue to suffer such attacks, the Euro-American child defends itself by creating a white racial identity for itself. It begins to think and act like its community's ideal of a white self."[10] For Glen, this move toward creating a white racial identity in response to mentally harmful encounters is the turn toward pride in the tension between freedom and finitude. White racial identity is a deformed one; it is caused by white shame. Racism is a common response to white shame as white folks come into contact with their inadequacies through collective engagement with white adults in the wake of the brutal history of whiteness. With Thandeka, the process of overcoming racism begins with reforming whiteness for white people and addressing its catalytic white shame.

BONHOEFFER AND RACISM

One of Glen's most influential mentors, Dietrich Bonhoeffer, offers what was for Glen the definitive theological description of engagement with shame. Bonhoeffer's description of Jesus as *Stellvertretung*,

---

9. Thandeka, *Learning to Be White: Money, Race, and God in America* (New York: Continuum Press, 1999), 1.

10. Ibid., 18.

a word that Glen defined as empathic representative action, is both a depiction of God's interaction with our shame and a mandate for Christian social interaction with one another. Christ as empathic representative moves through our walls of shame, *eintreten*, or entering into the places where we hide our inadequacies, and there Christ accepts the self we seek to hide. Christ as *Stellvertretung* sees us in our shame, accepts us as we are, and turns our heart toward God and our real neighbor, thus enabling us to love our real sisters and brothers by participating with God in God's ongoing empathic work in Christ. Glen sees the *Stellvertretung* move as incarnational, and it is followed with concrete norms rooted in the way of Jesus. In America, entering through the barriers of shame means dealing with the history of distorted humanity that is the root of racism to repentance and into life together.

Race and Just Peacemaking

Glen follows his analysis of racism with practical engagement to address the byproducts of sin and shame that are central to practices of domination and authoritarianism, of which racism is a popular form. In his defining work of ten just peacemaking initiatives, initiatives number four, five, and six identify necessary responses.[11] Number four states that "we must acknowledge responsibility for conflict and injustice; seek repentance and forgiveness." Turning our gaze away from the history of racism in America abdicates responsibility and leaves the walls of shame in place, which in turn safeguards the prideful practices of domination and authoritarianism. In that arrangement, white supremacy remains the de facto norm for social interaction. This is how Glen understood racism. He argues for white acknowledgement and acceptance of complicity in ongoing injustice, which should lead to repentance. Initiative number five says that we must "promote democracy, human rights, and religious liberty." The Civil Rights Movement was a movement in America for

---

11. For each of these initiatives, see Glen Stassen, *Just Peacemaking: A New Paradigm for the Ethics of Peace and War* (Cleveland: Pilgrim Press, 2008).

rights that belong to every person by virtue of being born a human and having U.S. citizenship. Promoting rights and democracy serves the interests of peacemaking because it involves recognizing co-humanity in everyone and working together to promote mutual well-being rather than practicing injustice. The fifth initiative leads inevitably to the sixth, "fostering just and sustainable economic development." This sixth initiative requires that we see and be as concerned for the concrete demands of justice in another's context as for those in our own, while collectively working to ensure that our practices can sustain justice for future generations. Glen's advocacy for justice is what gave him the impression that a recovery of the way of Jesus for Christians would inevitably cover the problem of race as well.

Analysis

Glen was right about justice; there is no helpful dialogue about race without it. His emphasis on shame was also very helpful. There is something meaningful to an engagement with shame in the dialogue about racism, as it identifies distorted humanity at the core of the embrace of idealized humanity. Yet the entire structure of his theory about race begins with a significant shortcoming. Glen's model suggests that loving confrontation is the appropriate and Christian thing to do. One must confront the injustice, but simultaneously acknowledge the need for recognition and affirmation for racist white folks because racism, for Glen, was fundamentally about affect. Although he recognized that racism is an ideology that is exclusively for whites only (which is the title of another book that he was fond of on the topic),[12] one nefarious result of his model is that black people are tasked with the need to help white people stop hating them by affirming the shamed white self that hides behind emotional walls.

Given Glen's context in a white evangelical world, his race analysis was progressive. It was radical to claim that white supremacy harms white people, and that a healthy response to white supremacy demands a move into concrete social engagements and peacemaking

---

12. Robert W. Terry, *For Whites Only* (Grand Rapids, MI: Eerdmans, 1975).

initiatives, with justice as normative for Christian discipleship. That claim was radical in its context, but it was also harmful. The claim that people of color help to fight racism by affirming white people through their shame merely reinforces the subordinate role of black people as "help" in a white racist world, working for white people. Racism trains black people and white people to expect roles as appropriate for their status in a society with a hierarchy of racial beings. Black obeisance is one of those presumed roles. A better solution begins with a better diagnosis. The problem is that racism is not about affect; it's about anthropology.

Whiteness and Anthropology

Whiteness is the product of Enlightenment efforts to name and to classify all human life on the planet.[13] In the development of anthropology, whiteness serves as a discursive mechanism, developed in large part by European intellectuals, for organizing society according to the concept of a biological norm. Whiteness is not a direct reference to white people; the division of people into categories of race is the product of the discursive mechanism of whiteness that serves to arrange society biologically, according to an idealized aesthetic type. Whiteness provides the physical prototype that simultaneously serves as the divine representation of God with us. It turns Christ into an aesthetic representation of the ideal human, a white masculine sovereign who is risen with all power, and the category of human being is distributed in society and the world according to norms set in place by that organizing aesthetic. An individual's humanity is recognized by aesthetic proximity to that divine ideal. With the Enlightenment creation of aesthetics, white men endowed themselves with godlike power and authority to name and to organize all of human life in aesthetic relationship to themselves, in an act that resembles the first creation narrative in Genesis, "Let us make humankind in our image, according to our likeness" (Gen. 1:26a). This is more than

---

13. See Emmanuel Chuckwudi Eze, *Racism and the Enlightenment: A Reader* (Hoboken, NJ: Wiley Blackwell, 1997).

pride covering shame; it is a financially incentivized anthropology fashioned from a fetish of religious devotion. Idealized White Man does much more than secure relief from shame. He is a mechanism by which to manufacture and maintain systems and structures for whites only. It was in the context of the transatlantic slave trade that white masculinity became the template for humanity, as well as the one for whom heaven and earth was made.

The problem of a thin Jesus who distorted Christianity at the beginnings of the United States is thus not merely that he is thin, but that he is white. White Jesus is the template, and he does more than advance concepts that could be adjusted by reforming whiteness; God's image on the earth has been identified with white men, and the Bible interpreted through that lens supplies essential reinforcement for that view. We must address this distortion. A slaveholding society was also a deeply religious one, and its corresponding Christian traditions persist. White slaveholders once viewed themselves as defending the ways of God to the world as they fashioned a death-dealing social order with the racist analytical tools of whiteness.[14] The paradigm continues today.

The Creation of an Aesthetic

What then does it mean to say that God is sovereign over all life, that the character of God is revealed in a thick interpretation of Jesus to provide Christian norms for daily living, and that the Holy Spirit calls us to be free from ideological entanglements? How are we to discern between a thick Jesus and a white Jesus in light of the demands for black servanthood within both? What are we to make of the claims of an incarnational discipleship in light of the demands that racism makes of those of us who are baptized as Christian?

Whiteness is also a system of belief that structures a deviant discipleship. It is not enough to say that we need a thicker Jesus when

---

14. Elizabeth Fox-Genovese and Eugene D. Genovese, "The Divine Sanction of the Social Order: Religious Foundations of the Southern Slaveholders' Worldview," *Journal of the American Academy of Religion* 55, no. 2 (July 1987): 211–34.

your Jesus is white; we must address the way that the Jesus of whiteness represents an ideology of human difference as a fetish of hegemonic power. The white Jesus must die and we must also be undone. The encounter between the word of the white masculine god-man and the Word of God must bring the death of the god-man and the undoing of his created order. Our discipleship must be formed and shaped by the Word made flesh, rather than follow the flesh made word, to be captured within an alternative creation narrative.

Whiteness has so blended Christianity and a hegemonic Western anthropology that to problematize one is to interact with the other. Scholars like W. E. B. Du Bois made a frontal attack on the white racist Christ, with its subsequent idealized humanity. The social encounters between black people and racist Christians in the overtly racist United States demonstrate that if they do not problematize their influential history of racism, white Christian traditions have nothing to offer society beyond racist dreams of an idealized humanity for an idealized community. Their faith tradition prioritizes right belief over social interaction, which makes it possible to be cruel while claiming to be Christian. In such cases, discipleship is about pedagogy rather than embodied obedience to "love your neighbor."

Jesus and Opaque Theology

What Charles Long describes as theologies of the opaque may help to explain this claim.[15] Opaque is contrasted with transparent, which is what people and cultures on the lower rungs of the white racial hierarchy are made to become in a world structured by whiteness. Long refers to Paul Tillich's interpretation of the crucifixion as a graphic illustration of transparency. According to Tillich, on the cross, Jesus becomes transparent as believers look to God. The suffering body is rendered invisible, and what is seen is a theological abstraction. Theologians of opacity will not allow this suffering body to be ignored, which is the historical treatment it receives from hegemonic

---

15. Charles Long, "Significations: Signs," in *Symbols and Images in the Interpretation of Religion* (Aurora, CO: Davies Group, 1995), 7.

anthropologies associated with Western Europe. Theologians of opacity work to make apparent the lives of people relegated to invisibility and non-being as their suffering goes morally unaccounted for in the process of doing theology and ethics. Biological markers like skin color, within a sick theological anthropology, signify different levels of social worth and moral responsibility within the theological academy and in Christian churches. Theologies of the opaque, like those highlighted by a black Jesus, help facilitate the necessary deconstruction of harmful ideologies by making suffering apparent.

Theologians of the opaque, or rather, black theologians and intellectuals, offer a theo-ethical accounting for the body as an intervention against the history spun in motion with the transatlantic slave trade, to facilitate the deconstruction of racial ideologies by recalibrating our understanding of the human and the moral. A healthier theological ethics must turn our gaze toward our bodies as the point of departure for interpreting the way of Jesus, and it must work to undo whiteness.

The turn toward the body is an act of re-membering that recalls an interaction with Holy Communion and reception of the body of Christ as a gift. The gift of Holy Communion invites us to an encounter with one another that re-members the body that carries the marks of physical and epistemological violence. M. Shawn Copeland argues for living Holy Communion as discipleship in a "Eucharistic Praxis" of solidarity against oppression.[16] By orienting our lives in this way, in a praxis of Holy Communion as solidarity, we open ourselves to doing the incarnational work of embodied encounter that helps to remove obstacles that prevent us from joining in solidarity with one another, in communion and community.

Conclusion

Glen was my professor, but he was also like a father to me. Once he shared with me a story about his childhood, a story both revelatory

---

16. Shawn M. Copeland, *Enfleshing Freedom: Body, Race, and Being* (Minneapolis, MN: Fortress Press, 2009), 107.

and deeply embarrassing. Glen was one of two children and the only son of the exceptionally important Harold Stassen. His small Minnesota town was all white, with the exception of one black resident, a man whose name he didn't know. The town called the man "Snowball." Think about how casually offensive that is.

One day, Glen's mother was walking home with her head down when she noticed her husband's shoes walking in front of her. She looked up expecting to see her husband, only to see "Snowball" wearing the same shoes as Harold. Glen's mother thought the encounter was hilarious, and she said so to her son in retelling the experience. For Glen's mother, it was comical because of a broad gulf between the humanity of Harold Stassen and Snowball. Imagine Snowball wearing Harold Stassen's shoes!

In her story, Snowball became a kind of minstrel caricature. He was the comic Negro who tried wearing the clothing of white people and using big words only to demonstrate that he was significantly distant from whites in his capacities for civilized, intellectual, and even moral living. As a child, Glen was unnerved by his mother's story of that encounter. Somehow, even then, he knew that she was wrong; he was ashamed of her, and of himself as well. The experience of hearing that story from his mother left a mark on him that he worked for years to address. It may partly account for how he centered shame in his treatment of white racism.

Needless to say, both of us had stories about racism. Glen was working with a set of tools far too limited for the work that needs to be done with regard to race in Christian ethics. Incarnational discipleship must include recalibrating our common understanding of human being, from a harmful ideal to a healthy reality, in its claims about social engagement for the recovery of Jesus. That would be consistent with the direction of Glen's work. He was moving as though Jesus was serious about justice, and Glen was his disciple.

TWELVE

An Enduring Legacy for Christian Ethics

David P. Gushee

The reader will recall that the purpose of the collective inquiry that concludes with this chapter is to consider Glen Stassen's late work in Christian ethics, his final proposal of a thicker Jesus and an incarnational discipleship ethic. Some of the contributors to this colloquy have done precisely that, focusing tightly on a parsing of what Glen Stassen meant by incarnational discipleship as he articulated it most fully in *A Thicker Jesus*,[1] considering what can be gleaned from that concept today. But other authors, perhaps inevitably, have moved into a broader retrospective on Glen's contributions to Christian ethics, considering how his work looks now, five years after his untimely death.

This conclusion will move from the latter to the former; that is, I will summarize the nature of Glen's project in Christian ethics prior to the 2012 publication of *A Thicker Jesus*, and then consider more fully his late articulation of incarnational discipleship, aided in critical engagement by the contributions of the scholars who have so graciously participated in this project. Further, because Glen's work is inextricable from his life, I will draw upon our thirty years of friendship and colleagueship to place his work in the context of his life's deepest commitments and concerns as we understand them.[2]

---

1. Glen Harold Stassen, *A Thicker Jesus: Incarnational Discipleship in a Secular Age* (Louisville, KY: Westminster John Knox Press, 2012).

2. Longer accounts of Glen's life and work can be found in David P. Gushee, "Glen Harold Stassen (1936–): Baptist Peacemaker in a Conflicted World," in

Background

American Democracy, Liberal Reformism, and the Influence of Harold Stassen

A place to start in understanding Glen Stassen's life and work may be to compare his journey with that of his famous father, Harold Stassen (1907–2001).[3] Harold Stassen was a phenomenon: the youngest governor in Minnesota history, a decorated Navy captain and chief of staff to Admiral Halsey in the Pacific during World War II, a key organizer of the United Nations and a drafter of the UN Charter, very nearly the Republican nominee for president in 1948 and again a serious candidate in 1952, a cabinet secretary in the Eisenhower Administration, founder and first head of what became the Arms Control and Disarmament Agency, president of the University of Pennsylvania, and a committed American Baptist layman who served as president of the denomination, in which role he offered strong support to Martin Luther King Jr. and the Civil Rights Movement. The fact that in his later years Harold Stassen kept making fruitless runs for president was most unfortunate, for it obscured the fact that he had been a national-level talent and for three decades a major figure in American public life. Glen believed that if it had not been for his father's determined opposition to Richard Nixon from the 1950s forward, he might well have become an even more significant figure in the Republican Party and in national politics, possibly even president of the United States.

One might say that Glen Harold Stassen (don't miss the middle name, which Glen increasingly claimed when naming himself toward

---

Twentieth-Century Shapers of Baptist Social Ethics, ed. Larry L. McSwain and William Loyd Allen (Macon, GA: Mercer University Press, 2008), 244–63; David P. Gushee, "Glen Harold Stassen: Baptist Peacemaker, Global Christian Ethicist," *Perspectives in Religious Studies* 40, no. 2 (Summer 2013): 101–5; Michael L. Westmoreland-White, "Glen Harold Stassen (1936–): Follower of a Thick Jesus," in *Ethics As If Jesus Mattered: Essays in Honor of Glen H. Stassen*, ed. Rick Axtell, Michelle Tooley, and Michael L. Westmoreland-White (Macon, GA: Smith & Helwys, 2014), 7–20.

3. For the first time, Glen made his debt to his father explicit in print in *A Thicker Jesus*, ix.

the end of his life) switched his father's major and minor chords. Glen majored in Christian ethics and minored in American politics, whereas his father did the reverse—but Christian ethics and American politics were ever present (and deeply intertwined) in both lives. The same is true of Glen's sister, Kathleen Stassen Berger, a Baptist, psychologist, textbook author, and activist. It is a clear family legacy.

In this volume, Lisa Cahill notes what she describes as Glen's sometimes undue optimism in relation to the possible achievement of Christian ethical goals through political action. Ron Sanders and Miguel De La Torre suggest that Glen had a too rosy view of the Christian people and movements (like the Free Church Puritans) that helped shape early American constitutional democracy. Sanders says Glen needed to achieve greater prophetic distance from our democracy, and Reggie Williams notes Glen's tendency to lean heavily on Martin Luther King Jr. for his ethics in relation to race, rather than attending to more radical voices like that of James Cone, whose critique of America tended to be more harsh and unrelenting.

These are all fair criticisms. They may be understood most fairly in light of Glen's background and era. Glen was deeply shaped by being the son of an effective liberal Republican governor and cabinet officer whose heyday occurred at a time when the United States was playing a constructive role in world affairs, who worked in arms control, who served in an administration led by grownups, and who later joined his son in supporting social change through activist democratic politics. Glen, like his father and sister, believed deeply in American democracy, a critical patriotism, and faith-inspired political and social reform toward liberal ends, which he practiced in numerous arenas, including race, poverty, and peacemaking. This was an unshakable part of Glen's character, vision, and practice throughout his career, and he passed it on to his students through his teaching and example.

German Authoritarianism, Nazism, and the Holocaust

Reggie Williams notes that Glen often emphasized opposition to authoritarianism and domination, making it a central organizing category in his ethics, even to the extent, asserts Williams, of obscuring the saliency of white racism. I often heard Glen refer to German authoritarianism of the late-nineteenth century as a formative factor in his family's decision to come to America, and in his own brand of ethical and political thinking.[4] Add to that the collapse of liberal democracy in Germany in the late 1920s and early 1930s, the rise of Hitler to power in 1933, the immediately criminal nature of the Nazi regime, its aggressive launching of World War II in 1939, and its ultimate crimes against humanity, notably the mass annihilation of the Jewish people. Partly due to his German background, and partly due to having lived through much of the period of Nazism, Glen never strayed very far from consideration of the lessons to be learned from that era. This included the collapse of democratic politics and human rights; the pitiful, faithless, cowardly submission of a majority of the German churches and German Christians to Hitlerism; and the brave, discerning witness of exceptional scholar-churchmen-activists such as Karl Barth and Dietrich Bonhoeffer.

It might be said that these European debacles provided a primary contextual grounding for Glen's ethics, as well as some of the most influential figures in his thought, most notably Dietrich Bonhoeffer. If one then adds Glen's decision to complete his bachelor of divinity in the late 1950s at Union Theological Seminary in New York, another piece of the puzzle comes into place.[5] It was at Union where Dietrich Bonhoeffer experienced two momentous visits (1930–31, summer 1939), and where his legacy remains keenly felt even today. It was at Union that social-ethics giant Reinhold Niebuhr was teaching while Glen was a student, thus initiating a life-long critical engagement with the ethics both of Reinhold and of his brother H. Richard Niebuhr. It was at Union, and then at Duke for his PhD, where Glen became fully immersed in the mainline white Protestant social-ethics tradition at its mid-century peak.

Later, of course, Glen began to read the more diverse array of thinkers who eventually emerged in Christian ethics, including womanists and feminists. But the vast body of texts that he read during the

---

4. David P. Gushee, "An Interpretation of the Christian Ethics of Glen Harold Stassen: Incarnational Discipleship for Apocalyptic Times," *Perspectives in Religious Studies* 40, no. 2 (Summer 2013): 181–82.

5. Gushee, "Glen Harold Stassen," 103.

most formative years of his education were found in the mainline Protestant, white, male, social ethics tradition represented by such giants as Dietrich Bonhoeffer and the brothers Niebuhr. Like so many of us, including myself, Glen was shaped by both the keen insights and the blind spots of the white, male, European American (quite literally) Christian theological ethicists of this era. He was also shaped by the central crises of the twentieth century, at least as experienced by dominant European and American cultures—World War I, the rise of authoritarianism then totalitarianism, Hitler and Nazism, World War II, and the Holocaust. The fact that all these evils occurred in ancient, purportedly Christian lands, notably Germany, raised acute questions as to what exactly Christianity had been doing in Europe for two millennia.

One of the most valuable aspects of the collection of essays gathered here is the contribution of scholars of color—Miguel De La Torre, Stacey Floyd-Thomas, Hak Joon Lee, Peter Paris, and Reggie Williams. Reading their searching critiques of Glen's work reminds us that for most in the two-thirds world, and for people of color in Europe, America, and (other) colonized areas, the great historical drama central to history is the five-hundred-year history of white colonial racism, not the mid-twentieth-century WWI-Nazism-WWII-Holocaust drama. This makes a huge difference in how the context for undertaking Christian ethics is understood. I will say more about the specific critiques these scholars offer in a later section, but for now it is these different *historical dramas* (a favorite phrase for Glen) that we will highlight.

Nuclear Weapons, Pacifism, and Peacemaking

Then came Hiroshima, Nagasaki, the Cold War, and the threat of nuclear annihilation. Glen often remarked that not only was his father in the Pacific in the summer of 1945, but for a time the family did not know whether he was alive or dead. His life might well have been among those saved when the American atomic bombing of Japan brought an end to the war in the Pacific, thus forestalling an American invasion of mainland Japan. Glen also wrote of being deeply affected, as a child, by the vision of the mushroom cloud and the threat that now existed for humanity.[6] Thus, Glen and his family fully participated in that particularly paradoxical historical drama—atomic bombs saved many American lives while incinerating hundreds of thousands of Japanese and introducing a fearsome new threat into human and planetary life.

These new weapons of mass destruction continued to shadow Glen. Harold Stassen became founder and head of the Arms Control and Disarmament Agency as diplomats sought to control the spread and prevent any further use of these horrific weapons. Glen attended a Quaker high school in Philadelphia and came under the influence of Quaker pacifism and other social-justice and simple-living commitments. Glen studied nuclear physics as an undergraduate at the University of Virginia and watched the splitting of the atom while working summers at the Naval Research Lab in Washington. By the 1960s and thereafter, he became a serious peace activist, protesting the Vietnam War and becoming heavily involved in the anti-nuclear movement. He eventually became a board member for the Nuclear Weapons Freeze Campaign (later called SANE/Freeze, and then Peace Action), and served as one of their chief strategists during the height of the Cold War. I remember his many activities in this regard during the Reagan years in the mid-1980s.

Glen was certainly what was sometimes called a *nuclear pacifist*, joining the Catholic Church and most other sensible individuals and groups in rejecting any threat or use of nuclear weapons. The horrifying Cold War context also helped to shape Glen's overall just peacemaking ethic, which is mentioned several times in this collection and which many Christian ethicists would still understand to be Glen's largest contribution to the discipline. In the context of a possible nuclear war between the United States and any other nation, the old debate between pacifism and just war theory makes little sense and carries little practical interest. Glen's proposal of concrete peacemaking practices that can help reduce tension and move nations away from the brink of war arose in a context in which any "hot war" between nuclear-armed nations risked hundreds of millions of

---

6. Westmoreland-White, "Glen Harold Stassen," 8.

casualties and the ruin of the environment. Some ethics casuist somewhere might be willing to call a nuclear exchange a "just war," but for everyone else it would just be incineration.

This context may respond to criticisms from both Lisa Cahill and Miguel De La Torre in this volume, both of whom point out that Glen never seemed to embrace any form of coercion, let alone violence, as an option for a faithful Christian ethics. Cahill says this is unrealistic in human affairs, and De La Torre says that nonviolence cannot be mandated onto the suffering bodies of those who are routinely the victims of structural violence in society. Even though Glen championed just peacemaking as an alternative to both just war and pacifism, I do not recall that he ever publicly articulated support for any military action, and I believe that he could at least functionally be described as a pacifist. Michael Westmoreland-White clearly documents the influence of Anabaptist, Quaker, and Mennonite traditions and individuals in Glen's development, including the titanic effect of his engagement in the 1970s with the ethics of John Howard Yoder.[7] In this volume, Peter Sensenig embodies the continued influence of Glen in Mennonite circles.

Jesus, Scripture, and Hermeneutics

It would be quite wrong to suggest that Glen Stassen's ethical commitments were entirely driven by the circumstances of his family background, the apocalyptic crises of the twentieth century, and the influence of Christian pacifists. These were all factors in Glen's development, but the heart of the commitments themselves could be found in his understanding of Jesus Christ.

Glen liked to repeat Dietrich Bonhoeffer's famous question, "Who is Jesus Christ for Us Today?" If we now ask, who was Jesus Christ for Glen Stassen, we have plenty of material with which to work, most extensively in the book that Glen and I labored over for so long, *Kingdom Ethics*,[8] but really throughout his work.

---

7. Ibid., 13.

8. David P. Gushee and Glen H. Stassen, *Kingdom Ethics: Following Jesus in Contemporary Context*, 2nd ed. (Grand Rapids, MI: Eerdmans, 2016).

For Glen, Jesus Christ was everything the Christian Church says he is, but dogma about Jesus must never obscure obedience to Jesus—as it so often has in church history. Glen never challenged traditional orthodox christology, though he was not a systematic theologian and rarely lingered over dogmatic details, with the exception of a late burst of work on the meaning of the cross.[9] Glen, instead, emphasized Jesus' Jewishness and the particular historical context in which he appeared. Jesus was the Messiah sent by God to Israel as promised in the Hebrew Bible. His message and ministry were situated within the tradition of the prophets of Israel, notably Isaiah. He came preaching the kingdom of God, an ancient Jewish hope of God's restored and renewed reign over Israel and the world. He not only preached the kingdom, he also inaugurated it, bringing at least glimpses of the kingdom's seven marks: salvation, justice, peace, deliverance, healing, inclusive community, and joy—all promised by the prophets. The church as Jesus intended it is to be a pioneering, kingdom-advancing community, established as a beachhead in the world. The kingdom of God is surely coming, as certainly as mustard seeds sown in the ground become mustard trees. But the kingdom is participative. To be a true disciple of Jesus is to choose to invest one's life in participating in the reign of God and its concrete practices.[10] The nature of this reign, and the practices required, can be seen most clearly in the largest single block of Jesus' teaching, the Sermon on the Mount—to which Glen devoted massive study and publication in multiple essays and books.[11]

Step back a moment and notice a few things about Glen's account of Jesus and his use of scripture. Our team of scholars can help us here.

Notice that, like Lisa Cahill but unlike Miguel De La Torre, Glen expresses confidence that an accurate, usable, and reasonably

---

9. Stassen, "The Cross: Compassionate Presence and Confrontation," in *A Thicker Jesus*, 146–174.

10. David P. Gushee and Glen H. Stassen, "Jesus Began to Proclaim," in *Kingdom Ethics*, 3–20.

11. David P. Gushee and Glen H. Stassen, "Doing, Not Dualism," in *Kingdom Ethics*, 86–106; cf. Glen H. Stassen, *Living the Sermon on the Mount: A Practical Hope for Grace and Deliverance* (San Francisco: Jossey-Bass, 2006).

objective picture of the ministry and teaching of Jesus emerges from the New Testament. Glen's Jesus is not just a product of Glen's mind or culture, but instead can be reasonably discerned from scripture, especially if aided by historical-critical biblical scholarship, thorough knowledge of the Hebrew Bible, and immersion in the history of the Jewish people. For example, Glen works very hard to pinpoint what Jesus meant by the reign of God by testing all of Jesus' recorded utterances about God's kingdom against the Old Testament evidence, notably the prophet Isaiah, as well as materials from Second Temple Judaism.[12] Glen's Jesus is eschatological-moral, rather than apocalyptic-otherworldly. That is, Glen's Jesus comes as the bearer of the End of the Age, but instead of bringing judgment, doom, and an escape hatch to eternity, he brings restoration, renewal, and a moral praxis of justice, peace, deliverance, healing, and inclusive community fit for God's this-worldly reign.

Hak Joon Lee is correct that, though covenantalism plays a role in Glen's historical work and normative ethics, Glen rarely situates Jesus' ministry within a covenantal biblical frame, not tying Jesus to the Hebrew Bible via an Old Covenant/New Covenant paradigm, and not connecting Jesus to the succession of covenants depicted in the Old Testament (Noah, Moses, David, etc.). Larry Rasmussen and Ron Sanders are correct in noting that Glen's working canon relied very heavily on the synoptic Gospels and that Glen did relatively little with Paul, Peter, or John and their traditions, which for Rasmussen is especially problematic considering our current need for a Cosmic Christ for an era of climate crisis. Stacey Floyd-Thomas is also correct in suggesting that Glen's Jesus most often seems to come as Lord and Master, in contrast with her claim that for black women and other marginalized disciples, then and now, encountering Jesus often involves "taking Jesus on," as in challenging him. Glen's Jesus sounds much more like the invincible and invulnerable One, the One we obey, as in Barth and Bonhoeffer, than the one we "take on," the one who suffers alongside us as a slandered transgressor, as in Floyd-Thomas.

---

12. Gushee and Stassen, *Kingdom Ethics*, 4–10.

Miguel De La Torre also highlights a certain uncritical dimension to Glen's published work on scripture. To my knowledge, unlike De La Torre, Glen never challenges the character of God as depicted in passages like the Cain and Abel story or the conquest narrative; he doesn't wrestle with scripture in this way, or at least if he does, he doesn't reveal it to his readers, perhaps because it would only have hindered the reception of his work among the conservative Christians to whom he ministered for most of his career. Stacey Floyd-Thomas also demonstrates a freedom to wrestle with and interrogate scripture—even stories about Jesus in scripture—that is characteristic of womanist theology/biblical studies, emerging as it does out of a context in which scripture has so often been used to harm black women. It could also be noted that Glen doesn't talk about certain highly relevant historical-critical issues for his project, such as whether it was "Matthew" (or someone else, other than Jesus) who assembled the highly creative triadic structure of the Sermon on the Mount that Glen discovered in one of his career breakthroughs. He simply treats the Sermon as Jesus' teaching, full stop. Nor does Glen enter into dialogue with those historical Jesus scholars who suggest that Jesus was a Jewish apocalypticist who expected an imminent end of the world—which did not happen—and whose context and message were quite distant from the concerns of the modern world. Glen's Jesus is never described as either mistaken in any way or culturally distant from our experience.

Jacob Cook raises the possibility that Glen's project still partakes of the Western/European/evangelical tendency to seek certainty about our depiction and understanding of Jesus and to find (or strengthen) our identity in that certainty, rather than to accept the mystery of encounter with Jesus and the surprises it might bring in relation to others, ourselves, and Jesus himself. Cook would like to see Glen speak more about encounter with the living, risen Christ, as he sometimes did when describing his vivid personal spiritual life.[13] In general, the treatment of Jesus that both Glen and I offer is open to

---

13. I recall numerous instances of Glen describing what he believed he was learning from Jesus/Holy Spirit, especially through middle-of-the-night experiences of listening prayer and dreams.

the critique that we find a Jesus we are sure about, a Jesus we stake our claim to, one who is neatly usable for the kind of (liberal) reform efforts people like us are inclined to pursue in any case. This challenge then opens space to consider Miguel De La Torre's, Stacey Floyd-Thomas's, and Reggie Williams's more radical suggestion that, in the end, Glen's thicker Jesus is still a white Jesus, emerging from his privileged cultural context and remote from the needs and concerns of people of color.

The Historical Drama of the Faithless Church

Glen was deeply haunted by the failures of the churches and of regular Christians to follow Jesus. The theme is everywhere in his writings.[14] I have noted that one of his grounding contexts for understanding this failure was Nazi Germany. There the historical drama of the *Kirchenkampf* (the German Church Struggle) offered one of the best-documented examples of Christian faithlessness. Not even the grotesqueries of Adolf Hitler were enough to pry most German Protestant pastors and their people away from the seductions of uncritical nationalism, militarism, and racism, from submission to unjust totalitarian government, and even from complicity with and involvement in genocide when that eventually became government policy. Glen's life-long fascination with Dietrich Bonhoeffer was at least in part about finding out why Bonhoeffer was able to discern what following Jesus looked like while others were saying "Heil Hitler!" and marching off to war and Auschwitz.[15] "Who stands fast?" This was Bonhoeffer's question. "Who passes the test of history, being found faithful in crisis?" This was Glen's question, and Bonhoeffer was one who Glen believed did just that.

But, as Reggie Williams points out in his chapter, Glen's account of the roots of Christian faithlessness goes back much farther than

---

14. For example, Stassen, "Who Stands the Test of History? The Ground is Shifting," in *A Thicker Jesus*, 3–15; Gushee and Stassen, *Kingdom Ethics*, 86–94.

15. Bonhoeffer is mentioned thirty-four different times in *Kingdom Ethics* and seventeen times in the much shorter *A Thicker Jesus*.

Nazi Germany. He regularly cites examples of major church leaders and movements drifting away from the real, historical Jesus, from his way of life and ministry, from his message of the kingdom and his concrete teachings in the Sermon on the Mount. Glen, for decades, spoke of the ingenious strategies that Christians as far back as Justin Martyr and Clement of Alexandria developed for rationalizing faithlessness to Jesus.[16] In *Kingdom Ethics* these are summarized primarily as *evasions and dualisms*, and that language appears in *A Thicker Jesus* as well. When encountering "thick," "concrete," specific, demanding teachings of Jesus that required what Christians did not want to offer, like forgiveness, peacemaking, or enemy-love, as far back as the second century CE, we began evading them. We accepted spurious claims that these "hard sayings and high ideals"[17] apply only to clergy and not to laypeople; or only in Jesus' time (his first or second coming) and not to our time; or only to the church and not to the world; or only in private life and not in public life; or only in our hearts and not in our hands or in relation to our weapons.

We thinned out Jesus, Glen liked to say. We made Jesus a totem, a symbol, the magic key to eternal salvation rather than the living Lord of Christians in our everyday lives. We took the incarnate Son of God who claimed all of a disciple's life and made him a disembodied Savior figure who required nothing but our elaborate belief systems and worship rituals. Glen concurred with Bonhoeffer that this was "cheap grace," and that it was deadly.[18] Throughout his career, Glen sought a recovery of the Jesus we meet in the synoptic Gospels and especially the Sermon on the Mount as an antidote to Christian faithlessness, and as a recovery of the ethos of the early church.

Events in Glen's religious context and career made this ancient historical drama of Christian faithlessness seem altogether too real. Glen taught from 1976 to 1996 at Southern Baptist Theological Seminary in Louisville. (I was there from 1984 to 1987 as his student, and

---

16. Gushee and Stassen, *Kingdom Ethics*, 89–90.
17. Ibid., 93–94.
18. Ibid., 25, 94, 130, 176.

from 1993 to 1996 as his colleague, so I know whereof I speak.)[19] His career at Southern began just before the birth of the Christian Right and its eventual takeover both of the Republican Party and the Southern Baptist Convention. Glen had been raised in a very different understanding of what it meant to be a faithful Baptist Christian and had entered Southern Seminary at a time when it was relatively open and progressive—more like (say) Duke and less like Jerry Falwell's Liberty University. But from 1979 to 1991, the political fundamentalists in the Southern Baptist Convention executed a strategy to gain control of the large denomination and all its agencies, including the seminaries. After 1992, they had gained a working majority on the Southern Seminary board. By spring 1993, they had pushed out Glen's ethics colleague Paul Simmons (ironically, I was his replacement), and later that spring they selected the young, quite conservative R. Albert Mohler Jr. as president. From 1993 to 1996, the older Southern faculty were pushed out or fled in droves. Larry Rasmussen points out in his chapter that, like Bonhoeffer, Glen agonized over whether his call was to stay to the bitter end in a darkening context at Southern, or to leave for safer and more hospitable climes. Bonhoeffer's example helped to keep Glen in Louisville far longer than most of his colleagues. Finally, in 1996, we both left.

Glen didn't believe that Southern Baptist political conservatives just held convictions that differed from his preferences. This must be clearly understood. Glen instead believed that they had imbibed a wide range of massively counter-biblical, obviously contrary-to-Jesus beliefs and ideologies, including militarism, nationalism, laissez-faire capitalism, sexism, support for capital punishment, and indifference to creation and the poor. The Convention had been taken over by people whose version of Christianity involved direct disobedience to Jesus' clear teachings. This was what Glen believed.

Glen felt the need to fight back hard, using the tools of Christian ethics. He did not want to fight them on their preferred battle-

---

19. David P. Gushee, "Loving the Question, but Not Always the People: College and Seminary" and "Finding a Voice While Not Losing a Soul: Young Professor at Southern Seminary (1993–1996)," in *Still Christian: Following Jesus out of American Evangelicalism* (Louisville, KY: Westminster John Knox Press, 2017), 23–38, 61–78.

grounds of abortion and sexuality, and he did all that he could to avoid addressing those issues in print. You may have noticed that George Hunsinger, in his chapter, does not cite any comments by Glen in Hunsinger's own effort to make sense of the ethics of same-sex relationships. That's because Glen did not write about this issue, even though he did all he could otherwise to support LGBTQ students. (It is not evident, by the way, that Glen's late articulation of incarnational discipleship offers much that is relevant to sexual ethics; certainly, no indisputable conclusions can be drawn that are relevant to contemporary debates.) Glen did want to challenge the ascendant conservatives on just about everything else, because at least on those classic issues of Christian social ethics like war, poverty, and the death penalty, Glen believed that he clearly had the substance of Jesus' teachings with him. Glen was certain that Southern Baptists were living through their own *Kirchenkampf*, in which faithfulness to Jesus was at stake. I agreed, and still agree. As usual, our side lost.

When Glen escaped to Fuller Seminary in 1996, he bought himself nearly two full decades of relative freedom to teach and write the Christian ethics in which he believed, and to nurture numerous doctoral students in the tradition he represented. But even there, especially toward the very end of his life, he began to believe that the political conservatism that had swept Southern Baptists was crowding out space for his kind of vision at Fuller. Glen perceived that space for Jesus-and-justice evangelicals like himself was narrowing, and that (especially) white evangelicals were hunkering down into reflexive political conservatism.[20] I am grateful, in one sense, that Glen did not live to 2016, and so did not have to witness the surrender of white evangelicals to Donald Trump. He would have been beside himself with grief.

A Summary

Before publishing *A Thicker Jesus* in 2012 at the age of 76, Glen Stassen had already made several profound contributions to Christian

---

20. My account of that development is found in Gushee, "Every Christian's Least-Favorite Liberal (2014–2015), in *Still Christian*, 131–44.

ethics. His most substantial research breakthroughs were just peacemaking, the triadic structure and transforming initiatives of the Sermon on the Mount, and the seven marks of the kingdom of God in both Isaiah and Jesus. His most profound activist contribution was in the area of peacemaking, where his efforts were both national and global. He undertook activism on all kinds of other issues as well, including racism, civil rights, disability rights, poverty, and ecology. He straddled the ecumenical and evangelical worlds and served as a scholar, lecturer, and teacher in both worlds. As Stacey Floyd-Thomas notes, he was a fixture at professional meetings such as the Society of Christian Ethics, as well as the American Academy of Religion, and others. He was a beloved resistance figure within white Southern Baptist and evangelical worlds as these gave in to political conservatism. He went above and beyond the call of duty in admitting, funding, and serving doctoral students, with special commitment to mentoring students from marginalized communities, as well as international students, whom he later visited and helped on his international travels. His graduates dot the landscape of the world church and remain grateful to him for his commitment to them. He was nurtured in mainline Protestant social ethics but undertook his own ethics with a Jesus-centered vision. One might say that he had the Jesus and Sermon on the Mount focus of the Anabaptists (without succumbing to sectarian disengagement) combined with the politically engaged social ethics of the mainline Protestant and liberal Catholic ethics communities (without succumbing to neo-Augustinian compromises, as Cahill suggests). He was a serious scholar of Dietrich Bonhoeffer, of German history, and of Christian ethics. He read widely in political science as part of a commitment to learning multiple discourses and authors. I am sure that I have missed a half a dozen other research interests. It was quite a career. Quite a life!

Incarnational Discipleship

Is this not a formidable enough, and clear enough, contribution? Why did Glen also need incarnational discipleship? What did Glen think he was doing when, near the end of his life, he emphasized that he was naming his ethic by this term and seeking wide support for its adoption?[21]

The Content of the Ethic

In all presentations of incarnational discipleship, Glen proposed what really amounted to a Trinitarian, or three-strand paradigm. We see it in the selections in this volume, as in *A Thicker Jesus*,[22] and elsewhere.

First, incarnational discipleship involves the *submission of the disciple to the holistic sovereignty of God over all of life, without evasion or dualism*. Glen also included here, somewhat confusingly, language of the Lordship of Christ. When he speaks the language of the sovereignty of God over all of life, he appears to be drawing upon Reformed theology—let us not forget that his dissertation was on H. Richard Niebuhr. He might also be critiquing the neo-Reformed theology of the resurgent Calvinist Southern Baptists, who emphasize the sovereignty of God mainly to refer to divine determinism, especially in the arena of human spiritual salvation. In speaking of the Lordship of Christ, Glen appears to be connecting more to Baptist piety, including the Anabaptist strand.

This is *discipleship* because it involves total submission to the Lordship of Christ/sovereignty of God, without evasion or dualism or brackets or exception clauses. It is *incarnational*, in the sense that it is embodied holistically in life and practice, not just ethereally in emotion and belief—first by Jesus, now by us. If God is sovereign/Christ is Lord, the entire body/person is claimed, at all times and in all places. No sector of life is excluded. Thus, for example, one cannot embrace a politics that is Machiavellian because God is sovereign over the political arena as well as in personal life.

---

21. In correspondence with me, Michael Westmoreland-White, another beloved student of Glen's, claims that he coined the term "incarnational discipleship," first introducing it in a PhD colloquium at Southern Baptist Theological Seminary in 1992, and then defining and expanding on it in his dissertation, "Incarnational Discipleship: The Ethics of Clarence Jordan, Martin Luther King, Jr. and Dorothy Day." In light of this information, it seems that Glen should have mentioned this intellectual origin of "incarnational discipleship" in *A Thicker Jesus*.

22. Stassen, "The Three Dimensions of Incarnational Discipleship," in *A Thicker Jesus*, 16–41.

Second, incarnational discipleship means *attending closely and obediently to a thick Jesus, who is God revealed in flesh*, embodied in real history, part of a particular (Jewish) people, and who offered realistic this-worldly teaching as to how life is to be lived according to God's will. Thickness here has to do with taking Jesus' every word and act seriously, assuming that his teachings are meant to be embodied in real life, and understanding him, and the biblical record about him, in a concrete historical/Jewish context.

This is *discipleship*, the straightforward meaning of following Jesus and doing what he says. It is *incarnational* in perhaps four senses: Jesus as the incarnation of God in flesh; Jesus as incarnating and revealing God's love and will; Jesus as empathically entering into the situation of suffering humanity, in the incarnation and all the way to the cross; and the disciple as incarnating in his or her life lived in obedience to Jesus Christ the incarnate God. (Peter Sensenig offers some very thoughtful reflections on the theme of incarnation in his essay, including in the cross, demonstrating how a serious incarnational missiology, theology, and ethic could be developed from the clues Glen left behind.)

Third, *incarnational discipleship means responding to God the Holy Spirit in repentance and conviction of sin, notably the sin of surrender to the world's powers, authorities, and ideologies*. Anything that tempts the disciple to faithlessness; anything that confuses the disciple about who is Lord and to whom service is required, must be repented. The role of the Holy Spirit in Glen's model is to convict of such sin, bring such repentance, and motivate a renewed commitment to faithful incarnational discipleship.

It is not very easy to see how this theme connects to incarnation for Glen, and I cannot say that he ever articulates it clearly. Perhaps one might say that embodied persons are the site of ideological combat, the struggle for identity and loyalty, and the work of the Holy Spirit in repentance and change. Glen and I had already argued in *Kingdom Ethics* that continuous repentance is constitutive of the Christian moral life. Glen offers in his late work a more developed pneumatology, in which it is the Holy Spirit, alive in the life of the Christian, who convicts of sin, including the central sins of surrendering to alien idols, loyalties, ideologies, passions, and trusts.[23]

As Jacob Cook perceptively observes, Glen strongly emphasizes identity in *A Thicker Jesus*. I think he is right in suggesting that, at one level, Glen's incarnational discipleship is a proposal about how to protect faithful Christian identity amid the maelstrom of competing idols, all claiming the (purported) disciple's loyalty, even worship. How shall faithful Christian identity and moral practice be protected? By acknowledging that God is sovereign over every aspect of life, that Jesus Christ is Lord of all, without evasion or dualism. By studying and obeying the teachings and imitating the life of Jesus of Nazareth, God incarnate, the Jewish Messiah. By stripping oneself bare before the Holy Spirit for conviction of sin and repentance of anything that weakens one's identity and fidelity as a disciple of Jesus. These are powerful claims—especially when packaged together, they pack a considerable punch.

Perhaps because of a certain opacity in Glen's use of the term "incarnational" to modify discipleship, his meaning is not always entirely clear, and it is not obvious that incarnational discipleship is the best term to name what Glen is trying to describe. As well, as several authors point out, including George Hunsinger and Larry Rasmussen, the incarnation is a central and much disputed term in the Christian dogmatic tradition, and to introduce it as a modifier for "discipleship" may bring unneeded confusion and complexity. If I were talking with Glen about what to call this vision now, I would probably suggest that he simply call it a *Trinitarian discipleship ethic*, in which roles of each Person of the Triune God are mobilized to enable those who claim Christian identity and commitment to know and do God's will and to stay clear of faithless ideologies and practices. Before God the Father, we submit. Before God the Son, we obey. Before God the Spirit, we repent.

---

23. Gushee and Stassen, "Extracting Logs, Examining Fruits," in *Kingdom Ethics*, 169–93.

Is There an Incarnational Discipleship Tradition?

As can be seen in the essay that serves as the prologue to this volume, Glen offers a roll call of Christian moral exemplars whom he says represent a tradition of incarnational discipleship. This was characteristic of both his writing and teaching throughout his career, and it seems to have been an essential part of what he meant by incarnational discipleship. Glen was always looking for people whom he believed passed the test of history, whose "fruits" were good and therefore validated the ethical approach they had adopted. Perhaps the urgency of Glen's search for faithful, fruit-bearing Christians makes more sense now in light of the narrative of Christian faithlessness that so haunted him. Perhaps more than anything else, Glen wanted to know—he needed to know—who stood fast, who held firm, who was faithful, and how they got there. He believed that Jesus taught that good fruits were the validation of Christian identity—"You will know them by their fruits" (Matt 7:16a). He knew deeply the disastrous consequences of faithlessness. In his last book, *A Thicker Jesus*, he engaged philosopher Charles Taylor's *A Secular Age*, asking how the God-drenched Western world ended up with secularism.[24] One answer, for Taylor and Stassen, was that faithless Christianity very much helped to produce it. Any Christian seeking to respond to secularism needs therefore to deal with Christian faithlessness.

So, arguing like the Jesus-following scientist that he was, Glen treated incarnational discipleship as a hypothesis that had been tested repeatedly in history. Grouping people like André Trocmé, Dietrich Bonhoeffer, Dorothy Day, Clarence Jordan, and Martin Luther King Jr., he first sought to show that they were all practicing incarnational discipleship. He did this with reference to their books, speeches, and actions, looking for one or more of the three strands he had identified. When he believed he had documented that, he was then sure

---

24. Charles Taylor, *A Secular Age* (Cambridge, MA/London: Belknap Press of Harvard University Press, 2007). As Jacob Cook notes, Taylor discusses the theme of the incarnation, and incarnational Christianity, extensively in this book, which Glen found very important. It would be a mistake, however, to believe that this is where Glen found his phrase "incarnational discipleship." See note 21.

that they could be situated within the newly named, but not new in fact, incarnational discipleship tradition. At the end of his life, he was hoping to get a wide variety of Christian ethics scholars to embrace this newly named tradition, to flesh out its characteristics further, and to embrace it for themselves.

It is fair to say that no one in our consultation believes that Glen quite succeeded in this effort. Ron Sanders in this volume already points out (ironically) the relative thinness of what Glen says about the three strands of his ethic, and its susceptibility to being turned in a variety of directions. Moreover, it is simply questionable to group together disparate individuals, groups, and movements in history that one admires and retrospectively call them practitioners of incarnational discipleship. I personally am far more skeptical than Glen was about the existence of any kind of formula or paradigm for Christian ethics that can offer reliable good fruits, even while deeply valuing the threefold model that Glen finally arrived at. It is far easier to name what can and often does go wrong in the lives of Christian people than it is to develop a sure-fire paradigm for making it all come out right. There is a certain mystery to moral goodness, no guarantees are available, and people's lives can come out quite right or quite wrong from a variety of traditions, Christian and non-Christian.

In the end, one can concur with the significance of the elements of what Glen called incarnational discipleship without agreeing that he had identified a tradition or named a coherent paradigm that could be transmitted to the future under that name.

Radical Critiques for a Radical Era

Every scholar is a product of her or his culture and era. After even the greatest scholars die, time marches on while the scholar's work does not. Therefore, each era needs its own scholarship, including scholarship in Christian ethics.

This effort to bring Glen Stassen's late work into a 2019–2020 conversation has, for me at least, offered an extraordinarily clear illustration of the three claims in the above paragraph.

Glen's intellectual lineage stretches deep into the history of European and American Christian theology and ethics. His most formative experiences occurred from 1940 to 1990. The political ethic he produced was a progressive, communitarian, social-democratic, peaceable vision that is still widely held on the American left and in Europe. The Christian theological sources for his political ethic were found in an Anabaptist reading of scripture, a red-letter reading running back and forth between the prophets and the historical Jesus. He was deeply affected by the major voices in white mid-century Protestant ethics. His primary paradigms for ethical integrity were found among the anti-Nazis, human rights activists, peacemakers, dissidents, civil rights marchers, and anti-nuclear activists of his era. Finally, he served in an era in which churches were at times major constructive players in public life.

We live in very different times, even radical times, including here in the United States. In Glen's heyday the crises seemed mainly to be "over there." But now they are *right here*. The rise of white ethnonationalist populism in the United States and around the world, the election and quite possible reelection of Donald Trump, the related weakening of the rule of law and accountable government here, and the worsening climate change crisis to which the United States so greatly contributes are now among the dominant factors of our time, and these developments are having a profound effect on contemporary Christian ethics. Amid these very American crises, Glen's ethic somehow seems not quite radical enough.

Consider again, for example, Glen's treatment of race. Many of the scholars in this collection argue or suggest that Glen never quite arrived at a serious enough encounter with white supremacist racism. The theme is one of the most remarkable things about this collection of essays. Not to be too dramatic, but one could describe it as driving the final nail in the coffin of white American Christian ethicists' liberal reformism on race. Together, in various moods and modes, authors in this collection demonstrate that white supremacism is America's greatest and most poisonous ideology, that it has entirely infected American politics and religion from colonial days, and that it is an idol that white people must kill, as Peter Paris so evocatively suggests and Reggie Williams simply states. In other words, the radicals of the 1960s, folks like James Cone, Malcolm X, and James Baldwin, are the more relevant voices on race in our era—more relevant than Dr. King, which feels like a shocking statement to come from any student of Glen Stassen's. Yet Glen never appears to have seriously engaged these more radical voices. For that matter, neither did I until after 2016, and neither have most white Christian ethicists.

The people who, in 2016, just knew that Donald Trump would be elected, precisely because of (and not despite) the fact he was the most radically and openly racist GOP candidate, these are the people who prove to have understood America with the critical historical realism that Glen Stassen so prized. I was not one of those people, so I am among those who are in the process of being hastily educated about the depth and toxicity of white American Christian racism. I believed in a better America than that, and so did Glen. Our understanding of white America and its racism proved far too superficial. As De La Torre and Williams both say, the problem unveiled in 2015–2016 was not that the American Christian Jesus was too thin, but that he was too white. This pale Jesus is a participant in and underwriter of white Christian supremacism, both in virulent ethno-nationalist form at Trump rallies and in milder form in white ethicists who don't focus on or just don't understand the full horror, depth, and centrality of white racism.

Greater radicalism than what Glen offered is required in thinking about American democracy and American Christian political ethics as well. As Peter Paris and Miguel De La Torre state quite matter-of-factly, the ideals and visions of the French and American revolutions were never intended to apply to anyone other than white men. This touches upon one of the oldest arguments in American politics. Did the Declaration of Independence mean what the Constitution negated a few years later, that all (men) are created equal? Is healing our national soul just a matter of bringing law and practice into line with our founding principles, or were the principles racist (and sexist) in the first place?

Glen accepted the more hopeful answers to those questions. But how does it look now, on the brink of the 2020 election? Doesn't it look more like what Malcolm X said in the 1960s, and what Peter Paris says in his chapter? Should we not now see the multi-racial egalitarian democracy envisioned by Dr. King and American liberals, and barely brought to birth in this nation (over many dead bodies) during the Civil Rights Movement, as essentially foreign to the four-hundred-year history of the United States? Is it not more accurate to see white ethnopopulist reaction against these recent "strides toward freedom" as actually reflecting the oldest, truest, sickest soul of America? What impact might such sorrowful realism have on Christian political engagement? Is optimistic liberal activist reformism sufficient under these circumstances? But again, this problem does not just belong to Glen. I am speaking of an entire social-ethics tradition that was premised on the basic goodness of America and the prospects for nonviolent, morally inspired reform.

Furthermore, where exactly are we to find the faithful Christians who are to bring the teachings of Jesus and the Lordship of Christ into American public life in order to create such reform? As Peter Sensenig suggests so painfully from a context of Muslim-Christian dialogue in Africa, with their support for the anti-Muslim Donald Trump in the election and ever since, evangelicals in the United States are again egregiously failing the fruits test, in full view of a watching world.

So, again, where might we find faithful American Christians? How shall we understand the church situation in the United States? Resistance to Donald Trump is mainly found among Christians of color, a smallish group of white Christian allies, and a whole lot of secular folks who find (largely white) Christianity hopelessly compromised in this country. Are they wrong? Stacey Floyd-Thomas simply states as fact, in her chapter, that white and black Christians have never really worshiped the same God. It is very hard to imagine Glen accepting that claim in 2014, but it makes far more sense to me today than it would have five years ago. We are by now a very, very long way from the idea that massive concerted Christian influence can make America a better country. After all, what are we to make of all these people who claim Christian identity in this country while wearing their MAGA hats and chanting "send her back" at Trump rallies? Perhaps our moment is most akin to the fading Weimar Republic, circa 1931, rather than the Civil Rights Movement, circa 1963. If so, where is today's Confessing Church, and where is today's Dietrich Bonhoeffer?

Then there is climate change. Larry Rasmussen, our best Christian ethicist working on climate change, suggests that humanity is slowly cooking itself to death as we refuse to respond to a problem that the world's climate scientists have been telling us about since at least 1990. Rasmussen proposes that we need a bigger Jesus (the Cosmic Christ) and a bigger ethic (creation justice), than Glen was able to produce—again, as a product of his era, in which "environmental problems" seemed fixable with proper reformist effort in personal, ecclesial, and public life. Certainly, today, many in progressive Christian theology and ethics are attempting to respond with more far-reaching proposals, but who is listening? A climate hoaxer is in the White House and may be there for six (or more) years, and the entire GOP has become a climate-denial party.

These are indeed radical times. As Miguel De La Torre illustrates, some are losing confidence that the arc of the universe bends toward justice, and instead are embracing hopelessness. But Lisa Cahill demurs, saying that in hope, even from the most desperate corners of the world, Christians must remain engaged as faithful witnesses and obedient participants in the practices of God's reign as inaugurated in Jesus Christ.

Glen Stassen lived through the radical evils of apocalyptic mid-century Europe. But he did so from here, from America, which he believed in, and which he believed would, or could, be responsive to faith-based justice movements such as many in which he participated. What if that is not who we are now? What kind of Jesus, and what kind of Christian ethic, is needed for such a time as this? At this moment, it seems that the baton is being passed to those with a deeper radicalism of moral vision, often rooted in their radical suffering of oppression in America. There are people in this country, including Christian ethicists, who do not need to be stripped of their illusions about white Christian America, because they never had any illusions in the first place. These voices from the margins, these fugitive saints, people like Harriet Tubman and Ida B. Wells-Barnett, have always embodied a more radical kind of incarnational discipleship in faithless white Christian America. Perhaps it is to them, and their current successors, that we should look for moral leadership today.

CONTRIBUTORS

Glen Harold Stassen, 1936–2014 (PhD, Duke University) served for eighteen years as Lewis B. Smedes Professor of Christian Ethics at Fuller Theological Seminary in Pasadena, California, after teaching for twenty years at Southern Baptist Theological Seminary, and a few years before that at Berea College and Kentucky Southern. His works included *Just Peacemaking* (in several versions and approaches), *Kingdom Ethics* (2003), *Capital Punishment* (1998), *Living the Sermon on the Mount* (2006), *Authentic Transformation* (1995), and *A Thicker Jesus: Incarnational Discipleship in a Secular Age* (2012), the focus of this collection. He was a scholar-activist, deeply engaged in domestic and global peacemaking and social justice movements throughout his life.

Lisa Sowle Cahill (PhD, University of Chicago Divinity School) is J. Donald Monan, SJ, Professor at Boston College. She is a past president of the Catholic Theological Society in America (1992–93) and the Society of Christian Ethics (1997–98). Her books include *Blessed are the Peacemakers: Just War Theory, Pacifism, and Peacebuilding* (2019); *A Theology and Praxis of Gender Equality* (2019); *Global Justice, Christology, and Christian Ethics* (2013), and *Theological Bioethics* (2005).

Jacob Alan Cook (PhD, Fuller Theological Seminary) teaches theology and philosophy and works with the Apprentice Institute for Christian Spiritual Formation at Friends University. He is currently revising his first book, *Evangelicals and Identity Politics,* for publication, and studying questions of Christian identity. During his doctoral residency, Jake worked with Glen Stassen as the associate director of Fuller's Just Peacemaking Initiative, which supported critical thinking about, and creative engagement with, practices that make for peace.

Miguel A. De La Torre (PhD, Temple University) is Professor of Social Ethics and Latinx Studies at Iliff School of Theology. A Fulbright scholar, he has served as president of the Society of Christian Ethics, co-founder and executive director of the Society for the Study of Race, Ethnicity and Religion, and in numerous leadership roles at the American Academy of Religion. The author of thirty-five books, five of them winners of national awards, he also wrote the screenplay for the award-winning documentary *Trails of Hope and Terror*.

Stacey M. Floyd-Thomas (PhD, Temple University) is the E. Rhodes and Leona B. Carpenter Chair and Associate Professor of Ethics and Society at Vanderbilt University Divinity School. She is the executive director of the Black Religious Scholars Group, past executive director of the Society of Christian Ethics, and co-founder/past president of the Society for the Study of Race, Ethnicity and Religion. She has published seven books, most recently *The Altars Where We Worship* (2016), and serves as the editor of book series with Abingdon Press and New York University Press.

David P. Gushee (PhD, Union Theological Seminary, New York) is Distinguished University Professor of Christian Ethics and Director of the Center for Theology and Public Life at Mercer University. He has served as president of both the American Academy of Religion and Society of Christian Ethics. He is author or editor of twenty-four books, including *Righteous Gentiles of the Holocaust* (1994), *Kingdom Ethics* (2003/2016), *The Sacredness of Human Life* (2013), *Changing Our Mind* (2014), and *Moral Leadership for a Divided Age* (2018).

George Hunsinger (PhD, Yale) is the McCord Professor of Theology at Princeton Theological Seminary. A recognized Karl Barth scholar, he has a long history of ecumenical activity and social involvement. In 2006, he founded the National Religious Campaign Against Torture. In 2010, he was awarded the International Karl Barth Prize. In 2019, he served as a visiting professor at the Pontifical Gregorian University in Rome. Among his books is *The Beatitudes* (2015), endorsed by Archbishop Desmond Tutu and awarded first place in spirituality by the Catholic Press Association.

Hak Joon Lee (PhD, Princeton Theological Seminary) was named Lewis B. Smedes Professor of Christian Ethics at Fuller Theological Seminary in September 2015, having served on the Fuller faculty since 2011 as professor of theology and ethics. Lee's research focuses on covenant ethics, public theology, and Asian American theology and ethics. His publications include *The Great World House: Martin Luther King, Jr., and Global Ethics* (2011), and *Intersecting Realities: Race, Identity, and Culture in the Spiritual-Moral Life of Young Asians* (editor, 2018).

Peter J. Paris (PhD, University of Chicago) is the Elmer G. Homrighausen Professor Emeritus of Christian Social Ethics at Princeton Theological Seminary. He has served as president of the American Academy of Religion, the Society of Christian Ethics, the Society for the Study of Black Religion, and the American Theological Society. He is the author or editor of numerous books, including *Black Religious Leaders* (1991), *The Social Teaching of the Black Churches* (1998), *The Spirituality of African Peoples* (1994), *Virtues and Values* (2004), and *African American Theological Ethics* (2016).

Larry L. Rasmussen (PhD, Union Theological Seminary, New York) is Reinhold Niebuhr Professor Emeritus of Social Ethics at Union Seminary. He is the author or editor of many books, including two major award winners: *Earth-Honoring Faith: Religious Ethics in a New Key* (2012), which won the Nautilus Grand Prize for 2014, and *Earth Community, Earth Ethics* (1996), which won the 1997 Grawemeyer Award in Religion. He served as a member of the Science, Ethics, and Religion Advisory Committee of the American Association for the Advancement of Science, and as co-moderator of the World Council of Churches unit on Justice, Peace, and Creation.

Ron Scott Sanders (PhD, Fuller Theological Seminary) is an affiliate faculty in Christian Ethics at Fuller Seminary. A doctoral student of Glen Stassen, he is the author of *After the Election: Prophetic Politics in a Post-Secular Age* (2018). He teaches courses on Christian ethics, faith and politics, peacemaking, and diversity in unity in the church. He has also served for nineteen years as a campus minister at Stanford University, where he has been an active part of the religious life on campus.

Peter M. Sensenig (PhD, Fuller Theological Seminary) is a regional consultant for the Mennonite Board in Eastern Africa, serving in Zanzibar, Tanzania. A doctoral student of Glen Stassen, he has taught in the areas of peace and conflict studies, ethics, and Muslim-Christian relations at institutions across Africa and in the United States. The author of *Peace Clan: Mennonite Peacemaking in Somalia* (2016), he is an ordained minister in the Mennonite Church USA.

Reggie L. Williams (PhD, Fuller Theological Seminary) is Associate Professor of Christian Ethics at McCormick Theological Seminary. A doctoral student of Glen Stassen's program in Christian ethics at Fuller, he has served on the board of directors of the Society of Christian Ethics and the International Dietrich Bonhoeffer Society and is a member of the American Academy of Religion and Society for the Study of Black Religion. His groundbreaking book, *Bonhoeffer's Black Jesus: Harlem Renaissance Theology and an Ethic of Resistance* (2014), was selected as a Choice Outstanding Title.

INDEX

"A Time to Break Silence" (King), *xx–xxi*
Abyssinian Baptist Church, 47
agape vs. eros, 74–75
Ambrose of Milan, 129
Anabaptism, 184, 192, 193, 198
Angelou, Maya, 133
Anthropocene era, 68, 122–25, 131, 132, 134
Aquino, María Pilar, 14
archetype *vs.* prototype, 9–10
Aristotle, *xxiv*, 106
atonement theology, 29–30, 48, 67, 154
Authentic Transformation (Stassen), *xiv*
Autobiographie (Trocmé), *xx*

Baptists. *See* Southern Baptist faith
Barmen Declaration, 4, 85
Barth, Karl, 3–4, 71, 181, 186
Belew, Kathleen, 113–14
Benjamin, Walter, 49
Berger, J. M., 113–14, 180
Berlin Wall, *x, xi*
Berrigan, Daniel, 70
Berry, Thomas, 134
Bethel Confession, *xviii*
Biblical integrity, 80–83
Bievik, Anders Behring, 114
Black Lives Matter movement, 109, 121
Body Politics (Yoder), *xxiii*
Bonhoeffer, Dietrich
　basepoints of Christian faith, rethinking, 122–23
　on cheap grace, 47, 189

　christology of empathetic representative action, 154
　Discipleship, *xii, xiv*, 4
　as faithful in crisis, 188
　Harlem exposure to African American Christianity, 47, 155
　on incarnation *vs.* becoming human, 126–28
　incarnational discipleship, practicing, 3, 196
　on Jesus as the One We Obey, 186
　mainline Protestantism, representing, 182
　racism and, 170–71
　Sermon on the Mount, as centered on, 120, 121
　on shame in relation to race, 168
　Stassen, as a hero to, 119
　stay-or-go decision, struggling to make, 120, 190
　Union Theological Seminary, legacy felt at, 181
　"Who is Jesus Christ for Us Today" question, 121, 184
Bonhoeffer's Black Jesus (Williams), *xiv*, 2
Born from Lament (Katongole), 14
Bowers, Robert, 114
Brown, Michael, Jr., 109

Cahill, Lisa Sowle, 6, 180, 184, 185, 192, 201
Calvin, John, 78
Cannon, Katie, 68
celibacy, 82–83

chastity and fidelity, 74–80
Chávez, César, 53
cheap grace, 47, 189
Christ and Culture (Niebuhr, H. R.), *xvi*
Christ the Tree of Life (painting), 128
Christian ethics
    apocalyptic strands in, 23
    as Christ-centered, 9, 74
    consequentialist ethics as the measure of, 125
    despair and hope, considering, 9, 10, 11–13
    ecclesiocentric tendencies, avoiding, 12
    fellow-Christians, as solely meant for, 26, 70
    history of white colonial racism, in the context of, 182
    incarnational discipleship, as an addition to, 2, 19, 72, 83, 192
    marriage, renewing the understanding of, 71
    nonviolence, as embracing, 184
    race issues, needing work on, 177
    realism and honesty, in need of, 21
    Southern Baptist interpretation, 190–91
    Stassen, as a scholar of, 1, 120, 178, 180, 181, 191–92
    a thicker Jesus, bringing to, 135, 139
    three strands of, 197
    white supremacy in the U.S., effect on, 198
    See also sexual ethics
Christian faithlessness, 188–89, 196
Christian identity
    good fruits as the validation of, 196
    historical drama and, 6, 89
    identity in certainty, 36, 187
    in incarnational discipleship, 6
    incarnational theology of, 33–38
    protection of, 195
    the question of identity, 91, 151–54
    Stassen's quest for, 26–28
    the struggle for, 194
    in *A Thicker Jesus*, 25
    Trump supporters and, 200

Christian practices, defining, *xxii–xxiv*
Church for the World (McBride), *xix*
Civil Rights Memorial, 117
Civil Rights movement
    Brown v. Board of Education as impetus for, 108
    as foreign to the 400-year history of the U.S., 200
    Just Peacemaking, discussed in, 21
    misuse of covenant, as correcting, 103
    participation in, as a test of faithfulness, 3
    peacemaking, serving the interests of, 171–72
    Stassen, engagement with, 119, 138, 163, 179, 192, 198
    the cleaving of marriage, 75, 76–77, 78, 79, 80
Clement of Alexandria, *xv*, 189
climate change, 7, 17–18, 101, 121–26, 132, 198, 201
climate justice, 132–34
Clinton, Bill, 105
The Color Purple (Walker), 57–59
Cone, James, 41, 57, 60, 164, 180, 199
consequentialist ethics, 125
Cook, Jacob, 6, 187, 195
Copeland, M. Shawn, 157, 176
covenant doctrine
    covenantal democracy, 137, 141, 142–43, 146
    God as creator, 127
    historical drama of the Bible, 89–93
    in incarnational discipleship, 7, 87–89, 98–100, 103–104, 129
    New Covenant of Jesus, 99–100, 102, 186
    Puritan heritage of covenant, 42–43, 87, 89, 100–101, 102, 139, 140, 148
    in Sermon on the Mount, 95–97, 98
Critique of Judgement (Kant), 167

Davenport, Charles, 111
Davies, W. D., *xiv*
Day, Dorothy, 3, 4, 166, 196
De La Torre, Miguel, 6, 11, 12–13, 180, 182, 184

INDEX

Death Penalty (Megivern), *xv*
democracy
    covenantal democracy, 137, 141–43, 146–47, 148
    egalitarian democracy as foreign to U.S. history, 200
    German collapse of, 181
    just peacemaking, promoting, 171
    Puritan contribution to, 42–44, 87
    radical contemplation of, 199
    social-democratic ideals, 198
    Stassen, connection to American democracy, 7, 180
    as a tradition, 140
    after WWII, 20
Dorrien, Gary, 67
Douglas, Kelly Brown, 57, 67
Douglass, Frederick, 44
Du Bois, W. E. B., 111, 164, 175

ecclesiocentric theology, 11–12
Egan, Eileen, *xxi*
Embracing Hopelessness (De La Torre), 12
En la Lucha (Isasi-Díaz), 61
eros vs. *agape*, 74–75
Ethic for Christians and Other Aliens in a Strange Land (Stringfellow), 70
Ethics (Bonhoeffer), *xiv*, *xviii*
Ethics and Society in Nigeria (Wariboko), 118
Eucharistic Praxis, 176
eugenics movement, 110–13, 117

the faithless church, 188–91
fidelity and chastity, standard of, 74–80
Floyd-Thomas, Stacey, 6, 13, 182, 186–87, 188, 192, 200
For the Nations (Yoder), *xvii*
Ford, Gerald, 116
Foucault, Michel, 49
Francis, Pope, *xxiv*
Franklin, Benjamin, 43–44
Frost, Michael, 151–52
The Future of Ethics (Jenkins), 17–18

"A Genealogy of Modern Racism" (West), 105–106
God of the oppressors, 51–52, 58–59
Golden Rule, 72, 73, 82

Grant, Jacquelyn, 57, 157
Gushee, David P., 1, 7–8, 11, 12, 121

Harvey, Jennifer, 35–36
Hauerwas, Stanley, 11, 154–55
hero identity, 152
historical drama, 48, 89–93, 182–91
historical relativism, *ix*
Hitler, Adolf, 52, 111, 181, 182, 188
Holmes, Oliver Wendell, Jr., 112
Holocene era, 122, 123–24, 125, 131
homosexuality, 71, 72–73, 80–83
Horsley, Richard, 95
Hunsinger, George, 7, 191, 195

incarnation theme, 28–33
incarnational discipleship
    Christian ethics, as an addition to, 2, 19, 72, 83, 192
    covenantal basis for, 7, 87–89, 98–100, 103–104, 129
    in the current day, 121, 125
    ethics of, 33–34, 84, 86, 130, 193–95
    exemplars of, 3–4, 45–46, 63, 196, 201
    faithfulness, as an act of, 161
    identity, question of, 6, 151–54
    Jesus, seeing in the other, 154–57
    as a life ordered by justice, 165
    papers presented on, 5–8
    repentance as a dimension of, 152
    secularism, meeting the challenges of, 136
    social engagement claims, 177
    A Thicker Jesus, articulated in, 27, 40, 89, 178
    three dimensions of, 87, 135–37
    tradition of, 6, 27, 68, 196–97
    white America, created in the framework of, 10
    women, way of practicing, 64
Interfaith Just Peacemaking (Thistlewaite), 138
inverting perspectives, 156–57
Iroquois Confederacy, 43–44
Isasi-Díaz, Ada María, 60–61

Jeffress, Robert, 158
Jenkins, Willis, 17–18

INDEX

Jennings, Willie James, 150, 157
Jesus and Judaism (Sanders), xiv
Jesus and the Nonviolent Revolution (Trocmé), *xii*, 4
Jesus Christ
    Baptist devotion to, 25, 34, 190–91
    Cosmic Christ, 127, 134
    covenantal interpretation of, 103–104
    historical Jesus, 25, 27, 33, 37, 62, 187, 189, 198
    identifying with, 35–36
    in incarnational discipleship, 2, 27, 63, 135, 144, 167, 194–95
    Islamic interpretation of, 149–50
    Jesus, scripture, and hermeneutics, 184–88
    Jesus the refugee, 151, 161–62
    Jewish apocalyptic Jesus, 11, 22–23, 187
    justice, the way of Jesus as, 163, 164, 165, 168
    Lordship of Christ, 4, 10, 62–63, 148, 193, 200
    the new Exodus and, 93–94, 102
    as the new Moses, 96–97
    opaque theology and, 175–76
    in Orthodox iconography, 128
    PHAT Jesus, 6, 56–57, 59–68, 69
    reverence for Christ, 78, 79
    seeing in the vulnerable other, 150–51, 154–57, 161
    as *Stellvertretung*, 170–71
    See also Kingdom of God; Sermon on the Mount; thick Jesus; white Jesus
Johnson, Lyndon Baines, 108
Jordan, Clarence, 3–4, 166
just peacemaking
    as a breakthrough theory, 2, 192
    Cold War, as developed in the context of, 183
    covenantal approach to peacemaking, similarity to, 101
    democracy as a key practice in, 138
    ethos of impunity, avoiding, 21
    Just Peacemaking Institute invitation letter, 3–5
    pacifism and just war theory, as an alternative to, 135, 184
    race and, 163, 171–72
    repentance, leading to, 162
    white Jesus and, 52
Just Peacemaking: The New Paradigm (Stassen, ed.), 138
Just Peacemaking: Transforming Initiatives (Stassen), 21, 138
just violence concept, 53
just war tradition, 16, 135, 183–84

kairos moments and trajectories, 22
Kant, Immanuel, 167
Katongole, Emmanuel, 14–15
King, Martin Luther, Jr.
    as an incarnational disciple, 3, 196
    assassination of, 109
    covenant-based human rights, operating from, 103, 137
    egalitarian democracy, envisioning, 200
    Harold Stassen, receiving support from, 179
    holiday in honor of, 116
    Malcolm X, as compared to, 21, 199
    Revolution of the Candles as inspired by, *x–xii, xxii*
    Stassen, as influenced by, 166–67, 180
    Strength to Love, xii, 4
Kingdom Ethics (Stassen/Gushee), 1, 11, 121, 184, 189, 194
Kingdom of God
    in covenant theology, 103
    exclusion from, 146
    Exodus tradition, reign of God in, 94
    individuals, as drawn into, 32
    Jesus and the reign of God, 22–24
    as a kin-dom, 60–62, 67
    in *Kingdom Ethics*, 11
    the oppressed, the kingdom as near to, 35
    in redemption theology, 128
    Sermon on the Mount as elucidating, 97, 185
    seven marks of, in Isaiah and Jesus, 192

sinful, worldly projects, modern church identifying with, 26
Kingdom of God in America (Niebuhr, H. R.), *ix*
Kirchenkampf (German Church Struggle), 120, 188, 191
Koinonia Farm, *xxi, xxii*
Ku Klux Klan (KKK), 108

lament, 14–15, 16, 36, 152, 158, 162
Latinx community, 40–42, 46, 51–54, 61
Learning to be White (Thandeka), 169–70
Lee, Hak Joon, 7, 182, 186
Lester, Muriel, 3, 4, 166
Lincoln, Abraham, 44–45, 137
linear history concept, 49–50
Long, Charles, 65–66, 175
Luther, Martin, 82, 129

MacIntyre, Alasdair, 139–40, 143
marriage. *See* sexual ethics
Martin, Trayvon, 109
Massingale, Bryan, 21
Mateen, Omar, 114
McBride, Jennifer, xix
Megivern, James J., xv, xvi
Mennonites, 12, 45, 149, 160, 184
Milbank, John, 27
Mohler, R. Albert, Jr., 39, 190
Moltmann, Jürgen, 156
"More Justice in East Germany" conference, *x–xi*
Muhammad, Prophet, 161
mujerista theology, 60–61
Murphy, Nancey, 87, 88
Muslim refugee crisis, 157–62

natural law argument, 81–82
Niebuhr, H. Richard, 21–22, 181, 182, 193
Niebuhr, Reinhold, 19, 20, 47, 168–69
Nixon, Richard M., 109, 179

Obama, Barack, 109, 110, 117, 159
opaque theology, 175–76
Overton, Richard, 142

panentheism, 129
Paris, Peter, 7, 182, 198–99
Pequot War, 43
PHAT Jesus, 6, 56–57, 59–68, 69
Philpott, Daniel, 20–21
political Augustinianism, 11–12
Politics of Jesús (De La Torre), 41–42
Politics of Jesus (Yoder), *xii*
Politics of Repentance (Trocmé), *xix*
Powell, Adam Clayton, Sr., 47
Protestant social justice, 131–32
Puritans
  democracy, Puritan contribution to, 42–44, 87
  Free Church Puritans, 137, 139–42, 148, 180
  Puritan heritage of covenant, 42–43, 87, 89, 100–101, 102, 139, 140, 148

Quakers, *xv*, 183, 184

race and racism
  Bonhoeffer and racism, 170–71
  centrality of shame in white racism, 177
  Christian self-examination on, 84–85, 166, 174
  critical race theory, 7, 53
  Jim Crow racism, 108, 163
  just peacemaking and race, 171–72
  legacy of white colonial racism, 182
  Lincoln on racial equality, 44
  modern racism, 105–106
  in Nazi Germany, 188
  racism as sinful, 26, 141–42
  racist interpretation of covenant, 101–102
  repentance for, *xxi*, 4, 152
  responsibility of whites for racism, 15–17
  social power, ascribing on the basis of race, 34
  Stassen, stance on, 120, 163, 180, 192, 198–99
  thin Jesus and, 167–70
  toxicity of American Christian racism, 199

underestimating the problem of, 164
white supremacist racism, 114, 198
Radical Orthodoxy, 4, 27
Rand, Ayn, 45
Rasmussen, Larry, 7, 17, 99, 186, 190, 195, 201
refugee crisis, 157–62
reparations, 21, 112–13, 117–18
repentance
  Christian identity, as part of, 195
  continuous repentance, 85, 164, 194
  Holy Spirit, as prompting, 27, 34, 63
  for ignorance regarding homosexuality, 73
  in incarnational discipleship, 84, 136, 144
  as incumbent upon all, 85
  Jesus, calling for, 23
  just peacemaking, role in, 162, 171
  lamentation, as linked to, 15
  reparations, making part of, 36
  for social sin, *xx*, 4
  in *A Thicker Jesus*, 152
  of white supremacists, calling for, 16
Revolution of the Candles, *x*, *xi*, *xxii*, 3
Rice, Chris, 152
Roof, Dylan, 114
Rorty, Richard, 136, 140, 143–44

Sagan, Carl, 133
salvation history, 48–50
same-sex unions, 71–72, 80, 81, 83
Sanders, Ron, 7, 180, 186, 197
satanic christology, 41
Schliesser, Christine, 120
Schulte, Paul, 16
Schüssler Fiorenza, Elisabeth, 9–10
A Secular Age (Taylor), 26, 28, 87, 136, 196
Sensenig, Peter, 7, 184, 194, 200
Sermon on the Mount
  African American church tradition, embodying, 103
  Bonhoeffer, as a focus of, *xiv*, 120, 121
  Christian faithlessness, as an antidote to, 189
  as christology from below, 128
  as a covenantal renewal speech, 97
  as covenant-based, 87–88, 95–97
  ethics derived from, 102
  feminist critique, 98
  Kingdom of God, revealing nature of, 185
  peacemaking steps developed from, 138
  Stassen, as inspired by, 19, 118
  as transgressive, 67
  triadic structure of, 135, 187, 192
The Sermon on the Mount (Jordan), *xii*, 4
sexual ethics
  biblical integrity and, 80–83
  fairness, standard of, 72–73, 82
  fidelity and chastity, 74–80
  incarnational discipleship, little to offer, 191
  same-sex unions, 71–72, 80, 81, 83
sexual reorientation, 82
shame
  of colonized minds, 47–48
  racism, stemming from, 115, 168–69, 171, 174
  of same-sex desire, 72–73, 83
  white shame, 170, 172–73, 177
Simmons, Paul, 190
Sobrino, Jon, 19
Social Sources of Denominationalism (Niebuhr, H. R.), *ix*
Society of Christian Ethics, 5–6, 39, 55, 192
Southern Baptist Convention, 190
Southern Baptist faith
  altar calls as a typical marker of, 40
  Baptist preachers, silent reaction to social oppression, 59
  Baptist vision of a contemporary Jesus, 25, 34
  Calvinist Southern Baptists and divine determinism, 193
  Harold Stassen as president of the denomination, 179
  invitation to discipleship, Baptist pastors extending, 56
  paideia, Baptist heritage of, 55

INDEX

as politically conservative, 190–91
Stassen as a Baptist ethicist, 86, 192
Southern Baptist Theological Seminary, *xxi*, 1, 39, 120, 189
Stassen, Glen H.
   Bonhoeffer, as heavily influenced by, 119–21, 166, 188, 192
   Christian ethics, as a scholar of, 1, 120, 178, 180, 181, 191–92
   Christian identity, quest for, 26–28
   christology from below, preferring, 127–28, 129
   Civil Rights, engagement with, 119, 138, 163, 179, 192, 198
   fruits test concept, favoring, 151, 157–62
   Fuller Seminary professorship, 1–2, 7, 9, 39–40, 86, 120, 191
   historical patterns, mistaken notion of, 49–50
   as a pacifist, 183, 184, 192
   race, treatment of, 120, 163, 180, 192, 198–99
   Sermon on the Mount, as inspired by, 19, 118
   shame, emphasis on, 172, 177
   See also incarnational discipleship; *A Thicker Jesus*
Stassen, Harold, 119, 137, 177, 179–80, 182–83
Stassen Berger, Kathleen, 180
Stevenson, Bryan, 117
Strength to Love (King), *xii*, 4
Stringfellow, William, 70–71, 83
Syrophoenician woman, 10, 63, 69

Tarrant, Brenton Harrison, 114
Taylor, Charles, 25, 26, 28–33, 87, 136, 196
Thandeka, Rev., 168–90, 170
thick Jesus
   acceptance of, 39–40
   character of God revealed in, 174
   condemnation of God in the concept of, 50–52
   hermeneutical suspicion, concept as void of, 41
   incarnational discipleship as obedient to, 194

justice, as guided by the concept of, 164, 166
liberative methodologies, as stunting, 52–53
as needed for salvation, 47–48
prophetic stream of Israel, in continuity with, 135, 145–46
salvation history, resting on the illusion of, 48–50
saying no to, 40–41, 53–54, 57, 68
as too white, 6, 42–46
as unique, 83–84
A Thicker Jesus (Stassen)
   aliveness of creation, discussing, 129–30
   altar call, book ending with, 40
   amendments to, 134
   Christian ethics, contribution to the field of, 131, 135
   dedication details, 119, 137
   domination, on witnessing response to, 166
   on evasions and dualisms, 189
   as final book of Stassen, 118
   identity, spotlight on, 25, 152, 195
   on incarnational discipleship, 2, 27, 40, 89, 125, 139, 178, 193
   Jesus Christ for us today, looking at, 121
   Just Peacemaking, comparing to, 21
   publishing of, 191
   repentance and transformation, calling for, 126
   on secularism and Christian faithlessness, 196
   social ethics, emphasizing, 131
   title of book, finalizing, 86
   war and peacemaking practices, examining, 20
Tillich, Paul, 175
Townes, Emilie, 67, 147
Townsend, Anthony, 70–71
Tregubov, Andrew, 128
Trinitarian discipleship ethic, 195
Trobisch, Walter, 75–76
Trocmé, Andre, 3–4, 166, 196
Trump, Donald
   as a character, 62
   climate change, denying, 122

election of, 114, 198
resistance against, 200
Stassen, imagined reaction to era of, 121
white supporters of, 41, 159, 191, 199
xenophobia as associated with, 158
Tuskegee experiment, 105, 110–13

Underhill, John, 43
Uninhabitable Earth (Wallace-Wells), 124
Union Theological Seminary, 1, 47, 119–20, 181
United States
American exceptionalism, 109–10
American identity, 137, 139, 143, 145, 147
in the Cold War era, 183
democracy, Puritan contribution to, 42, 43, 137–142, 180
eugenics movement, 110–13
Paris Climate Accord, withdrawing from, 17
racism in, 16, 108, 171, 175
refugee crisis, attitude towards, 157–62
thin Jesus, purposefully creating, 165–66, 174
Tuskegee experiment, authorizing, 105
white privilege in, 48
See also Civil Rights movement; white supremacy

Vanhoozer, Kevin, 91
Visser't Hooft, Willem A., *xvi–xvii*
Volf, Miroslav, 155–56

Waldensians, *xv*
Walker, Alice, 57
Wallace-Wells, David, 124
Wallis, Jim, *xxiv*
Walzer, Michael, 140, 141, 145
War of the Lamb (Yoder), 138–39
Wariboko, Nimi, 118
Warner, Mark, 112
weddings in premodern Christianity, 75–76

West, Cornel, 105–106
Westfield, Nancy Lynne, 13
Westmoreland-White, Michael, 184
white Jesus
Jesús *vs.* white Jesus, 52, 54
no redemption for, 6, 41, 42
the oppressor, on the side of, 51
people of color, as remote from realities of, 188
rejection of, 46, 47
thick Jesus, discerning from, 13
thick Jesus as too white, 6, 42–46
universalization of as problematic, 48
white supremacy, connection with, 164, 199
See also thick Jesus
white supremacy
American Christian ethics, effect on, 198
collaborative activities of, 113–14
cultural ethos, eradicating, 115–16
idolatry, as a form of, 105
Ku Klux Klan, 108
modern racism, grounded in cultural ethos of, 106
nonviolence, no right to preach, 52
PTSD, causing in African Americans, 117
racism in a society based on, 15–16, 17
Tuskegee experiment, cultural ethos allowing for, 110
U.S. culture, as entrenched in, 7, 121, 160
white children as the first victims of, 170
white Christ, connection to, 164, 199
See also race and racism
whiteness and anthropology, 173–74
wicked problems, 18
Williams, Delores, 57, 67
Williams, Reggie
Bonhoeffer, works on, 2, 120
Christian faithlessness, on the roots of, 188–89
Fuller Theological Seminary, as a student at, 1

on Harlem experience of Bonhoeffer, 155
on MLK as a source for Stassen, 180
race, on Stassen's treatment of, 7
white supremacism, as strongly against, 198–99
womanist theology
  on divine co-suffering, 157
  incarnational atonement, as a source for understanding, 48
  PHAT Jesus concept in, 6, 56–57, 59, 63, 68–69
  ransom theory, rejecting, 67
  six key threads of the womanist prophetic voice, 147–48
  Stassen, little engagement with, 181, 187
  womanish women of the bible, 63–64, 66, 69

X, Malcolm, 21, 109, 199

Yoder, John Howard, 45, 52, 138–39, 184

Zeli, Danka, 14
Zimmerman, George, 109